HUMAN AND ARTIFICIAL INTELLIGENCE

DATE DUE			
Nov 11 '72			
Dec 13 '72			
Nov 21 '73			
Mar 10 '75			

CONTEMPORARY PROBLEMS IN PHILOSOPHY

George F. McLean, O.M.I., Editor

Situationism and the New Morality, Robert L. Cunningham

Human and Artificial Intelligence, Frederick J. Crosson

HUMAN
AND
ARTIFICIAL INTELLIGENCE

FREDERICK J. CROSSON

University of Notre Dame

APPLETON-CENTURY-CROFTS
EDUCATIONAL DIVISION
New York   MEREDITH CORPORATION

128.08
C88h
77578
Jan. 1972

Contents

Foreword

Today we seem to be enmeshed in paradoxes which are as exciting as they are menacing. The centuries of work directed toward dominating our environment now appear to have produced physical problems of doomsday proportions. The battle of this century to conquer famine threatens, by the very success of its "green revolution," to produce social problems of even greater consequence. Finally, the search of recent decades to expand mechanically and to replace electronically the human thought processes now raises the most fundamental of all questions: What does it mean to be a human being—a person—myself?

This volume by Frederick Crosson on the problem of *Human and Artificial Intelligence* is an integral part of the Appleton-Century-Crofts philosophy series CONTEMPORARY PROBLEMS IN PHILOSOPHY. As the problems treated in the series are actual ones, there can be no realistic hope of providing "the answer" or even "an answer." What is possible, however, and what each volume intends, is to shed light upon a key philosophical problem of the present age: first, by tracing its origin and analyzing its components; second, by studying recent approaches to the issue and providing samples of the most significant writing; and finally, by indicating those approaches which show the greatest promise for the future. With this in hand the reader can hope to reflect upon the fundamental issues of his day in a way which will enable his life to be more conscious and his decisions more free.

At first sight, one might expect the present topic, machines and computers, to be of marginal interest to such an overall project. It is a measure both of the significance of the work of cybernetics and of the depth of Dr. Crosson's truly humane analysis that this work sheds as much light on man as it does on machine. Certainly the volume discusses both the technological advances themselves and also whether they lead to a conception of man as a machine. But the volume is even more a study of two much more important issues: first, the way in which computer simulation of certain mental activities has made it possible to understand more clearly the place of these activities in human thought processes; and, second, the way in which the difficulties in simulating other dimensions of mental activity have shed great light on that nonconceptual, and perhaps nonconceptualizable ground of human thought and of personality itself.

To achieve this Dr. Crosson has effectively marshalled a mass of relevant research. In his introduction he traces the historical roots of this search in order to identify both the proper context and the specific orientation for this stage of man's attempt at self-understanding. Next, he clarifies the character of the technological advances and of the most significant work in machine simulation of human activities. He then draws from these contributions a more precise statement of the problem of man. Above all, he points out the way in which the extensive mathematical efforts which have gone into programming machines to simulate human processes have shed new light on what it means to be human.

With this as a guide the eleven selections from recent writings stand out in their full significance. Each is directed to a specific issue, but together they exemplify the manner in which the work of contemporary technologists, mathematicians, logicians, psychologists, and philosophers have converged in a massive project in order to make a distinctively contemporary contribution to man's oldest and most meaningful quest to "understand thyself."

G. F. McL.

Acknowledgments

The theme of this book reflects my association, over a period of seven years, with the Philosophic Institute for Artificial Intelligence at the University of Notre Dame. I am grateful to the Director of the Institute, Professor Kenneth Sayre, for the maieutic function which he has exercised on my thoughts and for his friendship throughout our philosophical disagreements.

I wish to acknowledge the financial assistance of the Institute for Interdisciplinary Studies of the St. Thomas Aquinas Foundation and the academic hospitality of the University of Chicago in making me a Research Associate while I was completing this book, especially the kindness of the Chairman of the Committee on Social Thought at Chicago, Professor James Redfield.

1   Introduction

I

Heliocentrism, evolution, psychoanalysis, cybernetics: each of these innovations has forced a rethinking of the nature and place of man in the universe. Two differences between the latest of these and the first three are noteworthy. First, a single individual can be identified as the major precipitator in the earlier instances: Copernicus, Darwin, Freud. No one person is similarly central in the cybernetic transformation, partly because it is more a climate in which we think and work, perhaps also because we are still in the developing stages of it, for the transformation has clearly not yet reached its peak. Second, the cybernetic transformation alone is intimately connected with technology. This means that, on the one hand, the questions raised by cybernetics could not have been sharply formulated before technological developments had opened them up to us, and on the other hand that the effects of those developments are rapidly diffused through our highly mechanized society. "Self-knowledge," a contemporary novelist has remarked, "is always bad news." These four innovations have certainly decisively influenced man's understanding of himself, and the shock of recognition has not been uniformly welcomed.

The questions raised by cybernetics have indeed been raised before, but without the precision and clarity with which they present themselves in our day. These questions concern the sense in which and extent to which organisms and in particular human beings can be understood as machines. The attempt so to understand them is generally called mechanism and is often unclearly if at all differentiated from materialism.

There are, however, clear differences between these two. Materialism is an ontological position, a theory about what there is, while mechanism is a theory about the organization of bodies. It is certainly possible to be a mechanist, in the sense of holding that all spatio-temporal processes are explicable in terms of mechanical principles, and not to be a materialist. Descartes [1] approaches this position but his notion of interaction holds him back. The views of Malebranche and Leibniz however appear to instantiate it. On the other hand, classical materialism which affirmed that only matter and the void exist never described living or nonliving bodies as machines.[2] In the modern period, some vitalists have formulated an anti-mechanistic materialism. E. Rignano, for example, describes the vital principle as "a new form of energy, always obedient to the general laws of energetics, but endowed with well-defined elementary properties different from those of any form of energy in the inorganic world."[3] Only if we assume that organic processes can be adequately explained by the same laws that explain inorganic processes (those of physics and chemistry) and further assume that the latter are mechanical principles, will it follow that all materialism is mechanistic. There is however an ambiguity involved in the term 'mechanical' here which needs to be clarified.

The Greek term *mēchanē* from which 'machine' comes meant any kind of contrivance or device: rhetorical artifice, siege machines, the deus ex machina of the tragedies, a bridge of boats. One who was *mēchanikos* was inventive, resourceful. There is a pseudo-Aristotelian treatise on mechanics, and the simple machines of Archimedes (lever, inclined plane, wheel and axle) are the basic elements of all subsequent machinery.

Another term which will be important in clarifying our problem is *automaton*. Paradoxically to our minds, the Greek term simply meant self-moving or self-acting, happening without apparent external agency, and was applied by Homer to men as well as inanimate objects.[4] Aristotle refers to *ta automata ton thaumaton*, marvelous little contrivances which were, in a sense, self-moving,[5] and employs the same term in a well-known passage of the *Politics* where he says that slaves would be unnecessary if the shuttle could move itself.[6]

These two terms may be related by saying that for the Greeks, and notably Aristotle, some machines are automata. Unlike the poets, Aristotle is concerned to note that genuine nonliving automata exist only in stories, while the marvelous little contrivances referred to earlier are only in an extended sense self-moving. The actual machines (in the modern sense) known to the ancients were of course all devices for the transmitting of energy originating outside them, so it is not strange that he does not seem to consider the idea seriously. The important and interesting point is that none of the ancient philosophers, materialist or not, affirms the proposition: *some living automata are machines.*

The man who does thus boldly characterize animals is that Prometheus of the modern world, René Descartes. Not even Hobbes, his materialist contemporary, who does (in terms of our stipulation) formulate a mechanistic theory of the world, couples machines and organisms together. In the *Discourse on Method,* after indicating how he can explain the movements of animals mechanically without introducing any reference to a soul or vital agent, Descartes adds:

This will not seem at all strange to those, who, knowing how many different *automata* [Descartes' emphasis] or moving machines can be made by the industry of man, without employing in doing so more than a very few parts in comparison with the great multitude of bones, muscles, nerves, arteries, veins and all the other parts which are in the body of each animal, will consider this body as a machine which, having been made by the hands of God, is incomparably better arranged . . . than any of those which can be invented by men.[7]

This is a very interesting passage, and contains indications of how Descartes came to such a conception. First of all, there exist in his time a number of different kinds of machines which present the appearance of self-motion. He mentions elsewhere water-driven statues [8] and clockworks.[9] The latter in fact exemplify a class of machines which not only transmitted but stored energy to be released at a later time, and hence were far more automatic than Aristotle's mechanisms.

Second, as his allusions to the parts of animate bodies indicate, a great deal more anatomy and physiology was known. Most suggestive here are probably the references to arteries and veins, for the great work of William Harvey, *de Motu Cordis* [10] had been published only eight years before the *Discourse*. Harvey's discovery that the motion of the blood was through a closed system of canals undoubtedly not only reminded Descartes of the tubes in the water-machines but also reinforced the impression of the autonomy of sufficiently complex organized bodies. Moreover the allusion to complexity of parts sounds a note with overtones in our day. Cyberneticists often speak of the need for "richly interconnected" systems if computer-based systems are to simulate the complexity of the brain: the *corpus callosum* which bridges the two halves of the cerebral cortex has 300 million separate conductors, for example. Quantitative complexity is a necessary condition for qualitatively different behavior.

But there is a deeper and more implicit element involved in the anatomical references. It is no accident that the one person who seems to have anticipated Descartes' suggestion was a Spanish physician,[11] and that his most famous follower in championing the automata theory was also a physician: La Mettrie, who published *L'Homme machine* is 1748. The body laid out or dissected before us is purely and simply an object in the natural world. All of its parts yield to the scalpel and seem to form an enormously complicated but self-enclosed system without any place for a soul to intrude itself.[12]

Third, and I believe most important, is the Christian context in which he places the argument. It appears that Descartes was led to his identification of automata (self-movers, one of Aristotle's criteria for animal life) as machines on the basis of an analogy between human and divine artificers.[13] If man, with few and gross parts, can make automata with the semblance of life, how much more can the infinite intelligence and unlimited power of God effect? I believe that this is why Descartes and not Hobbes, who does not discuss creation, makes the extrapolation.

There is a paradox here which has been a source of confusion up to our own day. Reference was made above to the common assumption that laws of matter and motion, i.e. laws of physics, are mechanical laws, i.e. explanatory of machines. But it seems clear that machines are and can be characterized only by including reference to their function, and that the function cannot be adequately specified by giving the physical-chemical topography of the machine. Machines constitute a class of objects which can be said to be adequate or deficient, successful or not successful in achieving their function.[14] They therefore require a two-levelled explicans, for while a physical-chemical analysis may tell us why a machine fails to function successfully, it cannot tell us what defines the successful operation of the machine.

The paradox, then, is that while Descartes acknowledges the purposiveness of man-made automata and argues by analogy to the automata-character of God-made animals, his critical eye is focussed on the elimination of an appeal to an animal soul to account for their behavior. He seems oblivious to the fact that if his analogy holds, even the bête-machine would require a level of explanation beyond that of physics. The elimination of Descartes' conceptual matrix through the replacement of the creator by natural selection does not, it seems to me, eliminate the need for a two-levelled understanding of automata.

What distinguishes machines, and hence constitutes a necessary condition for automata, is a unity of function—a unity exhibited in the operation of the machine, and implied when automata are characterized as *self*-moving. But consistent with his rejection of "final causes" (explanation by purpose), Descartes, although he expresses his admiration of the organization of living bodies, refuses to allow an appeal to an animal or vegetative soul to explain that unity, or even to say that the eye is made to see.[15] His program aims to account for apparently teleological behavior and structures on the basis of principles of physics, i.e. principles governing the motion of matter.

There is, however, an important exception made by Descartes to this program: man's linguistic behavior. Seen through a window, from a distance, men might be automata. But even if there were machines which resembled the human body, their inability to use language with all the flexibility with which human beings can would betray them.[16] It is, one might say, through exchange of speech that persons recognize each other.[17] This is not to deny that speech can be analyzed objectively, as verbal behavior. Descartes was familiar with talking parrots, but he thinks that such learned behavior will always be limited.[18] One of his disciples exclaimed, "to persuade me that a beast reasons, it would have to tell me itself." It is ironic that precisely this has been proposed by Scriven as a test for deciding whether a computer is conscious.[19]

What has given the whole question of machine automata or robots [20] a new lease on life has been, as in Descartes' time, a much greater knowledge of physiology, especially neurology, the extensive development of a formal analytic method (mathematical logic), and the appearance of a new kind of machine. The physiological advances are too extensive to survey here, but perhaps the most important have been the knowledge of the uniform electro-chemical character of neuron transmission of impulses throughout the nervous system, and the localization of brain functions.[21] The new genre of machines are those which store, transmit, and transform *information:* the computer.

COMPUTER SIMULATION

There are two basic types of computers: analogue and digital. An analogue computer represents the information which it stores and processes by a physical analogue of the magnitude of what it represents. For example, the velocity of a projectile may be represented by spatial distance on a scale or by the potential of an electrical sub-circuit. Summation or addition of velocities could then be represented by conjoining distances or by switching circuits into series alignment. The major distinctive advantage of analogue devices is that they can represent and deal with continuous variation in magnitude.

Digital computers, on the other hand, which are by far the more important and most common, represent and store the information which they process in terms of discrete elements, i.e. numerically. Any kind of specific information—the letters in a sentence, the items in an inventory, the shape of an object—can be symbolized by a numerical code. And any number-symbol can be correlated with a unique binary number. The binary number system employs as numerals only the digits '1' and '0' in place columns. It is apparent that any binary number, consequently, can be represented by a sequence of binary states, which may be switches (off-on), charges (positive-negative), etc. These in turn may be embodied in relays, vacuum tubes, transistors, magnets, etc.

Moreover the basic logico-mathematical operations—conjunction, disjunction, and negation—in terms of which the data thus represented can be processed or "worked on, can also be embodied in simple elementary circuits. An *or* gate or switch passes data when any of its input terminals are in the proper state; an *and* gate passes data when all of its input terminals are in the proper state; a *not* gate connects its input signal to the opposite state.

An easy but suggestive example of the similarity between these simple circuits and the neuron components of the nervous system is the comparison of the *or* gate with a synapse in which the superior neuron will fire (and relay information) if any of the inferior neurons which terminate at its base fire.[22] The formal structure of the synapse and the gate is the same. The hypothesis suggests itself that, since all of the logical operations of reasoning can be defined by the three mentioned, a sufficiently large and complexly interconnected computer ought to be able to process anything that can be processed by the nervous system, or more properly the brain. Let us call this the 'cybernetic hypothesis,' with the warning that by no means all cyberneticists would subscribe to it.

The cybernetic hypothesis will function in two directions: on the one hand, it will provide a model for neurological research which will, hopefully, integrate present knowledge into a coherent whole and suggest new areas of investigation. On the other hand, it suggests the possibility of simulating various kinds of human behavior by a properly programmed computer. Both directions of research are going on and a good deal of data has turned up to support the hypothesis. Our first concern in what follows will be with simulation.

A digital computer is a universal information processing machine, in the sense that it can simulate the information processing of any other system. The term 'simulate' is important here. We can describe the operation of any system—what it does—by specifying the input to the system, the transformation effected on the input by the system, and the output. The transformation effected is the computed function which the system executes on the basis of its internal state at the time of input. In the case of a computer, the internal state includes its memory and program, which contains instructions on what to do with input data.

As an example of this, take playing a game of checkers. The input here is the (visible) board with the pieces positioned on it; in memory are the rules of checkers; the instructions are to select each move so as finally to render the opponent unable to move; and the outputs are the successive moves. Both a man and a computer can compute this function: in fact Samuel's checker program [23] has been able to defeat a state champion. It is important to note that the processing of the input appears to be decidedly different in the two cases.

An indication of the difference already appears in the form of the input. The human player surveys the board at a glance, while the machine is fed the coded positions of the pieces serially. (This difference is more manifest if we think of playing only endgames.) Moreover in Samuel's program, the machine constructs all the relevant alternatives to each move to a depth of as much as twenty consequent moves, while the average human player probably articulates in imagination no more than five or six moves ahead, in the context perhaps of a vaguely anticipated sub-goal. While the machine *simulates* the (macro-) behavior of the human player, it does not *replicate* his conscious ratiocination, i.e. does not seem to process the information in the same way.

From the point of view of the method employed, computer simulation may be first divided (nonexclusively) into algorithmic and heuristic procedures. An algorithm is a rule for the solution of a problem, a rule whose application terminates in a definite answer: e.g. Euclid's algorithm for finding the greatest common divisor of two integers. Where to play at each move in tic-tac-toe so as to win or draw is a problem susceptible of algorithmic solution. Determining whether a well-formed formula in the propositional calculus is a theorem can be algorithmically determined by truth-tables.

In general, if the information relevant to the solution of a problem, including its statement, is specifiable in a finite number of unambiguous terms and a solution exists, then given sufficient time a solution can be "mechanically," i.e., algorithmically, determined. If the answer is required within a limited time, or if the relevant data are inexhaustible, or if a solution does not exist, or if, more practically, the data are finite but beyond the information-handling capacities of man and/or computer, then the problem cannot be algorithmically resolved.

For example, in principle chess is a game of "complete information," that is, we can specify unambiguously the goal, the rules governing the movement of pieces, etc., and so could theoretically calculate the ultimate consequences of each possible move in order to decide which move would lead most directly to winning. In practice, however, the number of possible alternatives obviates this possibility. The reason for this is that the number of paths of moves and countermoves to be traced increases rapidly—exponentially—into a "tree" of paths. Since there are, on an average over the game, about thirty possible moves (and countermoves) at each step, in a game of forty moves there will be 30^{80} paths to consider, and even if we assumed a computer which (apart from limitations of memory storage) could trace 10^{12} moves per second, it would take 10^{98} years to be ready to make the first move.

One of the earliest chess-playing programs cut this Gordian knot by 1) examining only seven out of the thirty possible continuations and 2) examining these only to a depth of four moves ahead. This reduced the number of moves for the machine to run through at each point to only 2401, a manageable number for the IBM 704.[24] As might be expected under these restrictions, although the machine played legal chess, it did not play too successfully. Nevertheless it was an important achievement because it attempted to circumvent the practical impossibility of an algorithmic solution by introducing strategies of simplification and selection of alternatives, i.e. by heuristics.

Moreover this program brings into view the three heuristic factors involved in nonalgorithmic solutions to such continuation problems: which alternatives to explore, how far to explore them, and, perhaps most elusive, how to recognize a good position when it is chanced upon.[25] Samuel was able to resolve the problem for checkers, in which the number of alternatives is of course much reduced, by a program which examined as much as twenty moves ahead and by an ingenious learning technique for the machine. Similar success is not yet in sight for chess programs.

Indeed in some areas it may be that the search for more efficient algorithms promises more than heuristics. Newell, Shaw, and Simon drew up a heuristic program for proving theorems from the propositional calculus which was able to find solutions for thirty-eight of the first fifty-two theorems of the *Principia Mathematica*, but involved large amounts of machine time. Hao Wang wrote an algorithmic program which easily found proofs for the same theorems in less than five minutes (including input-output time). If the heuristic program were powerful and general enough, its superiority would be clear, but the question is whether it can be made so.[26]

It is important to note that heuristic strategies are, in a sense, "truncated" algorithms. That is, they too involve a counting-out of steps and alternative paths, but coupled with a pruning of the paths and limitations on the number of steps explored. The counting-out or step-by-step character of these programs is due not only to the logic of analysis—i.e. dividing the problem into separate parts so as to attack each separately—but also to the requirements of the digital computer, which functions by a succession of discrete operations on discrete data. The results may be summed or integrated, but the logic of the analysis and of the machine requires a preliminary enumeration or articulation of the parts. The importance of this can perhaps best be seen in the areas of pattern recognition and automatic language translation.

Human beings, one might say, spend their cognitive lives in discriminating patterns: visual, musical, linguistic, etc. The way to begin simulating these achievements, it would seem, is by determining the features or criteria on the basis of which we recognize, say, a circle or a written number or letter. Figures or alpha-numeric characters may be poorly inscribed, but presumably there are some invariant features on the basis of which we identify the inscription. It quickly becomes apparent that such criteria, however easily we may use them in recognizing, are not easy for an individual to specify unless the range of possible variations is limited. Think of the varieties of handwriting, even apart from unusual "hands," such as Italic.

Nevertheless, if we cannot determine how we do it, we might try to discover invariant features on the basis of which we could recognize various kinds of patterns. For example, in the case of written alphabetic characters, we could try such features as closure, concavity or convexity, extension of lines above or below a "base line envelope" and so forth. The attempt could then be made to characterize letters on the basis of the presence of a differential set of such features. Actual writing often deviates considerably from any such standard, but if we take this into account by weighting the probability of finding certain features for a given letter and making the computer's decision depend on such a probabilistic assessment we can ameliorate though not resolve such departure. Programs have been written which exhibit eighty to ninety percent success in recognition in this way, especially if some limitations are placed on the inscriptions, e.g. that the lines are confined within a well-defined space.[27]

But there is a paradox which awaits the production of any successful program, even—indeed especially—one that achieved one hundred percent success. In fact, a letter which anyone would judge to be a "u," say, if it were isolated, might very well be seen as a "v" if it were in the context of a word whose meaning and hence whose spelling required a "v." We constantly unconsciously "adjust" such discrepancies in recognizing all sorts of patterns about whose overall sense we have no doubts. On reflection, it seems clear that we regularly recognize letters not only on the basis of the presence of invariant features, but by assessing features in the context of the word and even the sentence in which they are imbedded. Moreover the context referred to is in part determined essentially by the meaning of the word.

If these last observations are correct, then the problem of programming a computer to recognize a letter-pattern as a sum or set of discrete features, however successfully it may be solved, will constitute a simulation of human recognition at best only for isolated letters. In actual reading of script, the recognition of a word will not be through a one-by-one identification of the letters plus summation, but rather deviant letter-shapes will be assimilated in reading to what the context requires. A moment's thought will make clear that the same problems of individual letter recognition discussed above have now reappeared on the level of word recognition. Instead of deviant line-segments, we now have the difficulty of deviant letter-shapes on the one hand, and on the other instead of the surrounding letters as a partially determining factor we have the surrounding words as a partially determining context. At this level the problem is further complicated by the fact that words are units of meaning, so that a semantic dimension begins to appear as a datum of the task. We are thus led on to the area of language analysis.

Before discussing this, however, some additional comments and a look at other kinds of pattern recognition will be helpful.

As a corollary to the above considerations, it should be remarked that where the letter inscriptions are nearly standardized—e.g. as in the Palmer method—step-by-step identification and summation is perfectly feasible. A fortiori this is the case with printed letters where the typeface does have specifiable invariant features. (As we shall see, however, complications may appear here on the syntactic level.) In general, if we could make certain kinds of human behavior more machine-like, i.e. more standardized, a number of uses of computer-based recognition systems would become more practicable. For example, if people could be trained in school to write, say, the Palmer method with care and precision, or to form numerals in a standard way, automatic mail-sorting devices for the post office would be useable. We do adapt ourselves after all in similar ways already: think of multiple choice tests using chemically treated pencils for marking the answer. No doubt the future will involve similar kinds of adjustments of men to machine capabilities and machines to human capabilities.

The approach to letter recognition briefly described above has a limitation which is significant not only for pattern recognition but for simulation work in general. This is that the features to be employed by the computer in a recognition program are specified in advance by the programmer or analyst. It follows that the machine is restricted by the ingenuity of the latter. Two means of ameliorating this restriction have been slightly explored by programming self-adaptive or self-organizing systems. The machine can be allowed to combine or recombine the specified test features on its own, in a trial-and-error method which the programmer will "certify" as correct or incorrect. Consistently correct identification of the inscription by the machine would result in the consolidation of sets of features whose composition might be unexpected and even unknown to the programmer. Or alternatively, the machine may be programmed to generate test features of its own. Attractive as these might seem, especially the latter, they have not yet yielded much in the way of significant results.[28]

In another area of pattern recognition, a remarkable program has been written by Thomas Evans at Massachusetts Institute of Technology. Working with analogy-type topological drawings of the sort used in intelligence tests, Evans devised a program which enabled a computer to answer successfully—at "about the 10th grade level"—multiple choice questions of this kind. Consistent with what was said above about the logic of the computer, the program required that topological relations such as the inclusion of one geometric shape inside another be defined in terms of metric geometry, that is, of the linear relations of points or sets of points in Cartesian coordinates. Whereas we say that we "see at a glance" that one figure is included inside or outside another, and apply this relation to analogous figures, the machine had to define inside and outside, above and below, etc., in metric relations of numbered coordinate points and then explicitly infer the relation of topological inclusion or exclusion.

The gap between trial and error and "insight" is present here for human subjects as well as machines, for we, too, may have to try several possible relations before hitting on the best one. But some kind of heuristics or insight is present from the start for us, which allows us normally to eliminate several possible answers at once. The machine, on the other hand, must construct descriptions of all of the answers methodically before eliminating any of them.[29]

With respect to relatively simple geometrical forms, some experimental results in the psychology of perception have turned up promising-looking directions for further work. These experiments were carried out in terms of an information-theoretic analysis of certain simple patterns. In order to describe the results, some grasp of information theory is necessary.

Information theory is a recent discipline, first laid out and defined in the 1948 paper of Claude Shannon, *The Mathematical Theory of Communication*.[30] Concerned with the relation between the channel capacity of a communication and the reliable transmission of messages through the channel, Shannon proposed as a measure of information given by each symbol of a message the amount of uncertainty on the part of the receiver which the reception of the symbol removed. This amount can be quantified in terms of probability theory, so that, for example, if an unlikely symbol is received, it may be said to convey more information than one which was highly probable. Roughly, the more unexpected a symbol, the more information it yields.

If we know the elements of the source "alphabet"—whether these be letters, dots and dashes, musical notes, or whatever—and if, on the basis of a large number of messages, we can calculate the numerical probability of occurrence of each symbol, we can calculate the probability of each symbol's occurrence in a particular message, which will be the measure of the information it conveys. Note that there is no necessary connection here between information thus defined and "meaning." Whether a particular symbol or message makes sense is a separate and possibly subsequent question to its probability of occurrence.[31]

Working on the assumption that cognition can be thought of—modeled—in terms of information processing, a number of psychologists have attempted to analyze such functions as remembering and perceiving in terms of information theory. There is a problem here in determining what will serve as a source alphabet, and calculating its respective probabilities. One way of establishing such measures in the case of visual perception is to inscribe a figure on graph paper, identify the cells by Cartesian coordinates, and ask a subject (without showing him the figure) to guess, cell by cell, which cells the figure occupies. The number of wrong guesses provides a rough measure of the expectancy or probability of occupancy for each cell. It is as if we had a two-symbol code and no "noise," i.e. no distortion of the signal.

It turned out in a number of such experiments that principles of perceptual grouping such as "good continuation," "similarity," and related Gestalt qualities could be formulated in informational terms and hence quantified. In general the hypothesis was verified that "the probability of a given perceptual response to a stimulus is an inverse function of the amount of information required to define that pattern."[32]

This is an impressive and suggestive body of work. Its ultimate import, however, remains unclear for a number of reasons. Among these are the artificial character of the elements of the source alphabet and the subjective character of the estimated probabilities. Moreover there is good evidence that the notion of a *unit* of information, required for the application of theory, is ineluctably relative to the attitude of the subject, and hence cannot be defined independently or objectively.[33] If it could be so defined, a large step toward computer simulation of human perception would be taken. Until then, the application of information theory to psychological functions will remain of limited interest.

Let us turn now to the field of automatic language translation.

This has been, in terms of money (over sixteen million dollars) and time (the first concrete proposals go back twenty years) the most extensively explored area of artificial intelligence.

In the 1940's, inspired by the seeming analogy between decoding and translating, high hopes were entertained for machine translation of Russian (and other) texts into English. Warren Weaver wrote that a Russian text could be regarded as "really written in English" but "coded in some strange symbols." This view implicitly assumed that some kind of one-to-one correspondence exists between syntactic and semantic units in the two languages, and further that these correspondences could be made explicit, i.e. discovered and specified. It assumed, that is, that the computer could identify the syntactic units, the individual word-roots (i.e. separate off inflected word-endings) of the input language, then search a "mechanical dictionary" in its memory, and finally combine the thus translated units into an output language sentence via the syntactic rules of the latter language.

Instead of this achievement, what the work in automatic translation has resulted in is the disclosure of an unsuspected complexity and intermixture of syntax and semantics. Even apart from unsolved problems on the first level, it turns out that pairing a meaning with an identified word requires the determination of its syntactic function, and this has proven impracticable because of a very high degree of syntactic ambiguity in natural languages. Moreover frequently the only way to resolve this ambiguity is by recourse to the meaning of the sentence as a whole, which means that a circularity is involved in the program as described.[34]

For example, consider the sentence "Time flies like an arrow." [35] The word 'time' here may be either a noun, an adjective, or a verb, yielding three different syntactical interpretations. (To see how it could be the latter two, which are less perspicuous perhaps, compare: "fruit flies like a banana" and "time runners with a stop-watch.") The only way to choose among these possible interpretations is by recourse to the semantic context. This means that we cannot treat the semantic level as simply dependent on the syntactic.

As A. G. Oettinger comments,

No techniques now known can deal effectively with semantic problems of this kind. Research in the field is continuing in the hope that some form of man-machine interaction can yield both practical results and further insight into the deepening mystery of natural language. We do not yet know how people understand language, and our machine procedures barely do child's work in an extraordinarily cumbersome way.[36]

Even if the task of determining a unique syntactic and semantic structure were solved, further problems lie on the third level of the program described above, that of transposing the input sentence into a syntactically meaningful output language. A word-by-word translation of one natural language into another frequently if not generally results in either obscurity or loss of meaning. "Nous le leurs donnons" cannot be rendered as "We it them give"; the latter must be transformed into English order. The exploration of transformation rules by Noam Chomsky and his associates in recent years has resulted in a clear distinction between "surface grammatical structure" and "deep structure" which raises serious questions about the possibility of programming a computer with such transposition rules.

Surface structure analysis is the sort which most of us learned as paradigmatic in grammar school, and which analyzes a sentence by successive divisions or bracketings nested within one another: 1) subject phrase, 2) predicate phrase; 1a) noun phrase, 1b) prepositional phrase; 2a) verb, 2b) prepositional phrase, and so on down to nouns, verbs, adjectives, articles, etc.

Chomsky remarks,

With such a conception of language structure, it made good sense to look forward hopefully . . . to such projects as machine translation. But these hopes have by now been largely abandoned with the realization that this conception of grammatical structure is inadequate at every level, semantic, phonetic and syntactic.[37]

When sentences are transformed grammatically, e.g. from active to passive, the neat bracketings of surface structure are broken up. Successive transformations reveal structures which are hidden in the surface analysis, which are "deeper." Moreover there is experimental evidence which suggests that sentences are stored in memory in terms of these deeper structures.[38] Chomsky has been led by his work to a return to the "classical rationalist" account of knowledge and language which attributed to the mind a system of innate rules for the generation of linguistic and perceptual organizing schemata.

Our knowledge of language is not arrived at simply by exposure to repeated use of words: "Serious efforts have been made in recent years to develop principles of induction, generalization and data analysis that would account for knowledge of a language. These efforts have been a total failure." [39]

Presumably the innate properties which Chomsky is led to infer have a biological or more specifically a neurological foundation, and one may assume that these foundational structures have been acquired by the human organism over centuries of development. We are not yet able to isolate and identify them, and while it is "perfectly safe to attribute [them] to evolution," we should "bear in mind that there is no substance to this assertion—it amounts to nothing more than the belief that there is surely some naturalistic explanation for these phenomena." [40] If and until we can identify the innate structures, the project of building a machine which could learn a natural language, and a fortiori of programming a computer to converse in a natural language, must remain in abeyance.

Abeyance does not mean abandonment, however, and it would be inadequate to omit discussion of the grounds for confidence provided by recent work in physiological psychology, much of which can be seen as supporting the cybernetic model of the central nervous system.

MECHANICAL PROCESSES IN THE ORGANISM

Aristotle long ago observed that since the artifacts we make are better known to us than the works of nature, it is normal for us to understand the latter through the illumination of the former. Thus, for example, he compares the bones of the flexed arm with the arms of a catapult drawn back by the ropes.[41] Harvey was employing this principle in describing the valves of the veins as "lock-gates." It is only, as Claude Bernard pointed out, when we already understand the relation of a structure to its function that we can discern in an organ the analogous relation.[42] This is why technology not only supplies the instrumental means of access for scientific research, but is also a source of models for understanding what is investigated.

As we have seen earlier, it was just such a conception of "living machinery" which inspired the Cartesian program for mechanical biology. Not only the work of Harvey, but the water-driven automata lent support to the hypothesis that organic functions could be explained hydrodynamically. At the same time, as was noted, Descartes recognized that any such machine would have limited flexibility with respect to behavior, especially linguistic behavior. The problem, for him as well as La Mettrie, was in understanding the self-regulative and self-adapting character of behavior and organic function without appealing to animistic teleology.

Looking back, we can see the roots of the contemporary response to this difficulty in two discoveries made over a century and a half ago: Galvani's discovery of the electrical character of nerve action and Watt's invention of the govenor. Together with the concept of the reflex arc, formulated shortly thereafter, which linked together afferent and efferent systems by the same mode of electrical propagation of information, these disclosures have yielded an account of auto-regulation in terms of the model of electrical feedback circuits.

Let us look first at some examples of negative feedback circuits in the physiology of the organism.

A negative feedback circuit is one in which part of the output of a system is returned or fed back to diminish or negate the rate of output. A standard example is the room thermostat coupled to a furnace. The heat (output) of the furnace actuates the thermometer of the thermostat which, when it reaches a certain pre-set point, turns off the furnace.

The importance of this type of control device is apparent when we reflect that previously, the diminishing of the output of a furnace would have been accomplished by a human agent. When the room felt warm enough, or when the thermometer reached the desired temperature, one would "bank" or turn off the furnace by closing drafts, or pushing switches. It is not the muscles of man which the thermostat replaces, but his nervous system. In particular, due to the feedback structure, the heating circuit exhibits an apparent purposiveness in maintaining the temperature near a certain desirable level.

There are numerous sub-systems in the body which exemplify this type of control function, for example the oxygen level of the blood. As oxygen is burned by the muscles in exertion, the amount of carbon dioxide in the blood increases and the altered proportion stimulates a section of the brain stem which controls the chest muscles. Oxygen intake is increased by accelerated breathing and the rate of circulation is increased by accelerated heartbeats. As the oxygen level increases (and that of carbon dioxide decreases) toward a biologically pre-set normal level, negative feedback diminishes the breathing and heart rates to maintain that level. (This is somewhat oversimplified; actually a number of auxiliary processes play a role in achieving the equilibrium.)

Similarly, the concentration of salts in the blood and lymph is assayed by the kidneys. Excessive amounts of salt are eliminated with the urine, and deficient amounts are supplanted by withdrawing salt from storage in the skin. Analogous mechanisms maintain the homeostasis or equilibrium-levels of sugar, calcium, temperature, proteins, etc., in the blood. Apparently all the physiological necessities of the body are maintained by such self-regulating mechanisms, although the nature of all the components of the circuits are not known in some cases. Until they are, of course, we are only naming the methods of control in calling it negative feedback.

In addition to controls actuated by interoceptive stimuli, such as in the above examples, there are homeostatic controls actuated by exteroceptive stimuli which also aim at or result in internal equilibrium. For example, the well-known pupillar reflex which constricts the size of the pupil when too much light impinges on the retina. The homeostatic function of this and the other examples is "wired in," to use the language of our model.

It is relevant to note that such functions as have been mentioned are not wholly self-contained in the sense of being unchangeable. Attention has been drawn by some psychologists recently to the rather remarkable extent to which human subjects can learn to exercise an indirect but effective control over a wide range of "automatic" processes, from pulse beats to EEG alpha waves.[43]

Besides the reflexes alluded to above, there are numerous analogous tropisms in the simpler plants and animals. The sunflower appears to "aim at" the sun because the stem cells near the flower head are partially dried out by the sun's heat and shrink, thus pulling the flower over toward the sun. The "flame-seeking" moth is a victim of an evolutionarily acquired guidance system: its flight is oriented as a function of a constant angle of direction with respect to a source of light—in earlier times, the distant moon. A close source of light causes the fixed angle of flight to result in a spiral terminating at the flame.

Such fixed behavior patterns as the instinctive actions of animals represent another example of vital activities which have homologous similarities in the computer model. Specific stimuli can arouse an astonishingly large and diverse set of unlearned responses, often of great complexity. These responses function in the way that stored sub-routines do in a computer. They are "triggered"—perhaps a number of them in serial order—by appropriate pre-defined situations, and returned to storage for possible later use.[44] Nest-building, mating, egg-laying are among the many examples which may be cited.

It should be noted that the comparison here is limited by the fact that sub-routines in a computer are triggered interoceptively, so to speak, and not by environmental stimuli. Though there are simple robots which respond behaviorally to gross discriminations (e.g. strong light in Walter's tortoise [45]) we are very far from being able to build detection devices which could discriminate anything like the range of stimuli which trigger "adaptive" behavior in animals.

If we turn now to the case of learned behavior, we shift from periphery to central nervous system and to what seems to be the most promising aspect of the cybernetic model, the brain. If the previous examples are analogies to the model of computer-based systems, it is the brain which represents the computer of the model.

The basic structural similarity between the computer and the brain rests on the fact that both are composed of large numbers of digital-type, i.e. on/off elements which are intricately interconnected, and which process information by the transmission of discrete pulses. McCulloch and Pitts developed a logical model of such systems, called neural networks, and showed that it is possible in principle to construct such networks for any given input-output specifications, provided that the function to be computed can be completely specified in a finite number of unambiguous terms.[46] This means that it is not possible to claim that the nervous system is capable of any achievement which a computer cannot simulate, if the performance in question can be completely and logically described.

Once again, this is not to claim that the function would be computed in the same way. There are many differences between the brain and any present-day computers. For example while there is clearly some localization in the brain—centers of emotion, speech, afferent and efferent cortical areas, memory—it does not exhibit the individual-item-localization which exists in computers. Its "language" is different than that of the machines; it utilizes extensive redundancy in storage and communication and it is capable of repairing or transferring the function of damaged parts.[47]

Nevertheless, neurological and biological research continues to uncover resemblances (employment of feedback, linking of neural areas in learning, localization of more aspects of behavior, etc.) which argue for the mechanical nature of brain functions.[48] No verification of the claim that man is a machine is possible at the present time on the basis of the evidence available in the sciences— nor is a falsification possible on those grounds.

THE INTRINSIC LIMITATIONS OF SIMULATION

Mortimer Adler, in a recent book,[49] argues that the question of the difference of man is a "mixed question," partly scientific and partly philosophical. Referring to the development of computer technology and to the mathematical and neurological theories underlying work in artificial intelligence, he makes the following assertion:

. . . it is to the future development of the efforts represented by this [field] that we must look for any significant alteration in the state of the question about the difference of man, rather than to . . . paleoanthropology . . . ethologists . . . comparative [psychology] . . . or . . . biophysics and biochemistry. . . .[50]

The warrant for this statement has been indicated in our survey of the two sides of the cybernetic hypothesis. Both of the traditional problems of mind-body relationship and mechanism-vitalism, or better, mechanism-biologism (since vitalism is a dead issue, but the reducibility of biological to physio-chemical explanation is not) have been brought under a common roof by the computer-cybernetic model.

The implications of that model, as we have seen, are twofold. Its "anthropomorphic" import rests on the undisputable fact that computer-based systems can perform and indeed have taken over many of the tasks formerly discharged by the sensory-nervous systems of human beings. Its "mechanomorphic" aspect rests on the fact that many organic processes can be understood in terms of cybernetic concepts (programming, feedback, etc.) and hence the cybernetic model serves to organize and orient the experimental work in the biological fields.

The extrapolation of the "mechanomorphic" aspect leads to the thesis that men are machines. The extrapolation of the "anthropomorphic" aspect leads to the thesis that some machines are manlike, i.e. persons. The establishment of either thesis would of course diminish the unique status of human beings.

Taken together, the achievements of these two aspects of the model have led to philosophical reformulations of the traditional problems referred to. The most influential contemporary form of the mind-body problem is the so-called "neural-identity" theory, which holds that sensations, thoughts, and feelings *are* brain processes. The identity thus affirmed is held to be contingent, not logical, like the identity between the Morning Star and the Evening Star.[51] That is, the *meaning* of an introspective report and of a neurological report are different, but their referent is the same.

This theory is much debated at the present time. Two kinds of objections to it may be noted. First, although no one questions the possibility of establishing *some* kind of correlation between introspective reports and brain states, the clinching of the theory would require some definite description or specification of the mental experiences. But it is dubious that, perhaps apart from elementary and artificially induced phenomena, mental experiences are susceptible of the precise kind of delimitation and identification required. Second, even if such a unique correlation (one-one or one-many) could be established, how could one establish that it is more than a correlation, that it is an identity? Apart from sheer

behavioral criteria for the ascription of consciousness.[55] Even if we could design a machine to simulate human behavior, e.g. carry on a conversation, one might say that, after all, just because it behaves as if it were conscious, this doesn't prove that it is conscious, because it is only behaving as we designed it to. (Scriven has called this the "argument from design.") [56] Others respond that, after all, the only ground for the ascription of consciousness to another is what we observe, so that if consciousness cannot be attributed to another on this basis, one is logically forced back to solipsism.[57] Even if it is granted that behavioral criteria are only a necessary and not a sufficient condition, the possibility must remain open that the corroborative weight of accumulated achievement in simulation will render nugatory any residual hesitation. If, as our technical capacity and our neurological knowledge increase, our robots exhibit a wider and wider range of sustained intelligent performance, doubt may become profitless.[58]

This last argument makes the decision appear to be an empirical one, and the philosophical argument between cybernetic anthropomorphists and their opponents to be a stand-off. If some machines are or can be intelligent beings then those machines will be able to exhibit all of the—or at least the essential [59]—performatory characteristics which distinguish men from other animals. The verification of this argument-form would be retroductive: consistent verification of its consequent and consistent failures to falsify that consequent would establish its reasonable plausibility, like that of evolution. The falsification of the argument would require the falsification of its consequent, i.e. the specification of some typically human behavior which no machine could exhibit.

At first glance, this latter requirement would seem to clinch the case for the proponents of the anthropomorphic position. For the model of neural networks developed by McCulloch and Pitts showed that in principle a network could be constructed—by appropriate interconnection and threshold determination of elements—to compute any specific input-output function. In the words of John Von Neuman: "Any functioning in this sense which can be defined at all logically, strictly and unambiguously in a finite number of words can also be realized by such a formal neural network." [60]

Not only did this theorem foreclose earlier efforts to specify neurological functions which were "too complex" for machines to perform, it also undercut all future objections of the form: "One stipulation or linguistic convention, how could we confirm that when process A occurs in my brain the thought B which accompanies it also occurs in my brain? [52]

It would seem, then—and this is a tentative evaluation in a still lively controversy—that this form of solution to the mind-body problem runs up against a verifiability limitation. Note that this conclusion would not affect one possibility in the mechanism-biologism argument, namely that of synthesizing a human being on the basis of the genetic code. It simply means that any such artificially produced human would require the same kind of two-levelled explanation alluded to in the previous paragraph (or three-levelled, if the mechanism-biologism dispute were settled in favor of the latter).

If we set these considerations aside for the moment and turn to the anthropomorphic side of the cybernetic hypothesis, a different, though related, set of questions and problems comes into view. Can we build machines (or build machines which will build machines) which will be able to do all the things which men can do: converse, solve problems, feel, recognize the same range of patterns, etc.? And if we do, can we refuse such machines the status of being persons?

Some would say that such questions are nonsensical, that after all such hypothetical automata are *machines*, put together piece by piece by us (or by other machines), built to function in certain ways. It has been claimed that we should not even speak of a computer counting, because computers "*do not perform mathematical operations* but only physical operations which we coordinate with mathematical operations." [53] Others respond that in such circumstances our refusal to extend mentalistic and personal predicates to a machine is unwarranted, a linguistic inhibition which needs to be loosened by extending our terms. If it sounds odd or "deviant" now to speak of machines thinking or being persons, they add that this does not entail that it will never become proper as machines continue to develop (or be developed), so that some time a "linguistic decision" to do so may emerge. [54]

To put this same disagreement in different terms, we can express it as the question of the commensurability of experience (or consciousness) and behavior. Some claim that there is an incommensurability, in the sense that being conscious or experiencing is not something we *do* and that there are therefore no adequate thing a machine can never do is X," provided the objector can tell us precisely what behavior he has in mind.

But the term 'precisely' in the last sentence raises a difficulty. It refers to the qualifying clause in Von Neuman's statement, namely, that the function be definable unambiguously in a finite number of terms. That this may constitute a problem is generally recognized.[61] The question here, however, is about the meaning of our difficulty, or indeed our inability, to construct a formal description or definition of the patterned units which mark off kinds of named behavior, or the variety of patterns we perceptually discriminate. If such an inability is based on sheer ignorance, it has no logical import. Kenneth Sayre has taken it in this sense. Any act of which all men are capable, he argues, either is or is not clearly understood. "If it is not clearly understood, then no clear meaning can be attached to the claim that all men but no machines can accomplish it," while if it is clearly understood, i.e. logically specifiable, then it can be computed by a suitable finite automaton.[62]

As we have seen earlier, there is a recurring difficulty in the field of artificial intelligence which is related to this problem. It is that the attempt to articulate formal criteria in order to specify machine tasks and procedures (in game-playing, pattern recognition, translation, etc.) runs up against the fact that our ability to recognize patterns, transform sentences and so forth, relies on a tacit employment of cues and information which we are unable to reflectively spell out or describe. When we try to say how we do certain things, we produce at best hints or guidelines or piecemeal criteria. We can see what it is we do—e.g. read or parse a sentence—but we cannot say adequately how we do it.

For example, Von Neuman has remarked that nobody would attempt to define, in any practicable compass, the "general concept of analogy which dominates our interpretation of vision," say, as we move from badly drawn Euclidean triangles to convex and concave triangles, to triangles composed of dots, of different triangulated landscapes, etc. Consequently, he argues, it may be that

it is futile to look for a precise logical concept, that is, for a precise verbal description, or "visual analogy." It is possible that the connection pattern of the visual brain itself is the simplest logical expression of this principle.

Obviously, there is on this level no more profit in the McCulloch-Pitts result.[63]

Briefly stated, then, our problem is this: although the brain (nervous system) is, hypothetically, a neural network and therefore instantiates a formal system, our conscious experience of perceiving and doing appears to function informally, i.e. without explicit awareness of the elements which are integrated into its processes. We deal with similarities (analogous figures, novel sentences) which we are unable to express as identities, i.e. as elements of a formal system.

Claude Shannon has commented on this as an obstacle in simulation work:

. . . Efficient machines for such problems as pattern recognition, language translation and so on, may require a different type of computer than any we have today. It is my feeling that this computer will be so organized that single components do not carry out simple, easily described functions. . . . Can we design . . . a computer whose natural operation is in terms of patterns, concepts and vague similarities, rather than sequential operations on ten-digit numbers? [64]

But if to be a machine is to instantiate a formal system, with identity and substitutivity of elements and well-defined rules of formation and transformation, how could we define "vague similarities" for it? It is easy to see why Von Neuman was tempted to fall back on the neural connection pattern of the brain as the "simplest" response to such questions.

Although this disparity of "logics" of the mind and the brain represents a hiatus which no one at present sees how to overcome, it rests on more than simple ignorance of how we do what we do. We can see that the explicit, step-by-step procedures of a formal system cannot produce the results aimed at in machine simulation of human performance and that consciousness cannot therefore be conceived as a "purely passive property," a "display device" for what goes on in the brain.[65] On the contrary, conscious experience involves an activity of informal integration by which subsidiary and marginal elements are fused with focal elements to form a patterned awareness.

Recent work in psychology has drawn attention to a very wide range of such marginal components of consciousness, some of which can be experimentally isolated and identified by measuring devices, but which, although they clearly play a role in the voluntary behavior of subjects, are not susceptible of being brought to explicit consciousness. One investigator has spoken of such components as belonging to the "inferable conscious." [66] Michael Polanyi has for some years been developing the thesis that all human activity rests on such indefinable elements, and that without relying on such tacit awareness, no focal or explicit knowledge would be possible.[67] Let me try to explicate this distinction in terms of the contrast between tactile and visual perceptions.

Von Senden's work on patients born blind who were able to see after operations leaves no doubt that forms (*Gestalten*), are immediately discriminated by the patients in their visual fields. Although recognition, even of simple geometrical shapes, was slow and required learning, visual wholes were spontaneously apprehended. It appears true, in general, that in vision the total form represents the starting point for any analytic articulation of the parts. The total form guides the visual analysis into primary and subordinate parts and makes possible the discrimination between parts and "noise" (in the information-theoretic sense).

In tactile perception, on the other hand quite different conditions hold, as Revesz has emphasized in his notable study on *Psychology and Art of the Blind*. In tactile perception, "the structure, the spatial arrangement and mutual relationship of the parts have to be brought into consciousness intentionally by strenuous work." [68] Subordinate parts with special importance may become the center of attention because of their size or material peculiarities, since the parts are given sequentially and are more or less structurally independent. "Noise" cannot be excluded as irrelevant until an overall organization is achieved by synthesis. Indeed for this reason Revesz' blind subjects proved completely incapable of deciphering relief sculptures.

On the basis of his experiments, Revesz was led to distinguish between two kinds of perceptual wholes: synthetic or summated wholes and formal wholes. Since the summated whole "sums up the spatial arrangement of the examined parts as a result of intuition and intellectual work, that summing up presupposes an act of conscious arrangement, as becomes manifest in the eventual product." The formal whole however is "given spontaneously as an individual unity and does not require any conscious arrangement of structure"; rather it is "conditioned by unconscious formative factors." [69] Succession and synthesis govern tactile perception, simultaneity and spontaneous unanalyzed wholes dominate visual perception.

(From a physiological point of view, one might want to argue that, presumably, successivity is involved in vision also, perhaps something like scanning of the visual cortex. But this would not advance the task of simulation [as distinct from replication of the biological structure], since it leaves one with the problem of dealing with summated wholes and explicit criteria of recognition in order to discriminate wholes which we perceive physiognomically. As before, the question is whether we can do this without encountering the limitation envisaged by Von Neuman.)

Some of the most interesting programs which have been written —e.g. Evan's program for the recognition of analogical figures of the type used in intelligence testing—clearly exemplify what has been described above as tactile perception. [70] The topological relations of the figures are spelled out by explicit statements and similarities (partial identities) are matched. Marvin Minsky, in describing the program, remarks that "rules or procedures of the same general character are involved in any kind of analogical reasoning." [71] I agree with this, but I think it is just the reasoning (i.e. ratiocinative) character of the process which embodies its weakness as well as its power. Let me try to state what I mean here as clearly as possible.

I am not arguing that human beings reason in a better or "higher" way than a machine can. If anything I am rather inclined to the contrary view that insofar as machines approach human performance in recognition it will be through faster and more precise logical processes than men are capable of. It is precisely this that seems to me to be required in order to supplement the multitudinous character of sequential or "tactile" input. And it is this also that constitutes the intellectual challenge and excitement of simulation work, trying to find a structural and formal equivalent for tacit processes.

In discussing a person suffering from lesions in the occipital region and deficiencies of vision, M. Merleau-Ponty remarks on the subject's inability to understand simple verbal analogies unless he can find and state a middle term which establishes the identity of the two relationships. But, he adds, "if we describe analogy as the apperception of two given terms under a coordinating concept, we should be giving as normal a procedure which is exclusively patho-logical." ("Exclusively" overstates the case, since even in normal subjects explicit analysis may be necessary to confirm or discern analogies in complicated cases.) Merleau-Ponty's reason is that "It is easier for the normal patient to understand the analogy than to analyze it, whereas the patient manages to understand only when he has made it explicit by recourse to conceptual analysis." [72]

The fundamental problem, involved in this contrast between tactile and visual perception, and underlying all simulation work in the basal area of recognition, is that of assigning instances to a category. Until we can conceive of a machine which can deal with "vague similarities" (as digital computers cannot) there will be an elementary difficulty facing the machine simulation of such assign-ments.

This difficulty can be put as follows. Any attempt to specify ex-plicit criteria for membership in a class on the basis of a comparison of instances of the class must rely on the pre-criterial collection of such instances. Consequently, no set of criteria can ever be declared to be complete, since by virtue of the way in which it is constituted, it leaves open the possibility (short of stipulative definition) that other instances may be adduced on the same implicit grounds as those of the original collection. Recognition has an "open texture" [73] which resists the closure implied by criterial classification.

W. V. O. Quine, in a recent discussion of this "inscrutability of categorical," seems to follow Kant in attributing to undefined native powers the ability to identify specimens of a class.[74] More generally, Wittgenstein, arguing at length for the inexactness of our language, claimed that we cannot justify our uses of terms by grounding those uses on necessary and sufficient criteria. It is possible, he thought, to be justified in saying, e.g. on the basis of certain behavior that a man has a toothache, even though no strict entailment holds be-tween the behavior and having a toothache.[75] Such justification ap-pears to be based, in his view, on a fact of natural history: "Here we strike rock bottom, that is we have come down to conventions." [76]

R. W. Newell has explored the logical ground of this type of justification and argued persuasively for its validity, despite its lack of either inductive or deductive form.[77] But at best, it seems to me, he only establishes that we *do* accept as reasonable in such cases the offering of considerations which while not a proof in a strictly logical sense are still (to quote J. S. Mill) "capable of determining the intellect either to give or to withhold its assent," [78] and that we cannot not do so without abandoning our "form of life."

It is the merit of Polanyi to have faced the fact of our capacity to recognize specimens of an empirical class as something requiring an explanation and to have proposed one. Rejecting (as does Merleau-Ponty) the suggestion that identification which goes beyond the given guarantees (i.e. which is not strictly entailed by the explicit observational data) is grounded only on conventions or is only a "verbal recommendation," he contends that a multitude of unspecifiable clues may enter into an act of identification. Such an act represents a particular instance of "tacit knowing," which always involves the contribution of subsidiary elements to the meaning of the object to which we are attending. In many cases, the subsidiary elements cannot be isolated and rendered explicit—hence the term "unspecifiable."

I cannot review here the wide-ranging examples and arguments by which Polanyi seeks to validate the comprehensiveness of his analysis. [79] Nor is it necessary to do so for the sake of my argument here. The difficulty alluded to above concerning the manner in which a set of criteria is established stands on its own, I believe, whatever its explanation; and the evidence for the role that implicit information can play in behavioral discrimination is secure, whatever its scope may turn out to be.

Moreover, if we fall back on Von Neuman's proposal that at least the brain is an "existence-proof" for the possibility of a neural-network which could compute all human functions, a question remains. If any machine must instantiate a formal system, and if the behavior in question functions only by use of an informal logic, can we simply assume that when a finite automation is as complex and richly interconnected as the brain it will begin to function informally? Presumably this is what happened at some stage in man's evolution. But this presumption, of course, as Chomsky remarked, merely expresses our confidence that there is a naturalistic explanation for the apparent discontinuity.

Our inability to specify wide ranges of human behavior "at all logically, strictly and unambiguously in a finite number of words" is thus not due to sheer ignorance. It is not an unsolved problem which we might yet hope to unpack, relying wholly on formal and explicit procedures. It is, rather, a Socratic or learned ignorance which recognizes what human experience is not, while unable to render explicit what it is.

This Gordian knot of artificial persons may be severed, if not unravelled, by biologists working with germ cells artificially stimulated to replicate a given DNA code. We may indeed, that is, produce human beings artificially by working with biological materials. And we certainly will have automata which will simulate and hence take over many presently human functions. These automata will be, I suspect, like Aristotle's natural slaves: exhibiting some quasi-intelligent kinds of behavior, but without the flexibility and range of biological persons. Man will draw, partially at least, machines into the human community in the manner in which, thousands of years ago, he first domesticated and then drew some alien animals partially into the human world and "tamed" them to become his companions. The presence of intelligent machines will no doubt bring about a similar change in his way of life.

NOTES

1. Descartes, Principia Philosophie IV, 203; Les principes de la philosophie, trad. Picot, *Oeuvres de Descartes* vol III (Paris: Levrault 1824), p. 519: ". . . je ne reconnois aucune différence entre les machines qui font les artisans, et les divers corps que la nature compose . . ."
2. Lucretius refers once or twice to simple machines such as pulleys, and once extends the term to the cosmos as a whole: *machina mundi; De Rerum Natura,* V, 96.
3. E. Rignano, *Man not a Machine* (London: K. Paul, Trench, Trubner & Co., 1926), p. 17 quoted in A. Vartanian, *La Mettries L'homme machine* (Princeton, N.J.: Princeton, 1960), p. 133.
   Vartanian has an excellent survey of the history of this controversy since La Mettrie.
4. *Iliad* 2.408, 18.376.
5. *Generation of Animals,* II, 1, 734b10. These are also referred to in the treatise on mechanics attributed to him, and appear to have been devices in which one part, once put in motion, communicated its motion serially to a number of other parts, and so continued to "move itself" after the first part was stilled.

6. *Politics*, I, 4, 1253b36, a reference to the latter Homeric passage cited above and to the statues of Daedelos. Cf. *de Anima*, I, 3, 406b15–20 and Plato, *Meno*, 97d and *Euthyphro*, 11b.
7. René Descartes, *Discours de la methode*, V in *Oeuvres de Descartes*, ed. Adam-Tannery (Paris: L. Cerf, 1897–1910), VI pp. 55–6. Cf. the commentary of E. Gilson on Descartes, *Discours de la methode, Texte et commentaire*, avec introd. et notes par Etienne Gilson (Paris: J. Vren, 1935), pp. 420–25.
8. *Traité de l'homme* in *ibid*. XI, pp. 130–32.
9. *a Mersenne* in *ibid*., I, p. 25; *Princ. Philos.*, IV, 203 in *ibid*., VIII, p. 326.
10. Wm. Harvey, *Exercitatio anatomica de motu cordis et sanguinis in animalibus*, 1628.
11. Gomes Pereira, *Margarita-Antoniana* (Medina del campo, 1554), discussed briefly in F. Bouillier, *Histoire de la philosophie cartesienna* (Paris: C. Delagrave, 1868), I, p. 153. Descartes did not know this work.
12. The keenness of Descartes was to see and say once and for all that mind cannot be consubstantial with the body thus conceived.
13. When he is laying out his theory, and not simply responding to particular objections, he almost always couples its presentation with an allusion to the difference between God's handiwork and man's. Cf. for example *Princ. philos.*, *loc. cit.*
14. See the discussion of this in M. Polanyi, "Life Beyond Physics and Chemistry" in *Chemical and Engineering News*, XLV, no. 35 (Aug. 21, 1967), pp. 54–66 and the references there cited.
15. E.g. *Principles*, 1me partie, art. 28. Cf. Bouillier, *op. cit.*, p. 174. This question is embedded in a theological controversy about the immortality of the soul: cf. the references and discussion in Gilson, *op. cit.*
16. *Meditationes*, II. *Discours* V; A.–T., VI, pp. 56–58. Descartes adds a second criterion, the flexibility of human behavior in general, but I shall omit consideration of this for the present. La Mettrie suggests that Descartes really believed man is a machine too, but abstained from declaring this explicitly because of fear of persecution.
17. It is interesting that when Camus and Sartre want to stress the strangeness of human behavior, they utilize the instance of watching someone in a telephone booth, whose words cannot be heard, and that Sartre's famous analysis of *le regard* is a silent encounter with another.
18. Cf. *a Mersenne* 8 Oct. 1629, A.–T., I, p. 25. On language as verbal behavior cf. B. F. Skinner, *Verbal Behavior* (New York: Appleton-Century-Crofts, 1957) and the critique of this position in N. Chomsky, *Cartesian Linguistics* (New York, Harper & Row, 1966).

19. M. Scriven, "The Compleat Robot: A Prolegomena to Androidology," see *infra*, pp. 117–40. The Cartesian disciple is Chanet, quoted in Bouillier, *op. cit.*, p. 152, n. 3.

20. The term 'robot' entered into English in 1923 through the play of the Czech dramatist Karel Capek, *R.U.R.* (Rossum's Universal Robots). The Czech word 'robotnik' meant slave or serf.

21. For a superbly written survey of these points and their application to a computer model of the brain, see D. E. Wooldridge, *The Machinery of the Brain* (New York: McGraw-Hill, 1963).

22. For a lucid elementary presentation of the logical structure of neuron networks, cf. W. S. McCulloch "Finality and Form" in *Embodiments of Mind* (Cambridge: M.I.T. 1965), pp. 256–75. More technical discussions of this topic are contained in other essays in the same book. For a mathematical treatment accessible to the intelligent layman, cf. M. Arbib, *Brains, Machines and Mathematics* (New York: McGraw-Hill, 1964).

23. Cf. *infra*, pp. 81–115. Note that as the title of Samuel's article indicates, he was concerned with machine learning as well as game-playing.

24. Cf. A. Bernstein and M. de V. Roberts, "Computer vs. Chess Player," *Scientific American*, CXCVIII (1958), 96–105.

25. See the discussion and proposals in A. Newell, "The Chess Machine" in *The Modeling of Mind*, ed. K. Sayre and F. Crosson (Notre Dame: Univ. of Notre Dame Press, 1963), pp. 74–89.

26. Wang discusses the alternatives in "Toward Mechanical Mathematics" in *ibid.*, pp. 94–95.

27. Actually the problem as described has been shifted from that of recognition to that of classification. For a critical discussion of this and a survey of the field, cf. K. Sayre, *Recognition: A Study in the Philosophy of Artificial Intelligence* (Notre Dame: Univ. of Notre Dame Press, 1965).

28. Cf. L. Uhr, C. Vossler, "A Pattern-Recognition Machine that Generates, Evaluates and Adjusts its Own Operators" in *Computers and Thought*, ed. E. A. Feigenbaum and J. Feldman (New York: McGraw-Hill, 1963), pp. 251–268; O. G. Selfridge and U. Neisser "Pattern Recognition by Machine" in *ibid.*, pp. 237–50; W. M. MacKay, "The Epistemological Problem for Automata" in *Automata Studies*, eds. C. Shannon and T. McCarthy (Princeton, N. J.: Princeton, 1956). Marvin Minsky comments that a number of earlier experiments on self-organizing "failed because of excessive reliance on random trial and error"; "Artificial Intelligence" in *Scientific American*, CCXV (Sept., 1966), 260.

29. See the description of this program in Minsky, *art. cit.* and the

critical discussion in R. Arnheim, "Intelligence Simulated," *Midway*, VIII (June, 1967), 81–89.

30. Reprinted in C. Shannon and W. Weaver, *The Mathematical Theory of Communication* (Urbana: University of Illinois Press, 1963).

31. For a relatively nontechnical exposition of the ideas of information theory and a discussion of its relation to "meaning," cf. F. J. Crosson "Information Theory and Phenomenology" in *Philosophy and Cybernetics*, eds. F. J. Crosson and K. Sayre (Notre Dame: University of Notre Dame Press, 1967), pp. 99–136.

32. F. Attnaeve, *Applications of Information Theory to Psychology* (New York: Holt, Rinehart and Winston, 1959), p. 83.

33. G. A. Miller, "The Magical Number Seven, Plus or Minus Two," *Psychological Review*, LXIII (1956), 81–97.

34. As Mortimer Taubes observes, "In ordinary grammatical studies a sentence is analyzed to show *how* the meaning has been expressed, not to determine *what* the meaning is." M. Taubes, *Computers and Common Sense* (New York: McGraw-Hill, 1961), p. 36.

35. For the computer print-out of the analysis of this example and discussion of it, cf. A. G. Oettinger, "The Uses of Computers in Science," *Scientific American, loc. cit.*, p. 168.

36. *Ibid.*, p. 169. A recent survey has even called into question the practical value of man-machine interaction in translation: D. B. Orr and V. H. Small, "Comprehensibility of Machine-Aided Translation of Russian Scientific Documents," *Machine Translation*, X (March and June, 1967), 1–10.

37. N. Chomsky, "Language and the Mind," *Psychology Today*, I (February, 1968), p. 66. For further references cf. the bibliography, *ibid.*, p. 71.

38. H. Savin and E. Perchonock, "Grammatical Structure and the Immediate Recall of English Sentences," *Journal of Verbal Learning and Verbal Behavior*, IV (1965), 348–53.

39. Chomsky, *art. cit.*, p. 68. His argument is developed with reference to earlier theories of language in *Cartesian Linguistics* (New York: Harper & Row, 1966).

40. Chomsky, *art. cit.*, p. 68.

41. *On the Motion of Animals*, 707b9–10. For a discussion of this heuristic principle and numerous examples, cf. G. Canguilhem, "The Role of Analogies and Models in Biological Discovery" in *Scientific Change*, ed. A. C. Crombie (New York: Basic Books, 1963), pp. 507–20.

42. "It was already known by common experience what was meant by a reservoir, a canal, a level, or a hinge, when, as a simple comparison,

it was said that the bladder must be a reservoir for the purpose of containing liquids, that the arteries and veins were canals destined to conduct fluids, that the bones and joints played the part of scaffolding, hinges, levers, etc." C. Bernard, *Leçons de physiologie expérimentale appliquée a la medecine* (Paris: J. B. Bailliere, 1850), quoted in Canguilhem, *art. cit.*, p. 509.

43. For a survey, cf. R. F. Hefferline, "Learning Theory and Clinical Psychology—An Eventual Symbiosis" in A. J. Bachrach (ed.), *Experimental Foundations of Clinical Psychology* (New York: Basic Books, 1962), pp. 97–138.

44. For an elaborate theory of biological and psychological explanation, encompassing humor and scientific discovery, and built on this model of sub-routines triggered off by a code-signal, cf. A. Koestler, *The Act of Creation* (New York: Macmillan, 1964).

45. Cf. W. Grey Walter, *The Living Brain* (London: Duckworth, 1953).

46. W. S. McCulloch and W. Pitts, "A Logical Calculus of the Ideas Immanent in Nervous Activity," *Bulletin of Mathematical Biophysics,* V (1943), 115–33; "How We Know Universals—the Perception of Auditory and Visual Forms" in *ibid.*, IX (1947), 124–47.

47. For a discussion of such differences, cf. J. Von Neuman, *The Computer and the Brain* (New Haven: Yale, 1958).

48. These similarities are described and discussed in the excellent work of D. E. Wooldridge referred to earlier, *The Machinery of the Brain* and in his later book *Mechanical Man* (New York: McGraw-Hill, 1968). Herbert Feigl, in his comprehensive survey of the mind-body problem, lists ten unresolved central questions in psychophysiology: "The 'Mental' and the 'Physical' " in *Minnesota Studies in the Philosophy of Science,* Vol. II (Minneapolis: University of Minnesota Press, 1958), pp. 479–83.

49. *The Difference of Man and the Difference it Makes* (New York: Holt, Rinehart and Winston, 1967).

50. *Ibid.*, pp. 41–42.

51. Cf. H. Feigl, *art. cit.* for a presentation of this theory and M. Adler *op. cit.*, p. 335 for a recent bibliography of the controversy.

52. Cf. N. Malcolm, "Scientific Materialism and the Identity Theory," *Dialogue,* III (1964), 120: ". . . no one has any notion of what it would mean to test for the occurrence of the thought inside my skull independently of testing for a brain process. The idea of such a test is not intelligible."

53. M. Bunge, "Do Computers Think," *British Journal for Philosophy of Science,* VII (1956), 142. Cf. also M. Scriven, "The Mechanical Concept of Mind" in *The Modeling of Mind* and A. Danto, "On

Consciousness in Machines" in *Dimensions of Mind*, p. 168. (For Scriven's later views, cf. *infra*, pp. 117–40.)

54. Cf. the essays of Danto and Putnam in *Dimensions of Mind*, and A. R. Louch, *Explanation and Human Action* (Oxford: Blackwell, 1966), pp. 130–33.

55. E.g. M. Taubes, *op. cit.*, p. 35; N. Moray, *Cybernetics* (New York: Hawthorn, 1963), pp. 112–13.

56. Cf. "The Compleat Robot," *infra*, p. 137.

57. Cf. A. M. Turing, "Computing Machinery and Intelligence," *Mind*, LIX (1950), 433–60.

58. Scriven, *ibid.*

59. Adler, *op. cit.*, considers speech alone to be a decisive characteristic.

60. J. H. Von Neuman, "The General and Logical Theory of Automata" in *The World of Mathematics*, ed. J. R. Newman (New York: Random House, 1956), vol. IV, p. 2090.

61. E.g. D. M. MacKay, "On Comparing the Brain with Machines," *The American Scientist*, XLII (1954), 263; N. Moray, *op. cit.*, pp. 113–17.

62. K. M. Sayre, "Philosophy and Cybernetics" in *Philosophy and Cybernetics* (Notre Dame: Univ. of Notre Dame Press, 1967), p. 25.

63. *Art. cit.*, p. 2091.

64. *Computers and the World of the Future*, ed. M. Greenberger (Cambridge, Mass.: M.I.T. Press, 1962), pp. 309–10.

65. Wooldridge, *op. cit.*, pp. 219–20.

66. G. Razran, "The Observable Unconscious and the Inferable Conscious," *Psychological Review*, LXVIII (1961), 81–147. Cf. note 41, *supra*.

67. Cf. especially M. Polanyi, *Personal Knowledge* (Chicago: Univ. of Chicago Press, 1958) and *The Tacit Dimension* (London: Routledge and Kegan Paul, 1967).

68. G. Revesz, *Psychology and Art of the Blind* (London: Longmans Green, 1950), p. 84. Even where the object is small enough to fit in the hand, successivity of perceptions dominates: p. 61.

69. *Ibid.*, pp. 86, 87.

70. Cf. M. Minsky, "Artificial Intelligence," *Scientific American*, CCXV, Sept. 1966.

71. *Ibid.*, p. 250.

72. M. Merleau-Ponty, *Phenomonology of Perception* (New York: Humanities, 1962), p. 128. Note the protocols of the subject's identification of an object: he "runs his fingers over an angle several times: 'My fingers,' he says, 'move straight along, then stop, and then move off again in another direction; it is an angle, it must be a right angle.'

—'Two, three, four angles, the sides are each two centimetres long, so they are all equal, all the angles are right angles . . . It's a dice'." (For a similar report, cf. *ibid.*, p. 131), p. 107n. I have frequently observed such a spontaneous verbalizing of the analysis in experiments of my own with blindfolded subjects.

73. Cf. F. Waismann, "Verifiability," *Proceeding of the Aristotelian Society Supplement,* 1945.
74. In S. Koch (Chm.), "Logic and Psychology." Symposium presented at the meeting of the American Psychological Association, Washington, D.C., Sept. 1967. Cf. Kant, *Critique of Pure Reason*, A141.
75. Cf. R. Albritton, "On Wittgenstein's Use of the Term 'Criterion' " in G. Pitcher (ed.), *Wittgenstein: The Philosophical Investigation* (New York: 1966), p. 246.
76. L. Wittgenstein, *The Blue and Brown Books* (New York: Harper, 1958), p. 24.
77. R. W. Newell, *The Concept of Philosophy* (London: Methuen, 1967).
78. *Ibid.*, p. 132.
79. For a recent statement, cf. M. Polanyi, "Logic and Psychology," *American Psychologist*, XXIII, no. 1 (Jan., 1968), pp. 27–43.

2 Information processing in computer and man

HERBERT A. SIMON

ALLEN NEWELL

This paper, by two of the most prominent workers in the field of artificial intelligence, may be taken as a "position paper" which enunciates some of the basic assumptions underlying work in simulation. Among these assumptions are: that man is aptly characterized as an information processing system; that we can simulate human performance by identifying the input and output of the system, and hence determine the computed function which transforms input to output; that information (as Norbert Wiener put it) "is not matter and is not energy," and hence the possibility of simulation is independent of the material in which the processing is effected, so that simulation does not have to wait on replication of biological structure. The authors go on to make the stronger claim that the way in which the human being processes information is highly similar to computer procedures. Samuel has some comments on the problematic character of this similarity in his essay.

These assumptions or hypotheses are discussed with reference to chess-playing programs and the elementary processing procedures which seem to be involved.

Herbert A. Simon and Allen Newell are both at

Reprinted with permission from *American Scientist,* Vol. 52, No. 3 (1964), pp. 281–300.

Carnegie-Mellon University: the former is Professor of Administration and Psychology in the Graduate School of Industrial Administration, and the latter is University Professor of Systems and Communication Sciences.

Organizing a computer to perform complex tasks depends very much more upon the characteristics of the task environment than upon the "hardware"—the specific physical means for realizing the processing in the computer. Thus, all past and present digital computers perform basically the same kinds of symbol manipulations.

In programing a computer it is substantially irrelevant what physical processes and devices—electromagnetic, electronic, or what not—accomplish the manipulations. A program, written in one of the symbolic programing languages, like ALGOL or FORTRAN, will produce the same symbolic output on a machine that uses electron tubes for processing and storing symbols, one that incorporates magnetic drums, one with a magnetic core memory, or one with completely transistorized circuitry. The program, the organization of symbol-manipulating processes, is what determines the transformation of input into output. In fact, provided with only the program output, and without information about the processing speed, one cannot determine what kinds of physical devices accomplished the transformations: whether the program was executed by a solid-state computer, and electron-tube device, an electrical relay machine, or a room full of statistical clerks! Only the organization of the processes is determinate. Out of this observation arises the possibility of an independent science of information processing.

By the same token, since the thinking human being is also an information processor, it should be possible to study his processes and their organization independently on the details of the biological mechanisms—the "hardware"—that implement them. The output of the processes, the behavior of *Homo cogitans*, should reveal how the information processing is organized, without necessarily providing much information about the protoplasmic structures or biochemical processes that implement it. From this observation follows the possibility of constructing and testing psychological theories to explain human thinking in terms of the organization of information processes; and of accomplishing this without waiting until the neurophysiological foundations at the next lower level of explanation have been constructed.

Finally, there is a growing body of evidence that the elementary information processes used by the human brain in thinking are highly similar to a subset of the elementary information processes that are incorporated in the instruction codes of present-day computers. As a consequence it has been found possible to test information-processing theories of human thinking by formulating these theories as computer programs—organizations of the elementary information processes—and examining the outputs of computers so programed. The procedure assumes no similarity between computer and brain at the "hardware" level, only similarity in their capacities for executing and organizing elementary information processes. From this hypothesis has grown up a fruitful collaboration between research in "artificial intelligence," aimed at enlarging the capabilities of computers, and research in human cognitive psychology.

These, then, are the three propositions on which this discussion rests:

(1) A science of information processing can be constructed that is substantially independent of the specific properties of particular information processing mechanisms.

(2) Human thinking can be explained in information-processing terms without waiting for a theory of the underlying neurological mechanisms.

(3) Information-processing theories of human thinking can be formulated in computer programing languages, and can be tested by simulating the predicted behavior with computers.

LEVELS OF EXPLANATION

No apology is needed for carrying explanation only to an intermediate level, leaving further reduction to the future progress of science. The other sciences provide numerous precedents, perhaps the most relevant being nineteenth-century chemistry. The atomic theory and the theory of chemical combination were invented and developed rapidly and fruitfully during the first three-quarters of the nineteenth century—from Dalton, through Kekulé, to Mendeleev

—without any direct physical evidence for or description of atoms, molecules, or valences. To quote Pauling:

> Most of the general principles of molecular structure and the nature of the chemical bond were formulated long ago by chemists by induction from the great body of chemical facts. . . .
> The study of the structure of molecules was originally carried on by chemists using methods of investigation that were essentially chemical in nature, relating to the chemical composition of substances, the existence of isomers, the nature of the chemical reactions in which a substance takes part, and so on. From the consideration of facts of this kind Frankland, Kekulé, Couper, and Butlerov were led a century ago to formulate the theory of valence and to write the first structural formulas for molecules, van't Hoff and le Bel were led to bring classical organic stereochemistry into its final form by their brilliant postulate of the tetrahedral orientation of the four valence bonds of the carbon atom, and Werner was led to his development of the theory of the stereochemistry of complex inorganic substances.[1]

The history this passage outlines is worth pondering, because the last generation of psychologists has engaged in so much methodological dispute about the nature, utility, and even propriety, of theory. The vocal methodologically self-conscious, behaviorist wing of experimental psychology has expressed its scepticism of "unobserved entities" and "intermediate constructs." [2] Sometimes it has seemed to object to filling the thinking head with anything whatsoever. Psychologists who rejected the empty-head viewpoint, but who were sensitive to the demand for operational constructs tended to counter the behaviorist objections by couching their theories in physiological language.[3]

The example of atomic theory in chemistry shows that neither horn of this dilemma need be seized. On the one hand, hypothetical entities, postulated because they were powerful and fruitful for organizing experimental evidence, proved exceedingly valuable in that science, and did not produce objectionable metaphysics. Indeed, they were ultimately legitimized in the present century by "direct" physical evidence.

On the other hand, the hypothetical entities of atomic theory initially had no *physical* properties (other than weight) that could explain why they behaved as they did. While an electrical theory of atomic attraction predated valence theory, the former hypothesis actually impeded the development of the latter and had to be discredited before the experimental facts could fall into place. The valence of the mid-century chemist was a "chemical affinity" without any underlying physical mechanism. So it remained for more than half a century until the electron-shell theory was developed by Lewis and others to explain it.

Paralleling this example from chemistry, information-processing theories of human thinking employ unobserved entities—symbols—and unobserved processes—elementary information processes. The theories provide explanations of behavior that are mechanistic without being physiological. That they are mechanistic—that they postulate only processes capable of being effected by mechanism—is guaranteed by simulating the behavior predicted on ordinary digital computers. (See the Appendix, "Computer Programs as Theories.") Simulation provides a basis for testing the predictions of the theories, but does not imply that the protoplasm in the brain resembles the electronic components of the computer.

A SPECIFIC INFORMATION-PROCESSING THEORY: PROBLEM SOLVING IN CHESS

Information-processing theories have been constructed for several kinds of behavior, and undertake to explain behavior in varying degrees of detail. As a first example, we consider a theory that deals with a rather narrow and special range of human problem-solving skill, attempting to explain the macroscopic organization of thought in a particular task environment.

Good chess players often detect strategies—called in chess, "combinations"—that impose a loss of a piece or a checkmate on the opponent over a series of moves, no matter what the latter does in reply. In actual game positions where a checkmating possibility exists, a strong player may spend a quarter hour or more discovering it, and verifying the correctness of his strategy. In doing so, he may have to look ahead four or five moves, or even more.[4] If the combination is deep, weaker players may not be able to discover it at all, even after protracted search. How do good players solve such problems? How do they find combinations?

A theory now exists that answers these questions in some detail. First, I shall describe what it asserts about the processes going on in the mind of the chess player as he studies the position before him, and what it predicts about his progress in discovering an effective strategy. Then we can see to what extent it accounts for the observed facts. The actual theory is a computer program couched in a list-processing language, called Information Processing Language V (IPL-V). Our account of the theory will be an English-language translation of the main features of the program.[5]

The statement of the theory has five main parts. The first two of these specify the way in which the chess player stores in memory his representation of the chess position, and his representation of the moves he is considering, respectively. The remaining parts of the theory specify the processes he has available for extracting information from these representations and using that information: processes for discovering relations among the pieces and squares of the chess position, for synthesizing chess moves for consideration, and for organizing his search among alternative move sequences. We shall describe briefly each of these five parts of the theory.

The theory asserts, first of all, that *the human chess player has means for storing internally, in his brain, encoded representations of the stimuli presented to him.* In the case of a highly schematized stimulus like a chess position, the internal symbolic structure representing it can be visualized as similar to the printed diagram used to represent it in a chess book. The internal representation employs symbols that name the squares and the pieces, and symbolizes the relations among squares, among pieces, and between squares and pieces.

For example, the internal representation symbolizes rather explicitly that a piece on the King's squares is a Knight's-move away, in a SSW direction, from a piece on the third rank of the Queen's file. Similarly, if the King's Knight is on the King's Bishop's Third square (KB3), the representation associates the symbol designating the Knight with the symbol designating the KB3 square, and the symbol designating the square with that designating the Knight. On the other hand, the representation does not symbolize directly that two pieces stand on the same diagonal. Relations like this must be discovered or inferred from the representation by the processes to be discussed below.

Asserting that a position is symbolized internally in this way does not mean that the internal representations are verbal (any more than the diagrams in a chess book are verbal). It would be more appropriate, in fact, to describe the representations as a "visual image," provided that this phrase is not taken to imply that the chess player has any conscious explicit image of the entire board in his "mind's eye."

The chess player also has means for representing in memory the moves he is considering. He has symbol-manipulating processes that enable him, from his representations of a position and of a move, to use the latter to modify the former—the symbolic structure that describes the position—into a new structure that represents what the position would be *after* the move. The same processes enable him to "unmake" a move—to symbolize the position as it was before the move was considered. Thus, if the move that transfers the King's Knight from his original square (KN1) to the King's Bishop's Third square (KB3) is stored in memory, the processes in question can alter the representation of the board by changing the name of the square associated with Knight from KN1 to KB3, and conversely for unmaking the move.

The chess player has processes that enable him to discover new relations in a position, to symbolize these, and to store the information in memory. For example, in a position he is studying (whether the actual one on the board, or one he has produced by considering moves), he can discover whether his King is in check—attacked by an enemy man; or whether a specified piece can move to a specified square; or whether a specified man is defended. The processes for detecting such relations are usually called perceptual processes. They are characterized by the fact that they are relatively direct: they obtain the desired information from the representation with a relatively small amount of manipulation.

The chess player has processes, making use of the perceptual processes, that permit him to generate or synthesize for his consideration moves with specified properties—for example, to generate all moves that will check the enemy King. To generate moves having desired characteristics may require a considerable amount of processing. If this were not so, if any kind of move could be discovered effortlessly, the entire checkmating program would consist of the single elementary process: DISCOVER CHECKMATING MOVES.

An example of these more complex, indirect processes is a procedure that would discover certain forking moves (moves that attack two pieces simultaneously) somewhat as follows:

Find the square of the opposing Queen. Find all squares that lie a Knight's-move from this square. Determine for each of these squares whether it is defended (whether an opposing piece can move to it). If not, test all squares a Knight's-move away from it to see if any of them has a piece that is undefended or that is more valuable than a Knight.

Finally, the chess player has processes for organizing a search for mating combinations through the "tree" of possible move sequences. This search makes use of the processes already enumerated, and proceeds as follows:

The player generates all the checking moves available to him in the given position, and for each checking move, generates the legal replies open to his opponent. If there are no checking moves, he concludes that no checkmating combination can be discovered in the position, and stops his search. If, for one of the checking moves, he discovers there are no legal replies, he concludes that the checking move in question is a checkmate. If, for one of the checking moves, he discovers that the opponent has more than four replies, he concludes that this checking move is unpromising, and does not explore it further.

Next, the player considers all the checking moves (a) that he has not yet explored and (b) that he has not yet evaluated as "CHECKMATE" or "NO MATE." He selects the move that is most promising—by criteria to be mentioned presently—and pushes his analysis of that move one move deeper. That is, he considers each of its replies in turn, generates the checking moves available after those replies, and the replies to those checking moves. He applies the criteria of the previous paragraph to attach "CHECKMATE" or "NO MATE" labels to the moves when he can. He also "propagates" these labels to antecedent moves. For example, a reply is labeled CHECKMATE if at least one of its derivative checking moves is CHECKMATE; it is labeled NO MATE if all the consequent checking moves are so labeled. A checking move is labeled CHECK-MATE if all of the replies are so labeled; it is labeled NO MATE if at least one reply is so labeled.

The most promising checking move for further exploration is selected by these criteria: that checking move to which there are the fewest replies receives first priority.[6] If two or more checking moves are tied on this criterion, a double check (check with two pieces) is given priority over a single check. If there is still a tie, a check that does not permit a recapture by the opponent is given priority over one that does. Any remaining ties are resolved by selecting the check generated most recently.

A number of details have been omitted from this description, but it indicates the theory's general structure and the kinds of processes incorporated. The theory predicts, for any chess position that is presented to it, whether a chess player will discover a mating combination in that position, what moves he will consider and explore in his search for the combination, and which combination (if there are several alternatives, as there often are) he will discover. These predictions can be compared directly with published analyses of historical chess positions or tape recordings of the thinking-aloud behavior of human chess players to whom the same position is presented.

Now it is unlikely that, if a chess position were presented to a large number of players, all of them would explore it in exactly the same way. Certainly strong players would behave differently from weak players. Hence, the information-processing theory, if it is a correct theory at all, must be a theory only for players of a certain strength. On the other hand, we would not regard its explanation of chess playing as very satisfactory if we had to construct an entirely new theory for each player we studied.

Matters are not so bad, however. First, the interpersonal variations in search for chess moves in middle-game positions appear to be quite small for players at a common level of strength as we shall see in a moment. Second, some of the differences that are unrelated to playing strength appear to correspond to quite simple variants of the program—altering, for example, the criteria that are used to select the most promising checking move for exploration. Other differences, on the other hand, have major effects on the efficacy of the search, and some of these, also, can be represented quite simply by variants of the program organization. Thus, the basic structure of the program, and the assumptions it incorporates about human information-processing capacities, provides a general explanation for the behavior, while particular variants of this basic program allow specific predictions to be made of the behavioral consequences of individual differences in program organization and content.

The kinds of information the theory provides, and the ways in which it has been tested can be illustrated by a pair of examples. Adrian de Groot [7] has gathered and analyzed a substantial number of thinking-aloud protocols, some of them from grandmasters. He uniformly finds that, even in complicated positions, a player seldom generates a "tree" of more than fifty or seventy-five positions before he chooses his move. Moreover, the size of the tree does not depend on the player's strength. The thinking-aloud technique probably underestimates the size of the search tree somewhat, for a player may fail to mention some variations he has seen, but the whole tree is probably not an order of magnitude greater than that reported.

In forty positions from a standard published work on mating combinations where the information-processing theory predicted that a player would find mating strategies, the median size of its search tree ranged from 13 positions for two-move mates, to 53 for five-move mates. A six-move mate was found with a tree of 95 positions; and an eight-move mate with a tree of 108. (The last two mates, as well as a number of the others, were from historically celebrated games between grandmasters, and are among the most "brilliant" on record.) Hence, we can conclude that the predictions of the theory on amount of search are quite consistent with de Groot's empirical findings on the behavior of highly-skilled human chess players.

The second example tests a much more detailed feature of the theory. In the eight-move mate mentioned above, it had been known that by following a different strategy the mate could have been achieved in seven moves. Both the human grandmaster (Edward Lasker in the game of Lasker-Thomas, 1912) and the program found the eight-move mate. Examination of the exploration shows that the shorter sequence could only have been discovered by exploring a branch of the tree that permitted the defender two replies before exploring a branch that permitted a single reply. The historical evidence here confirms the postulate of the theory that players use the "fewest replies" heuristic to guide their search. (The evidence was discovered after the theory was constructed.) A second piece of evidence of the same sort has been found in a recent game between experts reported in *Chess Life* (December 1963). The winner discovered a seven-move mate, but overlooked the fact that he could have mated in three moves. The annotator of the game, a master, also overlooked the shorter sequence. Again, it could only have been found by exploring a check with two replies before exploring one with a single reply.

The "fewest replies" heuristic is not a superficial aspect of the players' search, nor is its relevance limited to the game of chess. Most problem-solving tasks—for example, discovering proofs of mathematical theorems—require a search through a branching "tree" of possibilities. Since the tree branches geometrically, solving a problem of any difficulty would call for a search of completely unmanageable scope (numbers like 10^{120} arise frequently in estimating the magnitude of such searches), if there were not at hand powerful heuristics, or rules of thumb, for selecting the promising branches for exploration. Such heuristics permit the discovery of proofs for theorems (and mating combinations) with the limited explorations reported here.

The "fewest replies" heuristic is powerful because it combines two functions: It points search in those directions that are most restrictive for the opponent, giving him the least opportunity to solve his problem; at the same time, it limits the growth of the search tree, by keeping its rate of branching as low as possible. The "fewest replies" heuristic is the basis for the idea of retaining the initiative in military strategy, and in competitive activities generally, and is also a central heuristic in decision-making in the face of uncertainty. Hence, its appearance in the chess playing theory, and in the behavior of the human players, is not fortuitous.

PARSIMONIOUS AND GARRULOUS THEORIES

Granting its success in predicting both some general and some very specific aspects of human behavior in chess playing, like the examples just described, the theory might be confronted with several kinds of questions and objections. It somehow fails to conform to our usual notions of generality and parsimony in theory. First, it is highly specific—the checkmating theory purports to provide an explanation only of how good chess players behave when they are confronted with a position on the board that calls for a vigorous mating attack. If we were to try to explain the whole range of human behavior, over all the enormous variety of tasks that particular human beings perform, we should have to compound the explanations from thousands of specific theories like the checkmate program. The final product would be an enormous compendium of "recipes" for human behavior at specific levels of skill in specific task environments.[8]

Second, the individual theories comprising this compendium would hardly be parsimonious, judged by ordinary standards. We used about a thousand words above to provide an approximate description of the checkmate program. The actual program—the formal theory—consists of about three thousand computer instructions in a list-processing language, equivalent in information content to about the same number of English words. (It should be mentioned that the program includes a complete statement of the rules of chess, so that only a small part of the total is given over to the description of the player's selection rules and their organization.)

Before we recoil from this unwieldy compendium as too unpleasant and unaesthetic to contemplate, let us see how it compares in bulk with theories in the other sciences. With the simplicity of Newtonian mechanics (why is this always the first example to which we turn?), there is, of course, no comparison. If classical mechanics is the model, then a theory should consist of three sentences, or a couple of differential equations.[9]

But chemistry, and particularly organic chemistry, presents a different picture. It is perhaps not completely misleading to compare the question "How does a chess player find a checkmating combination?" with a question like "How do photoreceptors in the human eye operate?" or "How is the carbohydrate and oxygen intake of a rabbit transformed into energy usable in muscular contraction?"

The theory of plant metabolism provides a striking example of an explanation of phenomena in terms of a substantial number of complex mechanisms. Calvin and Bassham, in their book on *The Photosynthesis of Carbon Compounds*,[10] introduce a figure entitled "carbon reduction pathways in photosynthesis" with the statement:

"We believe the *principal* pathways for photosynthesis of simple organic compounds from CO_2 to be those shown in Figure 2." (Italics ours) The figure referred to represents more than forty distinct chemical reactions and a corresponding number of compounds. This diagram, of course, is far from representing the whole theory. Not only does it omit much of the detail, but it contains none of the quantitative considerations for predicting reaction rates, energy balances, and so on. The verbal description accompanying the figure, which also has little to say about the quantitative aspects, or the energetics, is over two pages in length—almost as long as our description of the chess-playing program. Here we have a clear-cut example of a theory of fundamental importance that has none of the parsimony we commonly associate with scientific theorizing.

The answer to the question of how photosynthesis proceeds is decidedly longwinded—as is the answer to the question of how chess players find mating combinations. We are often satisfied with longwinded answers because we believe that the phenomena are intrinsically complex, and that no brief theory will explain them in detail. We must adjust our expectations about the character of information-processing theories of human thinking to a similar level. Such theories, to the extent that they account for the details of the phenomena, will be highly specific and highly complex. We might call them "garrulous theories" in contrast with our more common models of parsimonious theories.

ELEMENTARY INFORMATION PROCESSES

We should like to carry the analogy with chemistry a step further. Part of our knowledge in chemistry—and a very important part for the experimental chemist—consists of vast catalogs of substances and reactions, not dissimilar in bulk to the compendium of information processes we are proposing. But, as we come to understand these substances and their reactions more fully, a second level of theory emerges that explains them (at least their general features) in a more parsimonious way. The substances, at this more basic level, become geometrical arrangements of particles from a small set of more fundamental substances—atoms and sub-molecules—

held together by a variety of known forces whose effects can be estimated qualitatively and, in simple cases, quantitatively.

If we examine an information-processing theory like the check-mating program more closely, we find that it, too, is organized from a limited number of building blocks—a set of elementary informa-tion processes—and some composite processes that are compounded from the more elementary ones in a few characteristic ways. Let us try to describe these buildings blocks in general terms. First, we shall characterize the way in which symbols and structures of sym-bols are represented internally and held in memory. Then, we shall mention some of the principal elementary processes that alter these symbol structures.[11]

Symbols, Lists, and Descriptions: The smallest units of manip-ulable information in memory are *symbol tokens,*[12] or symbol oc-currences. It is postulated that tokens can be compared, and that comparison determines that the tokens are occurrences of the same symbol (*symbols type*), or that they are different.

Symbol tokens are arranged in larger structures, called *lists.* A list is an ordered set, a sequence, of tokens. Hence, with every token on a list, except the last, there is associated a unique *next* token. Associated with the list as a whole is a symbol, its *name.* Thus, a list may be a sequence of symbols that are themselves names of lists—a list of lists. A familiar example of a list of symbols that all of us carry in memory is the alphabet. (Its name is "alphabet.") Another is the list of days of the week, in order—Monday is next to Sunday, and so on.

Associations also exist between symbol types. An association is a two-termed relation, involving three symbols, one of which names the relation, the other two its arguments. "The color of the apple is red"—specifies an association between "apple" and "red" with the relation "color." A symbol's associations *describe* that symbol.

Some Elementary Processes: A symbol, a list, and an association are abstract objects. Their properties are defined by the elementary information processes that operate on them. One important class of such processes are the *discrimination* processes. The basic dis-crimination process, which compares symbols to determine whether or not they are identical, has already been mentioned. Pairs of com-pound structures—lists and sets of associations—are discriminated from each other by matching processes that apply the basic tests for symbol identity to symbols in corresponding positions in the two structures. For example, two chess positions can be discriminated by a matching process that compares the pieces standing on corresponding squares in the two positions. The outcome of the match might be a statement that "the two positions are identical except that the White King is on his Knight's square in the first but on his Rook's square in the second."

Other classes of elementary information processes are those capable of *creating or copying* symbols, lists, and associations. These processes are involved, for example, in fixating or memorizing symbolic materials presented to the sense organs—learning a tune. Somewhat similar information processes are capable of modifying existing symbolic structures by *inserting a symbol* into a list, by *changing a term of an association* (from "its color is red" to "its color is green"), or by *deleting a symbol* from a list.

Still another class of elementary information processes *finds* information that is in structures stored in memory. We can think of such a process, schematically, as follows: to answer the question, "What letter follows 'g' in the alphabet?," a process must find the list in memory named "alphabet." Then, another process must search down that list until (using the match for identity of symbols) it finds a "g." Finally, a third process must find the symbol *next* to "g" in the list. Similarly, to answer the question, "What color is the apple?," there must be a process capable of finding the second term of an association, given the first term and the name of the relation. Thus, there must be processes for finding named objects, for finding symbols on a list, for finding the next symbol on a list, and for finding the value of an attribute of an object.

This list of elementary information processes is modest, yet provides an adequate collection of building blocks to implement the chess-playing theory as well as the other information processing theories of thinking that have been constructed to date: including a general problem-solving theory, a theory of rote verbal learning, and several theories of concept formation and pattern recognition, among others.[13]

Elementary Processes in the Chess Theory: A few examples will show how the mechanisms employed in the chess-playing theory can be realized by symbols, lists, associations, and elementary information processes. The player's representation of the chess board is assumed to be a collection of associations: with each square is associated the symbol representing the man on that square, and symbols representing the adjoining squares in the several directions. Moves are similarly represented as symbols with which are associated the names of the squares from which and to which the move was made, the name of the piece moved, the name of the piece captured, if any, and so on.

Similarly, the processes for manipulating these representations are compounded from the elementary processes already described. To make a move, for example, is to modify the internal representation of the board by deleting the association of the man to be moved with the square on which he previously stood, and creating the new association of that man with the square to which he moved; and, in case of a capture, by deleting also the association of the captured man with the square on which he stood. Another example: testing whether the King is in check involves finding the square associated with the King, finding adjoining squares along ranks, files, and diagonals, and testing these squares for the presence of enemy men who are able to attack in the appropriate direction. (The latter is determined by associating with each man his *type*, and associating with each type of man the directions in which such men can legally be moved.)

We see that, although the chess-playing theory contains several thousand program instructions, these are comprised of only a small number of elementary processes (far fewer than the number of elements in the periodic table). The elementary processes combine in a few simple ways into compound processes and operate on structures (lists and descriptions) that are constructed, combinatorially, from a single kind of building block—the symbol. There are two levels of theory: an "atomic" level, common to all the information-processing theories, of symbols, lists, associations, and elementary processes, and a "macromolecular" level, peculiar to each type of specialized human performance, of representations in the form of list structures and webs of associations, and of compound processes for manipulating these representations.

Processes in Serial Pattern Recognition: A second example of how programs compounded from the elementary processes explain behavior is provided by an information-processing theory of serial pattern recognition.

Consider a sequence like:

ABMCDMEFM——.

An experimental subject in the laboratory, asked to extrapolate the series will, after a little thought, continue:

GHM, etc.

To see how he achieves this result, we examine the original sequence. First, it makes use of letters of the Roman alphabet. We can assume that the subject holds this alphabet in memory stored as a list, so that the elementary list process for finding the NEXT item on a list can find B, given A, or find S, given R, and so on. Now we note that any letter in the sequence, after the first three, is related to previous letters by the relations NEXT and SAME. Specifically, if we organize the series into periods of three letters each:

ABM   CDM   EFM

we see that:

(1) The first letter in each period is NEXT in the alphabet to the second letter in the previous period.

(2) The second letter in each period is NEXT in the alphabet to the first letter in that period.

(3) The third letter in each period is the SAME as the corresponding letter in the previous period.

The relations of SAME and NEXT also suffice for a series like:

AAA   CCC   EEE . . .

or for a number series like:

1 7 2 8 3 9 4 0 . . .

In the last case, the "alphabet" to which the relation of NEXT is applied is the list of digits, 0 to 9, and NEXT is applied circularly —i.e., after 9 comes 0 and then 1 again.

Several closely related information-processing theories of human pattern recognition have been constructed using elementary processes for finding and generating the NEXT item in a list.[14] These theories have succeeded in explaining some of the main features of human behavior in a number of standard laboratory tasks, including so-called binary choice tasks, and series-completion and symbol-analogy tasks from intelligent tests.

The nature of the series-completion tasks has already been illustrated. In the binary choice experiment, the subject is confronted, one by one, with a sequence of tokens—each a "+" or "V," say. As each one is presented to him, he is asked what the next one will be. The actual sequence is, by construction, random. The evidence shows that, even when the subjects are told this, they rarely treat it as random. Instead, they behave as though they were trying to detect a serial pattern in the sequence and extrapolate it. They behave essentially like subjects faced by the series-completion task, and basically similar information-processing theories using the same elementary processes can explain both behaviors.

A BROADER VIEW OF THINKING PROCESSES

A closer look at the principal examples now extant of information-processing theories suggests that another level of theory is rapidly emerging, intermediate between the "atomic" level common to all the theories and the "macromolecular" level idiosyncratic to each. It is clear that there is no prospect of eliminating all idiosyncratic elements from the individual theories. A theory to explain chess-playing performances must postulate memory structures and processes that are completely irrelevant to proving theorems in geometry, and vice verse.

On the other hand, it is entirely possible that human performances in different task environments may call on common components at more aggregative levels than the elementary processes. This, in fact, appears to be the case. The first information-processing theory that isolated some of these common components was called the General Problem Solver.[15]

Means-End Analysis: The General Problem Solver is a program organized to keep separate (1) problem-solving processes that, according to the theory, are possessed and used by most human beings of average intelligence when they are confronted with any relatively unfamiliar task environment, from (2) specific information about each particular task environment.

The core of the General Problem Solver is an organization of process for *means-end analysis*. The problem is defined by specifying a *given situation* (A), and a *desired situation* (B). A discrimination process incorporated in the system of means-end analysis compares A with B, and detects one or more *differences* (D) between them, if there are any. With each difference, there is associated in memory a set of *operators*, (O_D), or processes, that are possibly relevant to removing differences of that kind. The means-end analysis program proceeds to try to remove the difference by applying, in turn, the relevant operators.

Using a scheme of means-end analysis, a proof of a trigonometric identity like cos θ tan θ = sin θ might proceed like this:

The right-hand side contains only the sine function, the left-hand side other trigonometric functions as well. The operator that replaces tan by sin/cos will eliminate one of these. Applying it we get cos θ (sin θ/cos θ) = sin θ. The left-hand side still contains an extraneous function, cosine. The algebraic cancellation operator, applied to the two cosines might remove this difference. We apply the operator, obtaining the identity sin θ = sin θ.

Planning Processes: Another class of general processes discovered in human problem-solving performances and incorporated in the General Problem Solver are *planning* processes. The essential idea in planning is that the representation of the problem situation is simplified by deleting some of the detail. A solution is now sought for the new, simplified, problem, and if one is found, it is used as a plan to guide the solution of the original problem, with the detail reinserted.

Consider a simple problem in logic. Given: (1) "A," (2) "*not A or B*," (3) "*if not C then not B*"; to prove "*C.*" To plan the proof, note that the first premise contains A, the second A and B, the third, B and C, and the conclusion, C. The plan might be to obtain B by combining A with (AB), then to obtain C by combining B with (BC). The plan will in fact work, but requires (2) to be transformed into "*A implies B*" and (3) "*B implies C,*" which transformations follow from the definitions of "or" and "if . . . then."

Problem-Solving Organization: The processes for attempting subgoals in the problem-solving theories and the exploration processes in the chess-playing theory must be guided and controlled by executive processes that determine what goal will be attempted next. Common principles for the organization of the executive processes have begun to appear in several of the theories. The general idea has already been outlined above for the chess-playing program. In this program the executive routine cycles between an exploration (*search*) phase and an evaluation (*scan*) phase. During the exploration phase, the available problem-solving processes are used to investigate subgoals. The information obtained through this investigation is stored in such a way as to be accessible to the executive. During the evaluation phase, the executive uses this information to determine which of the existing subgoals is the most promising and should be explored next. An executive program organized in this way may be called a search-scan scheme, for it searches an expanding tree of possibilities, which provides a common pool of information for scanning by its evaluative processes.[16]

The effectiveness of a problem-solving program appears to depend rather sensitively on the alternation of the search and scan phases. If search takes place in long sequences, interrupted only infrequently to scan for possible alternative directions of exploration, the problem solver suffers from stereotypy. Having initiated search in one direction, it tends to persist in that direction as long as the subroutines conducting the search determine, locally, that the possibilities for exploration have not been exhausted. These determinations are made in a very decentralized way, and without benefit of the more global information that has been generated.

On the other hand, if search is too frequently interrupted to consider alternative goals to the one being pursued currently, the exploration takes on an uncoordinated appearance, wandering indecisively among a wide range of possibilities. In both theorem-proving and chess-playing programs, extremes of decentralized and centralized control of search have shown themselves ineffective in comparison with a balanced search-scan organization.

Discrimination Trees: Common organizational principles are also emerging for the rote memory processes involved in almost all human performance. As a person tries to prove a theorem, say, certain expressions that he encounters along the way gradually become familiar to him and, his ability to discriminate among them gradually improves. An information-processing theory (EPAM) was constructed several years ago to account for this and similar human behavior in verbal learning experiments (e.g., learning nonsense syllables by the serial anticipation or paired associate methods).[17] This theory is able to explain, for instance, how familiarity and similarity of materials affect rates of learning. The essential processes in EPAM include: (1) processes for discriminating among compound objects by sorting them in a "discrimination tree," (2) familiarization processes for associating pairs or short sequences of objects.

Discrimination processes operate by applying sequences of tests to the stimulus objects, and sorting them on the basis of the test results—a sort of "twenty questions" procedure. The result of discrimination is to find a memory location where information is stored about objects that are similar to the one sorted. *Familiarization processes* create new compound objects out of previously familiar elements. Thus, during the last decade, the letter sequence "IPL" has become a familiar word (to computer programers!) meaning "information processing language." The individual letters have been *associated* in this word. Similarly, the English alphabet, used by the serial pattern-recognizing processes, is a familiar object compounded from the letters arranged in a particular sequence. All sorts of additional information can be associated with an object, once familiarized. (For example, the fact that IPL's organize symbols in lists can be associated with "IPL".)

Because discriminaton trees play a central role in EPAM, the program may also be viewed as a theory of pattern detection, and EPAM-like trees have been incorporated in certain information-processing theories of concept formation. It also now seems likely that the discrimination tree is an essential element in problem-solving theories like GPS, playing an important role in the gradual modification of the subject's behavior as he familiarizes himself with the problem material.

CONCLUSION

Our survey shows that within the past decade a considerable range of human behaviors has been explained successfully by information-processing theories. We now know, for example, some of the central processes that are employed in solving problems, in detecting and extrapolating patterns, and in memorizing verbal materials.

Information-processing theories explain behavior at various levels of detail. In the theories now extant, at least three levels can be distinguished. At the most aggregative level are theories of complex behavior in specific problem domains: proving theorems in logic or geometry, discovering checkmating combinations in chess. These theories tend to contain very extensive assumptions about the knowledge and skills possessed by the human beings who perform these activities, and about the way in which this knowledge and these skills are organized and represented internally. Hence, each of these theories incorporates a rather extensive set of assumptions, and predicts behavior only in a narrow domain.

At a second level, similar or identical information-processing mechanisms are common to many of the aggregative theories. Means-end analysis, planning, the search-scan scheme, and discrimination trees are general-purpose organizations for processing that are usable over a wide range of tasks. As the nature of these mechanisms becomes better understood, they, in turn, begin to serve as basic building blocks for the aggregative theories, allowing the latter to be stated in more parsimonious form, and exhibiting the large fraction of machinery that is common to all, rather than idiosyncratic to individual tasks.

At the lowest, "atomic," level, all the information-processing theories postulate only a small set of basic forms of symbolic representation and a small number of elementary information processes. The construction and successful testing of large-scale programs that simulate complex human behaviors provide evidence that a small set of elements, similar to those now postulated in information-processing languages, is sufficient for the construction of a theory of human thinking.

Although none of the advances that have been described constitute explanations of human thought at the still more microscopic, physiological level, they open opportunities for new research strategies in physiological psychology. As the information-processing theories become more powerful and better validated, they disclose to the physiological psychologist the fundamental mechanisms and processes that he needs to explain. He need no longer face the task of building the whole long bridge from microscopic neurological and molecular structures to gross human behavior, but can instead concentrate on bridging the much shorter gap from physiology to elementary information processes.

The work of Lettvin, Maturana, McCulloch, and Pitts on information processing in the frog's eye,[18] and the work of Hubel and Wiesel on processing of visual information by the cat [19] already provide some hints of the form this bridging operation may take.

APPENDIX: COMPUTER PROGRAMS AS THEORIES

Since the use of computer programs as formal theories, in the manner described in this paper, is still somewhat novel, this appendix sketches briefly the relation between this formalism and the formalisms that have been used more commonly in the physical sciences.

In the physical sciences, theories about dynamical systems usually take the form of systems of differential equations. This is the form of classical Newtonian mechanics, of Maxwell's electromagnetic theory, and of many other theories of central importance. In the classical dynamics of mass points, for example, it is assumed that the initial positions and velocities of a set of bodies (mass points) are given, and that the forces acting on the bodies are known, instantaneous functions of the positions, say, of the bodies. Then, by Newton's Second Law, the acceleration (second derivative of position) of each body is proportional to the resultant force acting on it. The paths of the bodies over time are calculated by integrating twice the differential equations that express the Second Law.

More generally, a system of differential or difference equations is a set of conditional laws that determines the state of the system "a moment later" as a function of its state at a given time. Repeated application of the laws, equivalent to integrating the equations, then determines the path of the system over time.

A computer program is also literally a system of difference equations—albeit of a rather unorthodox kind. For it determines the behavior of the computer in the next instruction cycle as a function of the current contents of its memory. Executing the program is formally equivalent to integrating (numerically) the difference equations for a specified initial state of the computer. Thus, information-processing theories, expressed as programs in computer languages, are not merely analogous to more familiar kinds of dynamical theories; formally, they are of an equivalent type.

Very simple systems of differential and integral equations can sometimes be integrated formally, so that general properties can be inferred about the paths of the systems they describe, independent of particular initial and boundary conditions. There are no known methods for integrating formally systems of difference equations like those discussed in this paper. Hence, the principal means for making predictions about such systems is to simulate their behavior for particular initial and boundary conditions. This is the method of investigation that we have relied on here.

REFERENCES

1. *The Nature of the Chemical Bond* (Ithaca: Cornell University Press, 3rd edition, 1960), pp. 3–4.
2. The best-known exponent of this radical behaviorist position is Prof. B. F. Skinner. He has argued for example, that "an explanation is the demonstration of a functional relationship between behavior and manipulable or controllable variables," in T. W. Wann, (ed.), *Behaviorism and Phenomenology* (Chicago: Univ. of Chicago Press, 1964), p. 102.
3. A distinguished example of such a theory is D. O. Hebb's formulation in terms of "cell assemblies." *The Organization of Behavior* (New York: Wiley, 1949). Hebb does not, however, insist on an exclusively physiological base for psychological theory, and his general methodological position is not inconsistent with that taken here. See his *Textbook of Psychology* (Philadelphia: Saunders, 1956), Ch. 13.
4. A "move" means here a move by one player followed by a reply by his opponent. Hence to look ahead four or five moves is to consider sequences of eight or ten successive positions.
5. A general account of this program, with the results of some hand simulations, can be found in H. A. Simon and P. A. Simon, "Trial and Error Search in Solving Difficult Problems: Evidence from the Game of Chess." *Behaviorial Science*, VII (1962), 425–429. The theory described there has subsequently been programmed and the hand-simulated findings confirmed on a computer.

6. This is perhaps the most important element in the strategy. It will be discussed further later.

7. *Thought and Choice in Chess* (The Hague, The Netherlands: Mouton & Company, 1964).

8. The beginnings of such a compendium have already appeared. A convenient source for descriptions of a number of the information-processing theories is the collection by E. A. Feigenbaum and J. Feldman (eds.), *Computers and Thought* (New York: McGraw-Hill, 1964).

9. Of course, even Newtonian mechanics is not at all this simple in structure. See H. A. Simon, "The Axioms of Newtonian Mechanics," *Phil. Mag.*, Ser. 7, XXXVIII (1947), 888–905.

10. M. Calvin and J. A. Bassham, *The Photosynthesis of Carbon Compounds* (New York: W. A. Benjamin, Incorporated, 1962), pp. 8–11.

11. Only a few of the characteristics of list-processing systems can be mentioned here. For a fuller account, see A. Newell and H. A. Simon, "Computers in Psychology," in Luce, Bush, and Galanter (eds.), *Handbook of Mathematical Psychology*, Vol. I (New York: Wiley, 1963), especially pp. 373–76, 380–84, 419–24.

12. Evidence as to how information is symbolized in the brain is almost nonexistent. If the reader is assisted by thinking of different symbols as different macromolecules, this metaphor is as good as any. A few physiologists think it may even be the correct explanation. See Holger Hyden, "Biochemical Aspects of Brain Activity," in S. M. Farber and R. H. Wilson (eds.), *Control of the Mind* (New York: McGraw-Hill, 1961), pp. 18–39. Differing patterns of neural activity will do as well. See W. R. Adey, R. T. Kado, J. Didio, and W. J. Schindler, "Impedance Changes in Cerebral Tissue Accompanying a Learned Discriminative Performance in the Cat," *Experimental Physiology*, VII (1963), 259–81.

13. For examples, see Feigenbaum and Feldman, *op. cit.*, Part 2.

14. J. Feldman, F. Tonge, and H. Kanter, "Empirical Explorations of a Hypothesis-Testing Model of Binary Choice Behavior," in A. C. Hoggatt and F. E. Balderston (eds.), *Symposium on Simulation Models* (Cincinnati: South-Western Publishing Company, 1964), pp. 55–100; K. R. Laughery and L. W. Gregg, "Simulation of Human Problem-Solving Behavior," *Psychometrika*, XXVII (1962), pp. 265–82; H. A. Simon and K. Kotovsky, "Human Acquisition of Concepts for Sequential Patterns," *Psychological Review*, LXX (1963), 531–46.

15. A. Newell and H. A. Simon, "GPS, A Program That Simulates Human Thought," in Feigenbaum and Feldman, *op. cit.*, pp. 279–93.

16. Perhaps the earliest use of the search-scan scheme appeared in the
    Logic Theorist, the first heuristic theorem-proving program. See
    A. Newell and H. A. Simon, "Empirical Explorations With the Logic
    Theory Machine: A Case Study in Heuristics," in Feigenbaum and
    Feldman, *op. cit.*, pp. 153–63.
17. E. A. Feigenbaum, "The Simulation of Verbal Learning Behavior,"
    in Feigenbaum and Feldman, *op. cit.*, pp. 297–309.
18. J. Y. Lettvin, H. R. Maturana, W. S. McCulloch, and W. H. Pitts,
    "What the Frog's Eye Tells the Frog's Brain," *Proceedings of the
    Institute of Radio Engineers*, XLVII (1959), 1940–51.
19. D. H. Hubel and T. N. Wiesel, "Receptive Fields, Binocular Inter-
    action and Functional Architecture in the Cat's Visual Cortex," *Jour-
    nal of Physiology*, CLX (1962), 106–54.

3 Computers and the brain

DEAN E. WOOLDRIDGE

This is the concluding chapter of a book which reviews the biological evidence for what has been termed
earlier the mechanomorphic thesis: that organic processes are essentially machine-like and can be understood in terms of concepts such as feedback, storage of
information, and stimulus and response. While acknowl-
edging the gap between the model of the brain as a
computer and the present state of research, the author
is convinced that "the hole in the logical structure of
the mechanistic philosophy," namely consciousness, can
be plugged by a "passive theory of consciousness"
which conceives of it as "a sort of display device" for
what goes on in the brain's circuitry. In philosophical
terms, this is a variety of epiphenomalism, which views
awareness as a natural concomitant of a certain level
of mechanical complexity.

Dean E. Wooldridge was vice-president for research
and development of the Hughes Aircraft Company
when he left in 1953 to co-found the Ramo-Wooldridge
Corporation. In 1962 he resigned as president of the
enlarged Thompson Ramo-Wooldridge Corporation to
devote his time to scientific pursuits and writing.

Not long ago nearly everyone subscribed to the
concept of brain/mind dichotomy. According to this concept, even
the most complete and detailed understanding of the physical struc-

ture and operation of the brain could never suffice to explain mental activity. The mind was considered to be something nonphysical, outside the realm of the natural sciences; it was believed to make use of the brain as the agent for some of its activities, but was thought to possess properties and powers that could never be interpreted on the basis of any conceivable organization of cells and tissue.

In recent years the dualistic brain/mind concept has steadily lost ground to the mechanistic point of view. The development of machines capable of performing thoughtlike processes has aided this trend, although it would be unfair to attribute too much influence to electronic computer developments. The fact is that the change is mostly to be attributed to the successes of the traditional approach of medical research workers. Throughout the years they have learned that, whatever their philosophy, they make consistent progress in learning how living organisms operate by assuming that they are subject to the physical laws of nature and by painstakingly applying the techniques of scientific investigation. As a result, the history of medical research largely consists in repetitions of a single theme: the removal of one after another of the organs and functions of the body from the realm of the physically unknowable and unexplainable to which all living processes were once assigned. In former times the idea that the heart is no more than a complicated pump, which would one day be replaceable by a man-made device during a lengthy surgical operation, would have seemed as shocking to most people as the modern discoveries that the brain, too, operates in accordance with the physical laws of nature.

The practical approach to understanding a complex system of interrelated structures, whether it be a living organism or a man-made device, is to try to simplify the problem by breaking it down into smaller parts. This is why so much attention has been paid by research workers to the localization of functions in the brain. If it were impossible to find portions of this complex organ that are responsible for certain of its functions and other portions that seem to be related to other functions, not only would progress be impossible, but serious doubt would be cast on the validity of the mechanistic point of view. This is the reason for the importance of the discoveries that nervous tissue possesses neuronal building blocks whose individual properties largely account for the communication characteristics of the peripheral nerves, and that there are localized and determinable points of connection of the peripheral nerves to the cortex. Of similar importance are such developments as the isolation in the brain of the temperature-control mechanism and of neuronal circuits responsible for other reflex actions. Every time the control of some additional bodily process is traced to a specific part of the brain, there is a reduction by just that much in the amount of function that must be attributed to the "nonmaterial mind" and a corresponding increase in what can be accounted for by the machinelike brain.

Most impressive of all, of course, are the observations that reveal the physical basis of the "higher processes" of emotion and intelligence. The discovery of pleasure and punishment centers in the brain—discrete, localized, stable aggregations of neurons in which an electric current means a sense of well-being, hunger, sexual gratification, rage, terror, or pain—made it difficult for those whose thinking emphasized the dichotomy of the brain and the mind. This difficulty was further increased by the evidence for the controlling effect on personality of the integrity of the neuronal connections to the frontal lobes, as well as by the clear relationship established by Penfield between stimulating cortical currents and the "mental" processes of speech and memory. And evidence for the automatic, machinelike nature of some of the learning processes has further aggravated the plight of the brain/mind dualist.

In short, all the material of the preceding chapters has consisted of evidence for the applicability of the established physical laws of nature to the activities of the nervous system. The underlying thesis throughout has been, in essence, "The brain is a machine."

But if the brain is a machine, the next question is "What kind of machine?" Or, in more practical terms, "Is the brain so similar in its construction and operation to some known type of man-made machine that studies made on one are extensively pertinent to the other?"

Nowadays it is commonplace to emphasize the analogy between the human brain and electronic digital computers. Such popular terms as "artificial intelligence" and "electronic brains" underscore their real or imagined similarities. On the other hand, there are dissenting opinions. Competent life scientists sometimes point out that the brain is not electronic, only partially digital, and not really a computer at all. These divergent points of view lead to different conclusions as to the importance of collaborative work between the computer and brain scientists. There is practical value in a realistic appraisal of the essential similarities and differences of the two fields.

No one denies that many of the end results of the activities of computers and the brain are similar. Every chapter in this book has provided instances of brain or nervous-system performance that have operational characteristics analogous to those exhibited by man-made devices. And even when no evidence has been available to support a detailed computer analogy to brain function, the attitudes and kind of language that characterize computer science have seemed to be applicable; in spite of the present impossibility of completely accounting for the more complex operations of the brain in terms of established physical principles, there is a comfortable feeling about them—they seem to be the kinds of operations that we may hope to observe in later generations of more sophisticated computers.

Although there may be little argument about the existence of operational similarities, there is much less than complete agreement on the implications of such similarities with respect to the mechanisms involved. If we look only at the end result of the transport of passengers across the Atlantic Ocean, much is to be said for the resemblance between a steamship and a jet airplane. The two vehicles convey passengers from New York to London at a similar cost and at about the same rate, in terms of average number of passengers moved across the ocean per hour of travel time; in each case schedules must be set, tickets must be sold, reservations must be made, and passengers must be transported to and from terminal points. Yet, nearly identical though these operational features are, no one would suggest that the machinery employed is so much alike that steamship and jet-aircraft designers could profit extensively by looking over each other's shoulders. Could it be the same with computers and the brain? Is it possible that the similar operational results they achieve are obtained by mechanisms that are so dissimilar as to preclude any extensive usefulness of cross-fertilization of the two fields?

The differences are obviously great. Visual comparison of the brain and a modern computer would not be likely to suggest a strong family resemblance. But we should be as wary of placing undue weight on structural differences that may turn out to be superficial, as we are of being overly impressed by what may be superficial similarities in their operational results. We must recognize that the physical characteristics of an existing electronic digital computer are largely determined by economic considerations associated with the present and entirely transient limitations of the state of the art. In a modern computer installation, for example, there are likely to be motor-driven magnetic drums, complex tape-driving and -reeling mechanisms, two-dimensional arrays of magnetic cores, and the like. But it is only considerations of cost and size that prevent all these mechanical devices from being replaced by large numbers of electronically operated on/off switches, essentially similar to the "gates" and "flip-flops" employed for the actual computation and logical manipulation. In fact, it can be shown that a general-purpose electronic digital computer could be comprised in its entirety of suitably interconnected, electrically activated on/off switches. In such a computer, some of the switches would serve as storage elements for data and programs, and others as logic elements for the performance of the data-processing operations; certain combinations of switches would be employed to provide the necessary temporal sequencing of the circuit to cause the computer to go through the large number of elemental steps specified by its program for the accomplishment of its assigned tasks. But the result would be a network possessing all the computing and logic-processing capabilities of the most complex modern machines—all done with on/off switches, nothing more. And no great stretch of the imagination is needed to see a resemblance between a vast assemblage of tiny switching elements interconnected by wires and a vast assemblage of neurons interconnected by nerve fibers.

Thus we must search at a deeper level if we are to find really basic differences between computers and the brain. Let us consider one clear-cut difference: the principles of construction of nature's neuron and those of the computer engineer's transistorized electronic switch. Complex chemical processes in the one obviously have no close analogy in the other. But here again, the apparent importance of such a difference disappears under analysis. The computer scientist is essentially uninterested in the details of construction of his components; he is concerned primarily with their over-all performance characteristics. There is at least one "electronic-digital-computer" research program under way in which the computing elements are entirely hydraulic. Nevertheless the same general principles of design, analysis, and assembly govern this work as apply to all other work in "electronic" digital computers. To be sure, electronic components are employed in most computers, but only because no one has yet invented nonelectronic devices that can compete in size, weight, reliability, cost, and speed. If someone could devise a practical way of preparing organic neuronal material so that it possessed the over-all operating properties called for by digital-computer theory, it would find a ready market. In the term "electronic digital computer," the adjective "electronic" is essentially incidental.

If we cannot find differences between computers and the brain that we accept as essential by comparisons of their over-all system configurations or of the principles of construction of their components, we must move our investigations from the anatomical to the physiological level. Are the functions performed by the neurons in the brain closely similar to those performed by the component switches in the computer?

This question is more difficult to deal with than those we have considered. We know that the neuron possesses not only some of the characteristics of an on/off switch, but also other properties. The all-or-nothing-response feature of the neuron is exhibited only by its axon. The body of the neuron, in electronic terms, is more like a summing amplifier that adds the effects of a number of inputs and compares the sum with a threshold value to determine whether the axon is to fire and, if so, what is to be the frequency of its output pulse train. And the threshold value is usually adjustable by chemical or electrical changes in the surrounding tissue.

This is a description of a much more complex and sophisticated device than the simple on/off switch of the computer designer. A computer engineer, presented with such components for use in the construction of a control system, would have a choice to make. In implementing the pupillary-reflex mechanism, for example, he could arrange his circuit inputs and voltages so as to operate the neurons as simple on/off switches, wired into a configuration equivalent to a general-purpose digital computer, including suitable translating circuits for coupling to the afferent and efferent nerves. But he could get by with much less equipment by copying nature and utilizing some of the other properties of his neuronal building blocks. As we have seen earlier, he would have to do no more than pass the train of pulses indicating the measured level of retinal illumination to the input of a motor neuron that directly supplies, over its axon, the train of pulses that constricts the pupillary muscle. By a proper adjustment of the firing threshold of this neuron, it could then be made to transmit a constricting signal only when the measured quantity of radiation incident on the retina exceeded the desired value, and the amount of this constricting signal—that is, the frequency of the transmitted effector pulses—would increase with increasing brightness, as desired.

The equipment ratio of the two approaches would not be so large if we were dealing with a more complex intellectual process of the brain, but the essential point would remain. It is unlikely that nature would have provided herself with the capability for versatility and equipment simplification inherent in the properties of the neuron unless she planned to make extensive use of it. Not only logic, but the evidence from EEG and probe measurements, strongly suggest that there are no pure "digital" computing circuits in the brain, that is, circuits employing only the on/off switching capabilities of their components.

Here, finally, we appear to have a major difference between computers and the brain. Yet let us not conclude too quickly that the difference is so profound as to impose narrow limits on the areas of mutual relevance of brain and computer science. Completeness requires that we investigate the possibility that a valid case can be made for the point of view that the adjective "digital" is no more essential than "electronic" to the electronic digital computer. Improbable though it may seem, such a case can indeed be made!

What a computer does, and *all* that it does, is generate patterns of voltage at its output terminals by performing a precisely prescribed set of operations on the patterns of voltage supplied to its input terminals. These operations are simple, but frequently very numerous. In the basic computer that is composed entirely of interconnected electronic switches, each elemental step is a simple switching operation. Connections to the input terminals of one of the switches bring in voltages, either from the computer input data or from the output of earlier switching operations; the switch thus innervated assumes one electrical state or another in accordance with whether its pattern of input voltages meets the conditions for operation determined by its own internal design. The electrical result of each of these simple processing steps joins with the outputs from other similar operations, and perhaps with some of the computer input voltages, to provide the raw material for additional processing steps. Ultimately, the outputs of some of the switch processing elements provide the final answers to the problem being solved—the voltages on the output terminals.

The secret of the power of modern computers resides in the discovery that extraordinarily complex operations can be broken down into steps that can be handled by very simple processing elements. In mathematical calculations, any operation that the mathematician has invented can be broken down into such elemental steps and caused to control the generation of the voltages representing the output numbers. And in logic problems, the computer can deduce new conclusions from given propositions by the application of the rules of logic, which can be broken down into the same simple processing steps as those used in mathematical computations.

Now let us return to the point of this discussion—the properties required of the processing elements, the "neurons" of the computer. In actual computers they are usually purely digital elements—on/off switches. This contributes to the simplicity, increases the reliability, and lowers the cost of the computer components. Furthermore, the theory has been thoroughly worked out only for computers based upon such yes/no devices. This is a new field and a difficult one. It is natural that the early development of the field should be characterized by exploitation of the simpler principles of logical processes. Much of the theory to date emphasizes true/false choices as the elemental steps out of which complex problem-solving can be synthesized. The on/off alternatives of a simple switch nicely match the true/false alternatives of the steps of such theory. This is, in fact, the source of the "digital" operating characteristics of most modern computers.

However, there are other ways of solving logical problems. There is, for example, probabilistic logic, in which the basic elements are not positive yes/no answers, but estimates of the probability that the answer is yes or not. Simple on/off switches can be used as the components of computers based upon such logical schemes, but they are inefficient—much as devices such as variable-weight-factor summing amplifiers are inefficient when used as components of a computer designed around two-valued logic.

When we are wiser about these matters, it seems certain that we shall want processing elements for our computers that provide greater versatility in their performance characteristics than do simple on/off devices. In fact, the exploratory work now under way in various laboratories on different types of "electronic neurons" with variable-summing and adjustable-threshold features is probably a forerunner of this ultimate broadening of the spectrum of the elemental processing components that will be used by the computer circuit designer.

This brings us to the conclusion we were after: *the narrowly digital nature of its processing elements is not here to stay and hence is not a really essential characteristic of the electronic digital computer.*

But if the essence of the modern computer is not to be found either in the term "electronic" or in "digital," where does it lie? Are we engaged in a meaningless exercise in semantics, or is there some characteristic of electronic digital computers, not evident in the name, that possesses fundamental significance? There is indeed one such characteristic. It was referred to earlier as the secret of the power of modern computers—the discovery that complex computational and logical operations can be broken down into steps that can be handled by very simple processing elements. The individual processing steps, we have just seen, may be expected to develop with time. What will not change, what is really fundamental about the general types of machines that have been too narrowly described as "electronic digital computers," is that they get their amazing results by the performance of a very large number of very simple processing steps. *This would also appear to be a valid description of the essence of brain function.*

Thus our argument has finally led us to the conclusion that computers and the brain do not simply display superficial similarities in some of their operational characteristics. Instead, they are mechanisms of the same kind, in the sense that they obtain their similar results by essentially similar means. If this is true, then it is clear that the computer scientist and the brain scientist need one another badly for the future development of their respective fields. Consider the differences between the physical and biological approaches and how beautifully they supplement each other. We have seen that computer science is dominated by theory. The most intensive work is under way aimed at learning how intellectual processes can be broken down into simple steps. Computer programs have been worked out for the playing of games like checkers and chess, and for the automatic production of new theorems of geometry and the propositional calculus. Better understanding of the principles of learning is being gained continually by the physical scientists, who are developing techniques of programming existing machines, and of building new ones, that can do an increasingly effective job of learning from experience and modifying their performance accordingly. Progress is also being made in the theory of general problem-solving—the reduction to precisely specified sequences of simple steps of the processes that are described, when humans employ them, by such words as "originality" and "ingenuity."

It is from the work of these physical scientists that the theoretical techniques must come for explaining how the elemental processing steps of the neurons in the brain are capable of combining to produce the performance attributes of intelligence. Problems of the complexity of those arising in the brain cannot be solved by experiment alone; theory will be essential to point the way to meaningful experiments and to help interpret the results when they are performed. Since the biologist has neither the training nor the tradition for this kind of theoretical work, he needs the physical scientist—he cannot do the job without him.

But it works both ways. The task that has been undertaken by the physical scientist—that of developing quantitative and precise theoretical models of intellectual processes—is one that is too difficult for him to handle without clues from the life sciences. Any hint that "nature may do it this way" can be of inestimable value to the theoretical research worker in helping him choose a promising approach for his speculations from among the many blind alleys that confront him.   •

Fortunately, collaboration is under way and is increasing. From such interdisciplinary effort we may confidently expect great progress to be made in the coming years in our understanding of the operation of the brain. The human implications can be tremendous, in terms of relief of suffering from brain injury and disease, the better physical and psychological management of our mental health, and, ultimately perhaps, the development of electrical, chemical, and operative techniques for the practical enhancement of our intellectual capabilities.

Computer technology will be similarly rewarded. Increased understanding of the theory and practice of intellectual processes will lead inevitably to a steady evolutionary upgrading in the "intelligence quotient" of successive generations of computing devices. The application of lessons from the life sciences may be more effective than anything else in speeding the day when, by the availability of machines that truly "think," humanity will finally be able to enjoy the real fruits of automation.

These are foreseeable practical consequences of the cross-fertilization of computer and brain research. There is also a philosophic by-product of first magnitude that may well come out of this kind of activity. The convergence of computer and brain sciences will render untenable the studied avoidance of the phenomenon of consciousness that has characterized the science of the last fifty years. When it is established that there is a continuous gradation between the design features and performance characteristics of man-made machines and the intelligent living products of nature, scientists will be forced to come to terms in some way with this most vivid and real property of human experience.

To be sure, in considering consciousness, we defined a postulate, generally similar to that which underlies much modern thinking, that permitted us to get on with our physically based speculation. But our working hypothesis constituted no more than an untidy patching up of the hole in our logical structure that we hoped would permit it to hold together until we could finish our planned exploration of some of the current frontiers of brain research. We have evaded the main issue: why a philosophy with the spectacular and growing successes of mechanism should fail so completely to provide any means of dealing with the very real phenomenon of consciousness. Questions are already arising in increasing numbers, the answers to which now appear to require a completely unsatisfactory blending of physics and metaphysics. Consider, for example, Sperry's split-brain animals, which respond differently to external stimuli depending upon which half of the brain they are using. Have they been provided with two different senses of consciousness that are turned on or off in accordance with which eye they look through? If an affirmative answer is not yet required by the evidence, what will we say if Sperry succeeds in extending the split-brain technique all the way down through the brainstem and thereby makes possible the development of two clearly different personalities in the same body? And what is the significance of the remarkable fact, discovered by Magoun and coworkers, that the sense of consciousness is turned on or off by the presence or absence of suitable electric currents in the reticular activating system of the brainstem? What about the peculiar phenomenon of "double consciousness" experienced by Penfield's patients under temporal-lobe stimulation, in which they had the subjective sensation of living concurrently in the past and the present?

Questions arising out of a blending of physical and biological developments are even more compelling. Consider the following line of speculation: It is now known that there is no essential difference between living and nonliving matter. Living matter either has, or has almost, been synthesized in the laboratory out of inert ingredients, the statement depending upon just where the line is drawn in the very fuzzy region that separates life from nonlife. Rapid progress is also being made in breaking the genetic code; it is no longer purely science fiction to speculate that one day man may be able to synthesize the chromosomic content of cell nuclei and, by providing a suitable growth environment, thereby "build" living organisms of considerable complexity. Now, if the resulting animal is similar to a naturally created higher animal, will it be conscious? It would be hard to doubt that it will. What then if a creature of similar behavior and intelligence were to be fabricated from components of quite a different kind—with a nervous system and brain based on electronic components instead of neurons, for example? Would it too possess consciousness and the subjective feelings that go along with it? For all we know today, surely this has to be considered to be a possibility. And how about existing electronic digital computers? Is it possible that, somewhere among their wires and transistors, there already stirs the dim glimmering of the same kind of sense of awareness that has become, for man, his most personal and precious possession? Fantastic? Perhaps.

Such speculation is no longer pointless. It leads to what may well be the only sound procedure for permanently plugging the hole in the logical structure of the mechanistic philosophy: *to accept the sense of consciousness itself as a natural phenomenon suited to being described by and dealt with by the body of laws and methods of the physical sciences.*

This suggestion is really not particularly revolutionary. The immediate human reaction—that consciousness is by its very nature a mysterious and unexplainable phenomenon—is not very pertinent. All the laws and properties of nature are fundamentally mysterious and unexplainable; science can no more explain gravitational attraction or electric charge than it can the sense of consciousness. "Explanation" of the laws and fundamental particles of physics would involve exactly the same kind of crossing of the boundary into the realm of metaphysics as would "explanation" of the subjective sensations and feelings that constitute our personal sense of awareness.

All that is really required, for the sense of consciousness to constitute a reasonable candidate for admission into the structure of physics, is that it be orderly and lawful in its operation, and that techniques be conceivable for determining the relationships between its properties and the physical environment in which it occurs. Admittedly, the observations involved in any attempt to make consciousness scientifically respectable will have to depend mainly on variations in the personal sensations of human subjects, rather than on the objective readings of oscilloscopes and meters. This will make the matter more difficult, but certainly not impossible. We may never know just what is meant by a level of consciousness that is twice as intense as another, but there need be no ambiguity about the determination that all human subjects report themselves to feel conscious or unconscious in accordance with whether the electric potential at a certain point in a specific nucleus of the brainstem is greater or less than, say, 0.025 volt. Similarly specific relationships are already hinted at by some of the experiments connecting the electrical conditions of definite brain structures with such attributes of consciousness as fear and pleasure. Of course, this observation also underlines the fact that consciousness is not a simple property but possesses several attributes corresponding to the various sensations, perhaps in somewhat the same way as a fundamental particle of physics may possess not only mass but also charge and spin.

In interpreting consciousness as a physical property of matter, we do not really need to go back 300 years to the time of Spinoza. We have no reason to associate consciousness with all matter—only with the brain. And only with part of the brain, part of the time. We have learned that most of the work of the brain is done completely unconsciously, and we have come to have a healthy respect for the quality and the complexity of the computing/control functions that are carried out in this way. Even in what we consider to be our conscious mental activity, we are actually aware of only a part of what is going on in the brain. There must be intricate switching and scanning processes underway that move related thoughts successively into our consciousness; we are aware of the thoughts, but not of how they get there. Such unconscious activity sometimes appears to extend to complicated logical thinking—how else can we account for the sudden insight or solution of a difficult problem that sometimes comes to us when least expected? Even when it seems to us that our conscious processes are completely responsible for our mental activities, we may be wrong; the real work of the brain may be that which is going on quietly behind the scenes. The evidence as to the automatic, mechanical character of basic learning processes should have left the reader with a real question as to whether what his sense of awareness tells him he is doing in a learning situation is entirely to be trusted.

What is required to fit the facts, therefore, is not a theory that assigns a tiny bit of consciousness to every atom of matter. It does not even appear that consciousness is an inevitable property of complex computing/logic-processing structures. Instead, the evidence suggests that the property of consciousness is possessed only by very special organizations of matter (of types yet to be determined) when placed in a suitable electrochemical state (that is still unknown).

The relative rareness of the conditions necessary for the conscious state may, of course, be matched by its relative unimportance. No useful purpose has yet been established for the sense of awareness that illumines a small fraction of the mental activities of a few species of higher animals. It is not clear that the behavior of any individual or the course of world history would have been affected in any way if awareness were nonexistent. But this is a cosmic rather than a personal point of view. To a conscious person, anything pertaining to the property of consciousness must always seem of overriding importance. Of the greatest human significance, therefore, is the probability that our subjective sensations are ruled in a regular and predictable way by the processes of natural law. It will become progressively more difficult for this probability to be ignored as the matter is thrown into increased prominence by the convergence of the computer and brain sciences. The result may well be the transfer of the phenomenon of consciousness out of metaphysics and into the realm described by the physical laws of nature. It would be hard to imagine a development of more far-reaching importance to science and philosophy. Yet it could come as a consequence of increased collaborative research on computers and the brain.

Truly the convergence of the disciplines of computer research and brain research is a movement of the greatest importance. It is doubtful whether the history of science provides any example in which the merging of two technical fields provided a superior opportunity for major accomplishment. Although the collaborative effort is making good progress, it is still in its infancy. One prediction can be safely made: as understanding develops, promising new avenues of research will open up at a rapidly increasing rate. Whether or not the interdisciplinary effort is adequately manned today, it is very likely to be undermanned tomorrow, in relation to the importance and opportunities of the field.

This book has been written in the hope that, by calling attention to some of the interesting adventures available to those who explore the mysteries of the brain, it might help a few computer scientists make the decision to join the movement. There can be considerable doubt as to its attainment of the objective, but there can be no question as to the importance of the goal. The cause is a worthy one.

4   Some studies in machine learning using the game of checkers. II — Recent progress

ARTHUR L. SAMUEL

The first report on this program goes back ten years, and the following paper is a description of the state of the results as of 1967. Samuel's program is a landmark in artificial intelligence work. Its success—it has beaten a state champion and played to a draw with others—is less important than its ability to learn, both from books and from its own mistakes.

Although this is the most technical paper included here, it is lucidly written and provides the reward of a "front-line" view of research in artificial intelligence. Moreover the author carefully signals and discusses the major lacunae in the present state of the program. Perhaps most noteworthy here are his comments on the role of strategy in the game.

Arthur L. Samuel taught at M.I.T. and the University of Illinois, and worked at Bell Telephone Laboratories before joining IBM in 1949. After his retirement in 1966, he assumed a position in the Computer Science Department at Stanford University.

From Arthur L. Samuel, "Some Studies in Machine Learning Using the Game of Checkers. II—Recent Progress," *IBM Journal of Research and Development*, Vol. II, No. 6 (November 1967), pp. 601–17.

81

INTRODUCTION

Limited progress has been made in the development of an improved book-learning technique and in the optimization of playing strategies as applied to the checker playing program described in an earlier paper with this same title.[1] Because of the sharpening in our understanding and the substantial improvements in playing ability that have resulted from these recent studies, a reporting at this time seems desirable. Unfortunately, the most basic limitation of the known machine learning techniques, as previously outlined, has not yet been overcome nor has the program been able to outplay the best human checker players.[2]

We will briefly review the earlier work. The reader who does not find this review adequate might do well to refresh his memory by referring to the earlier paper.

Two machine learning procedures were described in some detail: (1) a rote learning procedure in which a record was kept of the board situation encountered in actual play together with information as to the results of the machine analyses of the situation; this record could be referenced at terminating board situations of each newly initiated tree search and thus, in effect, allow the machine to look ahead further than time would otherwise permit and, (2) a generalization learning procedure in which the program continuously re-evaluated the coefficients for the linear polynomial used to evaluate the board positions at the terminating board situations of a look-ahead tree search. In both cases, the program applied a minimax procedure to back up scores assigned to the terminating situations and so select the best move, on the assumption that the opponent would also apply the same selection rules when it was his turn to play. The rote learning procedure was characterized by a very slow but continuous learning rate. It was most effective in the opening and end-game phases of the play. The generalization learning procedure, by way of contrast, learned at a more rapid rate but soon approached a plateau set by limitations as to the adequacy of the man-generated list of parameters used in the evaluation polynomial. It was surprisingly good at mid-game play but fared badly in the opening and end-game phases. Both learning procedures were used in cross-board play against human players and in self-play, and in spite of the absence of absolute standards were able to improve the play, thus demonstrating the usefulness of the techniques discussed.

Certain expressions were introduced which we will find useful. These are: *Ply,* defined as the number of moves ahead, where a ply of two consists of one proposed move by the machine and one anticipated reply by the opponent; *board parameter value,** defined as the numerical value associated with some measured property or parameter of a board situation. Parameter values, when multiplied by learned coefficients, become *terms* in the learning polynomial. The value of the entire polynomial is a *score.*

The most glaring defects of the program, as earlier discussed, were (1) the absence of an effective machine procedure for generating new parameters for the evaluation procedure, (2) the incorrectness of the assumption of linearity which underlies the use of a linear polynomial, (3) the general slowness of the learning procedure, (4) the inadequacies of the heuristic procedures used to prune and to terminate the tree search, and (5) the absence of any strategy considerations for altering the machine mode of play in the light of the tactical situations as they develop during play. While no progress has been made with respect to the first of these defects, some progress has been made in overcoming the other four limitations, as will now be described.

We will restrict the discussion in this paper to generalization learning schemes in which a preassigned list of board parameters is used. Many attempts have been made to improve this list, to make it both more precise and more inclusive. It still remains a man-generated list and it is subject to all the human failings, both of the programmer, who is not a very good checker player, and of the checker experts consulted, who are good players (the best in the world, in fact) but who, in general, are quite unable to express their immense knowledge of the game in words, and certainly not in words understandable to this programmer. At the present time, some twenty-seven parameters are in use, selected from the list given in Ref. 1 with a few additions and modifications, although

---

* Example of a *board parameter* is MOB (total mobility): the number of squares to which the player can potentially move, disregarding forced jumps that might be available; Ref. 1 describes many other parameters.

a somewhat longer list was used for some of the experiments which will be described.

Two methods of combining evaluations of these parameters have been studied in considerable detail. The first, as earlier described, is the linear polynomial method in which the values for the individual parameters are multiplied by coefficients determined through the learning process and added together to obtain a score. A second, more recent procedure is to use tabulations called "signature tables" to express the observed relationship between parameters in subsets. Values read from the tables for a number of subsets are then combined for the final evaluation. We will have more to say on evaluation procedures after a disgression on other matters.

THE HEURISTIC SEARCH FOR HEURISTICS

At the risk of some repetition, and of sounding pedantic, it might be well to say a bit about the problem of immensity as related to the game of checkers. As pointed out in the earlier paper, checkers is not deterministic in the practical sense since there exists no known algorithm which will predict the best move short of the complete exploration of every acceptable [3] path to the end of the game. Lacking time for such a search, we must depend upon heuristic procedures.

Attempts to see how people deal with games such as checkers or chess [4] reveal that the better players engage in behavior that seems extremely complex, even a bit irrational in that they jump from one aspect to another, without seeming to complete any one line of reasoning. In fact, from the writer's limited observation of checker players he is convinced that the better the player, the more apparent confusion there exists in his approach to the problem, and the more intuitive his reactions seem to be, at least as viewed by the average person not blessed with a similar proficiency. We conclude [5] that at our present stage of knowledge, the only practical approach, even with the help of the digital computer, will be through the development of heuristics which tend to ape human behavior. Using a computer, these heuristics will, of course, be weighted in the direction of placing greater reliance on speed than might be the case for a human player, but we assume that the complexity of the human response is dictated by the complexity of the task to be performed and is, in some way, an indication of how such problems can best be handled.

We will go a step further and maintain that the task of making decisions as to the heuristics to be used is also a problem which can only be attacked by heuristic procedures, since it is essentially an even more complicated task than is the playing itself. Furthermore, we will seldom, if ever, be able to perform a simple test to determine the effectiveness of any particular heuristic, keeping everything else the same, as any scientist generally tends to do. There are simply too many heuristics that should be tested and there is simply not enough time to embark on such a program even if the cost of computer time were no object. But, more importantly, the heuristics to be tested are not independent of each other and they affect the other parameters which we would like to hold constant. A definitive set of experiments is virtually impossible of attainment. We are forced to make compromises, to make complicated changes in the program, varying many parameters at the same time and then, on the basis of incomplete tests, somehow conclude that our changes are or are not in the right direction.

PLAYING TECHNIQUES

While the investigation of the learning procedures forms the essential core of the experimental work, certain improvements have been made in playing techniques which must first be described. These improvements are largely concerned with tree searching. They involve schemes to increase the effectiveness of the alpha-beta pruning, the so-called "alpha-beta heuristic" [6] and a variety of other techniques going under the generic name of tree pruning. [7] These improvements enable the program to analyze further in depth than it otherwise could do, albeit with the introduction of certain hazards which will be discussed. Lacking an ideal board evaluation scheme, tree searching still occupies a central role in the checker program.

Alpha-beta pruning

Alpha-beta pruning can be explained simply as a technique for not exploring those branches of a search tree that the analysis up to any given point indicates not to be of further interest either to the player making the analysis (this is obvious) or to his opponent (and it is this that is frequently overlooked). In effect, there are always two scores, an *alpha value* which must be exceeded for a board to be considered desirable by the side about to play, and a *beta value* which must not be exceeded for the move leading to the board to have been made by the opponent. We note that if the board should not be acceptable to the side about to play, this player will usually be able to deny his opponent the opportunity of making the move leading to this board, by himself making a different earlier move. While people use this technique more or less instinctively during their look-ahead analyses, they sometimes do not understand the full implications of the principle. The saving in the required amount of tree searching which can be achieved through its use is extremely large, and as a consequence alpha-beta pruning is an almost essential ingredient in any game playing program. There are no hazards associated with this form of pruning.

A move tree of the type that results when alpha-beta pruning is effective is shown in Figure 1, it being assumed that the moves are investigated from left to right. Those paths that are shown in dashed lines need never be considered, as can be verified by assigning any arbitrary scores to the terminals of the dashed paths and by mini-maxing in the usual way. Admittedly the example chosen is quite special but it does illustrate the possible savings that can result. To realize the maximum saving in computational effort as shown in this example one must investigate the moves in an ideal order, this being the order which would result were each side to always consider its best possible move first. A great deal of thought and effort has gone into devising techniques which increase the probability that the moves will be investigated in something approaching this order.

The way in which two limiting values (McCarthy's alpha and beta) are used in pruning can be seen by referring to Figure 2, where the tree of Figure 1 has been redrawn with the uninvestigated branches deleted. For reasons of symmetry all boards during the look-ahead are scored as viewed by the side whose turn it then is to move. This means that mini-maxing is actually done by changing the sign of a score, once for each ply on backing up the tree, and then always maximizing. Furthermore, only one set of values (alpha

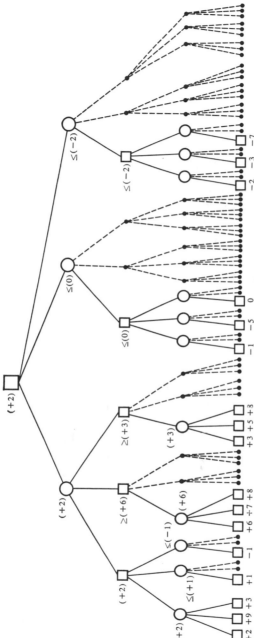

Figure 1 A (look-ahead) move tree in which alpha-beta pruning is fully effective if the tree is explored from left to right. Board positions for a look-ahead move by the first player are shown by squares, while board positions for the second player are shown by circles. The branches shown by dashed lines can be left unexplored without in any way influencing the final move choice.

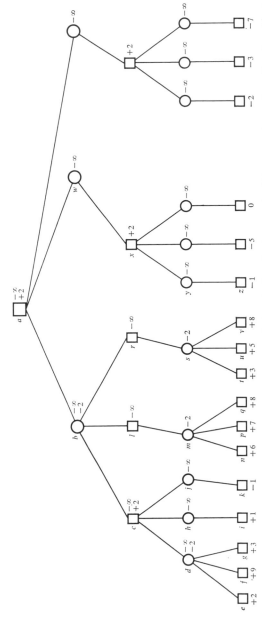

Figure 2 The move tree of Fig. 1 redrawn to illustrate the detailed method used to keep track of the comparison values. Board positions are lettered in the order that they are investigated and the numbers are the successive alpha values that are assigned to the boards as the investigation proceeds.

value) need be considered. Alpha values are assigned to all boards in the tree (except for the terminating boards) as these boards are generated. These values reflect the score which must be exceeded before the branch leading to this board will be entered by the player whose turn it is to play. When the look-ahead is terminated and the terminal board evaluated (say at *board e* in Figure 2) then the value which currently is assigned the board two levels up the tree (in this case at *board c*) is used as the alpha value, and unless the terminal board score exceeds this alpha value, the player at *board c* would be ill advised to consider entering the branch leading to this terminal board. Similarly if the negative of the terminal board score does not exceed the alpha value associated with the board immediately above in the tree (in this case at *board d*) then the player at *board d* will not consider this to be a desirable move. An alternate way of stating this second condition, in keeping with McCarthy's usage, is to say that the negative of the alpha value associated with the board one level up the tree (in this case *board d*) is the beta value which must not be exceeded by the score associated with the board in question (in this case *board e*). A single set of alpha values assigned to the boards in the tree thus performs a dual role, that of McCarthy's alpha as referenced by boards two levels down in the tree and, when negated, that of McCarthy's beta as referenced by boards one level down in the tree.

Returning to the analysis of Figure 2, we note that during the initial look-ahead (leading to *board e*) nothing is known as to the value of the boards, consequently the assigned alpha values are all set at minus infinity (actually within the computer only at a very large negative number). When *board e* is evaluated, its score ($+2$) is compared with the alpha at c ($-\infty$), and found to be larger. The negative of the score (-2) is then compared with the alpha at d ($-\infty$) and, being larger, it is used to replace it. The alpha at d is now -2 and it is unaffected by the subsequent consideration of terminal *boards f* and *g*. When all paths from *board d* have been considered, the final alpha value at d is compared with the current alpha value at *board b* ($-\infty$); it is larger, so the negative of alpha at d (now $+2$) is compared with the current alpha value at c ($-\infty$) and, being larger, it is used to replace the c value, and a new move from *board c* is investigated leading to *board h* and then *board i*. As we go down the tree we must assign an alpha value to *board h.* We cannot use the alpha value at *board c* since we are now interested in the minimum that the other side will accept. We can however advance the alpha value from *board b*, which in this case is still at its initial value of $-\infty$. Now when *board i* is evaluated at $+1$ this value is compared with the alpha at *board c* ($+2$). The comparison being unfavorable, it is quite unnecessary to consider any other moves originating at *board h* and we go immediately to a consideration of *boards j* and *k*, where a similar situation exists. This process is simply repeated throughout the tree. On going forward the alpha values are advanced each time from two levels above and, on backing up, two comparisons are always made. When the tree is completely explored, the final alpha value on the initial board is the score, and the correct move is along the path from which this alpha was derived.

The saving that results from alpha-beta pruning can be expressed either as a reduction in the apparent amount of branching at each node or as an increase in the maximum ply to which the search may be extended in a fixed time interval. With optimum ordering, the apparent branching factor is reduced very nearly to the square root of its original value or, to put it another way, for a given investment in computer time, the maximum ply is very nearly doubled. With moderately complex trees the savings can be astronomical. For example consider a situation with a branching factor of 8. With ideal alpha-beta pruning this factor is reduced to approximately 2.83. If time permits the evaluation of 66,000 boards (about 5 minutes for checkers), one can look ahead approximately 10 ply with alpha-beta pruning. Without alpha-beta this depth would require the evaluation of 8^{10} or approximately 10^9 board positions and would require over 1,000 hours of computation! Such savings are of course dependent upon perfect ordering of the moves. Actual savings are not as great but alpha-beta pruning can easily reduce the work by factors of a thousand or more in real game situations.

Some improvement results from the use of alpha-beta pruning even without any attempt to optimize the search order. However, the number of branches which are pruned is then highly variable depending upon the accidental ordering of the moves. The problem is further complicated in the case of checkers because of the variable nature of the branching. Using alpha-beta alone the apparent branching factor is reduced from something in the vicinity of 6 (reduced from the value of 8 used above because of forced jump moves) to about 4, and with the best selection of ordering practiced to date, the apparent branching is reduced to 2.6. This leads to a very substantial increase in the depth to which the search can be carried.

Although the principal use of the alpha and beta values is to prune useless branches from the move tree, one can also avoid a certain amount of inconsequential work whenever the difference between the current alpha value and the current beta value becomes small. This means that the two sides have nearly agreed as to the optimum score and that little advantage to either one side or the other can be found by further exploration along the paths under investigation. It is therefore possible to back-up along the tree until a part of the tree is found at which this alpha-beta margin is no longer small. Not finding such a situation one may terminate the search. The added savings achieved in this way, while not as spectacular as the savings from the initial use of alpha-beta, are quite significant, frequently reducing the work by an additional factor of two or more.

Plausibility analysis

In order for the alpha-beta pruning to be truly effective, it is necessary, as already mentioned, to introduce some technique for increasing the probability that the better paths are explored first. Several ways of doing this have been tried. By far the most useful seems to be to conduct a preliminary plausibility survey for any given board situation by looking ahead a fixed amount, and then to list the available moves in their apparent order of goodness on the basis of this information and to specify this as the order to be followed in the subsequent analysis. A compromise is required as to the depth to which this plausibility survey is to be conducted; too short a look-ahead renders it of doubtful value, while too long a look-ahead takes so much time that the depth of the final analysis must be curtailed. There is also a question as to whether or not this plausibility analysis should be applied at all ply levels during the main look-ahead or only for the first few levels. At one time the program used a plausibility survey for only the first two ply levels of the main look-ahead with the plausibility analysis itself being

carried to a minimum ply of 2. More recently the plausibility analysis has been applied at all stages during the main look-ahead and it
has been carried to a minimum ply of 3 during certain portions of
the look-ahead and under certain conditions, as will be explained
later.

We pause to note that the alpha-beta pruning as described might
be called a backward pruning technique in that it enables branches
to be pruned at that time when the program is ready to back up
and is making mini-max comparisons. It assumes that the analyses
of all branches are otherwise carried to a fixed ply and that all
board evaluations are made at this fixed ply level. As mentioned
earlier, the rigorous application of alpha-beta technique introduces
no opportunities for erroneous pruning. The result in terms of the
final moves chosen are always exactly as they would have been
without the pruning. To this extent the procedure is not a heuristic
although the plausibility analysis technique which makes it effective is certainly a heuristic.

While the simple use of the plausibility analysis has been found
to be quite effective in increasing the amount of alpha-beta pruning, it suffers from two defects. In the first place the actual amount
of pruning varies greatly from move to move, depending upon
random variations in the average correctness of the plausibility
predictions. Secondly, within even the best move trees a wrong
prediction at any one point in the search tree causes the program
to follow a less than optimum path, even when it should have been
possible to detect the fact that a poor prediction had been made
before doing an excessive amount of useless work.

A multiple-path enhanced-plausibility procedure

In studying procedures used by the better checker players one is
struck with the fact that evaluations are being made continuously
at all levels of look-ahead. Sometimes unpromising lines of play are
discarded completely after only a cursory examination. More often
less promising lines are put aside briefly and several competing
lines of play may be under study simultaneously with attention
switching from one to another as the relative goodness of the lines
of play appears to change with increasing depth of the tree search.
This action is undoubtedly prompted by a desire to improve the

alpha-beta pruning effectiveness, although I have yet to find a checker master who explains it in these terms. We are well advised to copy this behavior.

Fortunately, the plausibility analysis provides the necessary information for making the desired comparisons at a fairly modest increase in data storage requirements and with a relatively small amount of reprogramming of the tree search. The procedure used is as follows. At the beginning of each move, all possible moves are considered and a plausibility search is made for the opponent's replies to each of these plays. These moves are sorted in their apparent order of goodness. Each branch is then carried to a ply of 3; that is, making the machine's first move, the opponent's first reply and the machine's counter move. In each case the moves made are based on a plausibility analysis which is also carried to a minimum depth of 3 ply. The path yielding the highest score to the machine at this level is then chosen for investigation and followed forward for two moves only (that is, making the opponent's indicated best reply and the machine's best counter reply, always based on a plausibility analysis). At this point the score found for this path is compared with the score for the second best path as saved earlier. If the path under investigaiton is now found to be less good than an alternate path, it is stored and the alternative path is picked up and is extended in depth by two moves. A new comparison is made and the process is repeated. Alternately, if the original path under investigation is still found to be the best it is continued for two more moves. The analysis continues in this way until a limiting depth as set by other considerations has been reached. At this point the flitting from path to path is discontinued and the normal minimaxing procedure is instituted. Hopefully, however, the probability of having found the optimum path has been increased by this procedure and the alpha-beta pruning should work with greater effectiveness. The net effect of all of this is to increase the amount of alpha-beta pruning, to decrease the playing time, and to decrease the spread in playing time from move to move.

This enhanced plausibility analysis does not in any way affect the hazard-free nature of the alpha-beta pruning. The plausibility scores used during the look-ahead procedure are used only to determine the order of the analyses and they are all replaced by properly mini-maxed scores as the analysis proceeds.

One minor point may require explanation. In order for all of the saved scores to be directly comparable, they are all related to the same side (actually to the machine's side) and as described they are compared only when it is the opponent's turn to move; that is, comparisons are made only on every alternate play. It would, in principle, be possible to make comparisons after every move but little is gained by so doing and serious complications arise which are thought to offset any possible advantage.

A move tree as recorded by the computer during actual play is shown in Figure 3. This is simply a listing of the moves, in the order in which they were considered, but arranged on the page to reveal the tree structure. Asterisks are used to indicate alternate moves at branch points and the principal branches are identified by serial numbers. In the interest of clarity, the moves made during each individual plausibility search are not shown, but one such search was associated with each recorded move. While the tree of Figure 3 exhibits the combined effect of several forms of pruning, some yet to be explained, the flitting from path to path is clearly visible at the start. In this case there were 9 possible initial moves which were surveyed at the start and listed in the initially expected best order as identified by the serial numbers. Each of these branches was carried to a depth of 3 ply and the apparent best branch was then found to be the one identified by serial number 9, as may be verified by reference to the scores at the far right (which are expressed in terms of the side which made the last recorded move on the line in question). Branch 9 was then investigated for four more moves, only to be put aside for an investigation of the branch identified by the serial number 1 which in turn was displaced by 9, then finally back to 1. At this point the normal mini-maxing was initiated. The amount of flitting from move to move is, of course, critically dependent upon the exact board configuration being studied. A fairly simple situation is portrayed by this illustration. It will be noted that on the completion of the investigation of branch 1, the program went back to branch 9, then to branch 3, followed by branch 2, and so on until all branches were investigated. As a matter of general interest this tree is for the fifth move of a game following a 9–14, 22–17, 11–15 opening, after an opponent's move of 17–13, and move 15–19 (branch 1) was finally chosen. The 7094 computer took 1 minute and 3 seconds to make the move and to record the tree. This game was one of a set of 4 games being played simultaneously by the machine and the length of the tree search had been arbitrarily reduced to speed up the play. The alpha and beta values listed in the columns to the right are both expressed in terms of the side making the last move, and hence a score to be considered must be larger than alpha and smaller than beta. For clarity of presentation deletions have been made of most large negative values when they should appear in the alpha column and of most large positive values when such values should appear in the beta column.

Forward pruning

In addition to the hazardless alpha-beta pruning, as just described, there exist several forms of forward pruning which can be used to reduce the size of the search tree. There is always a risk associated with forward pruning since there can be no absolute assurance that the scores that would be obtained by a deeper analysis might not be quite different from those computed at the earlier ply. Indeed if this were not so, there would never be any reasons for looking ahead. Still it seems reasonable to assume that some net improvement should result from the judicious use of these procedures. Two simple forms of forward pruning were found to be useful after a variety of more complicated procedures, based on an initial imperfect understanding of the problem, had been tried with great effort and little success.

To apply the first form it is only necessary to limit the number of moves saved for future analysis at each point in the tree, with provisions for saving all moves when the ply is small and gradually restricting the number saved, as the ply becomes greater until finally when the maximum feasible ply is being approached only two or three moves are saved. (The decision as to which are saved· is, of course, based on the plausibility analysis.)

In the second form of forward pruning one compares the apparent scores as measured by the plausibility analysis with the current values of alpha and beta that are being carried forward, and terminates the look-ahead if this comparison is unfavorable. Rather than to apply this comparison in an unvarying way it seems reasonable to set margins which vary with the ply so that the amount of

Figure 3 An actual look-ahead move tree as printed by the computer during play.

```
                                                MOVE TREE                              ALPHA   BETA   SCORE
15 19,23-16,12-19   1                                                                                00014
 7 11,25-22, 5- 9   2                                                                               -00030
 8 11,25-22, 4- 8   3                                                                               -00016
15 18,25-22,18-25   4                                                                               -00032
14 17,21-14,10-17   5                                                                               -00036
12 16,24-19,15-24   6                                                                               -06404
 6 9,13- 6, 2- 9    7                                                                               -00037
14 18,23-14,10-17   8                                                                               -00044
 5 9,24-19,15-24    9                                                                                00021

 9  28-19, 8-11,25-22,11-15                                                                          00013

 1  24-15,10-19,26-23,19-26                                                                          00010

 9  22-18,15-24                                                                                      00010

 1  30-23, 8-12,25-22,14-18                                        **                                00034
       *12-16                                                                 00034                  00021
       *27-24                                                                -00034                 -00045
       * 5- 9                                                                 00034                  00024
      *31-22, 7-10,30-26                                                     -00034                 -00105
       *27-23                                                                -00034                 -00105
    *26-22, 7-10,27-23,19-26                                                         00034 00045
       *30-26, 3- 7                                                                  00034 00036
       *31-26, 3- 7                                                                  00034 00036
                                                                                     00034 00033
    *27-24, 7-10,24-15,10-19                                                 -00034                 -00034
       *27-24                                                                -00034                 -00045
      *31-22, 7-10,30-26                                                     -00034                 -00105
       *27-23                                                                -00034                 -00105
*24-15,10-19,23-16,12-19,26-23,19-26,30-23, 8-12,25-22                        00034         00034 00045
    *26-22, 7-10                                                              00034         00034 00033
    *27-24, 7-10,24-15,10-19                                        -00034-00010
       27-20                                                                                -00000
 9     *15-22                                                                 00034                 -00036
       * 4- 8                                                                 00034                 -00016
       *11-16                                                                 00034
      * 7-11,19-15,11-18,21-17                                               -00034-00007
       *10-19,23- 7                                                          -00034 00001
     *10-15,19-1C, 6-15,13- 6                                                -00034 00004
       * 1- 5                                                                 00034                 -00032
 3  22-18,15-22,26-17,11-16,30-26, 8-11                                       00034                  00024
       *10-15                                                                 00034                 -17341
       * 5- 9,24-20                                                                         00034 00005
      *14-18                                                                  00034                 -00041
     * 3- 8,22-17,15-19,24-15,11-18,28-24                                    -00034 16023
       *10-19,17- 3                                                          -00034                 -00037
       * 5- 9                                                                 00034                 -00105
       * 6- 9                                                                 00034                 -00105
      *14-18                                                                                00034 00031
    *14-17,21-14,10-17,24-15,15-24,28-19                                     -00034 00031
    * 6- 9,13- 6, 2- 9,29-25                                                 -00034 00032
```

2

22-17,15-18,26-22,18-25,29-22,11-15
* 2- 7,29-25
* 3- 7

          *12-16

```
                                                          00034    -00030
                                                          00034    -00034
                                                                   -00034 00023
                                                          00034    -00037
```

*11-16
* 3- 7,22-17,15-19,24-15,11-18,28-24
      *10-19,17- 3
* 5- 9
* 6- 9
*14-18
* 2- 7,24-19,15-24,28-19,14-17
      * 5- 9
*11-16,24-19
    *11-16

```
                                                          00034    -00030
                                                          00034    -00034 00031
                                                          00034    -00034 16023
                                                          00034    -00037
                                                          00034    -00105
                                                          00034    -00045
                                                          00034    -00045
                                                          00034    -00045
                                                                   -00034 00012
```

4

29-22,14-17,21-14,10-17,22-18, 6- 9,13- 6
         *17-21
* 5- 9,24-19, 8-11
* 1- 5
* 7-11
* 8-11,23-18
* 7-11

```
                                                          00034    -00034 00100
                                                          00034    -00030
                                                          00034    -00007
                                                          00034    -00032
                                                          00034    -00036
                                                          00034    -00034-00007
                                                          00034    -00030
```

5

24-19,15-24,28-19, 5- 9,25-21, 9-14
         *17-22
* 8-11,25-22

```
                                                          00034    -00017
                                                          00034    -07432
                                                                   -00034 00031
```

7

* 7-10

23-18,15-22,25-18,14-23,26-19, 8-11,29-25
      * 9-14
*14-23,27- 2,10-14,24-20, 8-11
* 9-13
*10-15,24-19
* 3- 7

```
                                                          00034    -00055

                                                          00034    -00030
                                                          00034    -00045
                                                          00034    -15617
                                                          00034    -15620
                                                                   -00034 11614
                                                          00034    -22205
```

8

21-14, 6- 9,13- 6, 1-17,25-21,17-22,26-17
      * 2- 6
* 2-18,26-23, 8-11,23-14
      *12-16
* 8-11,24-15,15-24,28-19, 6- 9
      * 4- 8
*15-18,26-22
* 7-10

```
                                                          -00034   10416
                                                          -00034   -00105
                                                                   -00034 10436
                                                          00034    -10370
                                                          00034    -00056
                                                                   -00034 00063
                                                          00034    06541
                                                          00034    -07410
```

6

28-12, 8-11,23-18,14-23,27-18, 5- 9,21-17
         *11-15
* 7-11,23-18,14-23,27-18, 5- 9
         *11-15
* 5- 9,23-18
* 6- 9

```
                                                          -00034   06404
                                                          00034    -07355
                                                          00034    -06446
                                                          00034    -07353
                                                          00034    06422
                                                                   -00034 -07364
```

	3	4	5	6	7	8	9	10	11	12	13	14	15	16	17	18	19	20	21	22	TOTAL
PLY	11	16	16	37	29	40	32	34	14	2	0	0	0	0	0	0	0	0	0	0	231
USAGE	0	8	1	12	12	5	11	24	13	2	0	2	0	0	0	0	0	0	0	0	88
ENDS			000342	1	1	1	9 29A21	16	15-19	8-11	15-18										
2,	15 19								7-11			2									

pruning increases with increasing ply. At low plies only the most unlikely paths can then be pruned, while fairly severe pruning can be caused to occur as the effective ply limit is approached. If the margins are set too high, then only negligible pruning will result, while if they are low or nonexistent, the pruning will be extreme and the risks of unwise pruning correspondingly large.

There are, then, several factors which may be experimentally studied, these being the magnitudes of the several forms of pruning and the way in which these magnitudes are caused to vary with the ply. The problem is even more complicated than it might at first appear since the various kinds of forward pruning are not independent. It seems reasonable to assume that the rate at which the margins are reduced in the last described form of forward pruning and the rate at which the number pruning is increased in the earlier described form should both depend upon the position in the plausibility listings of earlier boards along the branch under investigation. It is quite impractical to make a detailed study of these interdependencies because the range of possible combinations is extremely large and a whole series of games would have to be played for each combination before valid conclusions could be drawn. Only a very few arrangements have, in fact, been tried and the final scheme adopted is based more on the apparent reasonableness of the arrangement than upon any real data.

The problem of "pitch" moves

In both of the above forms of forward pruning serious difficulties arise with respect to the proper consideration of so called "pitch moves," that is, of moves in which a piece is sacrificed in return for a positional advantage which eventually leads at least to an equalizing capture if not to an actual winning position. In principle, one should be able to assign the proper relative weights to positional and material advantages so as to assess such moves correctly, but these situations generally appear to be so detail-specific that it is impossible to evaluate them directly in any way other than by look-ahead. Troubles are encountered because of the limited look-ahead distance to which the plausibility analysis can be extended; the equalizing moves may not be found and as a consequence a good pitch move may be pruned. A two-ply plausibility search in which the analysis is terminated only on a non-jump situation will correctly evaluate move sequences of the type P, J, J, where P stands for pitch and J for jump (with N used later for non-jump moves which are not forcing) but it is powerless to evaluate sequences of the P, J, P, J, J type or of the P, J, N, P, J type. Both of these occur quite frequently in normal play. A three-ply search will handle the first of these situations but will still not handle the second case. Unsatisfactory as it is, the best practical compromise which has been achieved to date seems to be to employ a two-ply plausibility search for the normal non-pitch situation and to extend the search to three-ply whenever the first or the second move of the plausibility search is a jump. As noted earlier a three-ply search is customarily employed during the preliminary multi-path phase of the analysis.

Several more complicated methods of handling this problem have been considered, but all of the methods tried to date have proved to be very expensive in terms of computing time and all have been discarded. One of these methods which seemed to be marginally effective consisted of a procedure for keeping a separate account of all pitch moves encountered during the plausibility search, defined in this case as sequences in which the first move in the search is not a jump and the second move is a jump. These pitch moves were sorted on the basis of their relative scores and a record was kept of the four best pitch moves. Of course some of these moves might have been also rated as good moves quite independently of their pitch status, either because most or all of the available moves were of this type or because the return capture was not delayed beyond the ply depth of the search. After the normal number of unpruned moves at any branch point had been explored, the best remaining pitch move (eliminating any already considered) was then followed up. Since most of the apparent pitch moves may in fact be sheer giveaway moves, it was quite impractical to consider more than a single pitch move but hopefully that apparent pitch which led to the highest positional score should have been the most likely move to investigate. This procedure causes a two-ply plausibility search to salvage one likely candidate per move which could be of the P, J, N, J, J, type and it increases the power of the three-ply plausibility search correspondingly. Unfortunately a rather high percentage of the additional moves so considered were found to be of no value and the bookkeeping costs of this procedure also seemed to be excessive.

As a further extension of this general method of handling pitch moves, it is possible to cause pitch sequences of the P, J, N, P, J type to be investigated using a two-ply plausibility search. One need only specify that the main tree not be terminated when there is a jump move pending. While the cost of this addition might seem to be small, in practice it leads to the exploration in depth of extended giveaway sequences, and as a consequence it is of very questionable value.

Look-ahead termination

Regardless of the form or amount of forward pruning the time arrives along each path when it is necessary to terminate the look-ahead and evaluate the last board position. It is rather instructive to consider the termination as simply the end of the pruning process in which the pruning is complete. The use of a fixed depth for this final act of pruning, as previously assumed, is of course not at all reasonable and in fact it has never been used. In the earlier work [1] much attention was given to the wisdom of terminating the look-ahead at so called "dead" positions. With the current use made of the plausibility analysis this becomes a restriction mainly applicable to the plausibility analysis and it is of but little value in terminating the main tree itself. A limit is, of course, set by the amount of storage assigned for the tree but since the tree storage requirements are not excessive this should normally not be allowed to operate. If the plausibility analysis is at all effective one should be able to ration the computing time to various branches on the basis of their relative probability of being the best. For example, the initial path which survives the swapping routine during the initial look-ahead procedure should certainly be carried quite far along as compared with a path resulting from investigating, say, the fourth choice as found by the plausibility, when this is again followed by a fourth choice, etc., all the way through the tree.

The procedure found most effective has been that of defining a parameter called the *branching count* which is assigned a value for each board encountered during the tree search. To insure that all of the possible initial moves are given adequate consideration, identical values are given to the counts for the resulting boards after these initial moves. As each move originating with one of these boards is made, the branching count for the originating board is reduced by one unit and the resulting board after the move is assigned this new value as well. This process is repeated at each branch point down the tree until the branching count reaches zero, whereupon the search down this path is terminated (more correctly steps are taken to initiate termination unless other factors call for a further extension of the search, as will be explained later). Along the preferred branch, the branching count will thus be reduced by one unit for each ply level. For the second choice at any branch point a two-unit reduction occurs, for the third choice a three-unit, etc. The net result is that the less likely paths are terminated sooner than the most likely paths and in direct proportion to their decreasing likelihood.

Actually, a slightly more complicated procedure is used in that the branching count is set at a higher initial value and it is reduced by one unit when the move under consideration is a jump move and by four units when it is a normal move. This procedure causes the search to be extended further along those paths involving piece exchanges than along those that do not. Also the search is not permitted to terminate automatically when the branching count reaches zero if the indicated score for the move under consideration implies that this is in fact a preferred path. In this case the search is extended until the same depth has been reached along this path as had been reached along the previously indicated preferred path.

Tree pruning results

It has been found singularly difficult to assess the relative value of the various tree-pruning techniques in terms of their effect on the goodness of play. Special situations can always be found for which the various forward pruning procedures are either very effective or quite inadequate. Short of very extensive tests indeed, there seems to be no very good way to determine the relative frequency with which these different situations occur during normal play. About all that has been done has been to observe the resulting game trees and to depend upon the opinions of checker masters as to the goodness of the resulting moves and as to the reasonableness in appearance of the trees.

As mentioned earlier, for each move that is tabulated in Figure 3 there was actually an auxiliary plausibility move analysis to a ply of 2 or more which is not shown at all for reasons of clarity. One can think of this as a fine brush of moves emanating from each recorded move. Examples of all types of pruning can be noted in this tree, although additional information is needed for their unambiguous identification. Checker experts all agree that such trees as these are much denser than they probably should be. Attempts to make them less dense by stronger pruning always seem to result in occasional examples of conspicuously poor play. It may well be that denser trees should be used for machine play than for human play, to compensate for deficiencies in the board evaluation methods.

EVALUATION PROCEDURES AND LEARNING

Having covered the major improvements in playing techniques as they relate to tree searching, we can now consider improvements in evaluation procedures, with particular reference to learning. We will first discuss the older linear polynomial scheme and then go on to consider the signature-table procedure.

Linear polynomial evaluations

While it is possible to allow for parameter interaction, for example, by using binary connective terms as described in Ref. 1 the number of such interactions is large, and it seems necessary to consider more than pair-wise interactions. This makes it quite difficult to depart very much from the linear case. Some improvement in performance resulted when the overall game was split, initially, into 3 phases (opening, mid-game, and end-game) and more recently into 6 phases with a different set of coefficients determined for each phase. Various procedures for defining the phase of the game were tested, the simple one of making the determination solely in terms of the total number of pieces on the board seemed as good as any tried, and there were indications that little was to be gained by going to more than 6 phases.

The total number of parameters used at any one time has been varied from a very few to as many as 40. It has been customary to use all of the currently assessed successful parameters during the learning phase. A number of attempts have been made to speed up actual play by limiting the number of parameters to 5, 10, 15, or 20, selecting those with the larger magnitude coefficients. Five terms in the learning polynomial proved definitely inadequate, an improvement in going from 10 to 15 terms appeared to be barely discernible, and no evidence could be found for improvements in using more than 20 terms. In fact, there seemed to be some indication that a fortuitous combination of many ineffectual parameters with correspondingly low coefficients could, on occasion, override a more effective term and cause the program to play less well than it would with the ineffectual parameters omitted. In a series of 6 games played against R. W. Nealey (the U. S. blind checker champion) using 15 terms, the machine achieved 5 draws with one loss. The six poorest moves in these games as selected by L. W. Taylor, a checker analyst, were replayed, using 20 terms with no improvements and then using only 10 terms with a distinct improvement in two cases. There is, of course, no reason to believe that the program with the fewer number of terms might not have made other and more grievous errors for other untested board situations. Twenty terms were used during the games with W. F. Hellman referenced in note 2. No further work has been done on the linear polynomial schema in view of the demonstrated superiority of the "signature-table" procedure which will now be described.

Signature-table evaluations

The impracticality of considering all inter-parameter effects and the obvious importance of such interactions has led to the consideration of a number of different compromise proposals. The first successful compromise solution was proposed and tested on the Project Mac computer by Arnold Griffith, a graduate student at M.I.T. In one early modification of this scheme, 8 subsets of 5 parameters each were used, initially selected from 31 different parameters with some redundancy between subsets. Each subset was designated as a signature type and was characterized by an argument computed in terms of the values measured for the parameters within the subset for any particular board situation. The arguments for each signature type thus specify particular combinations of the parameters within the subset and serve as addresses for entering signature tables where the tabulated values are meant to reflect the relative worth to the computer's side of these particular combinations. In the initial Griffith scheme the values read from the 8 different signature tables were simply added together to obtain the final board evaluation. Parameters which are thought to be somehow related were grouped together in the individual subsets. While it would have been desirable to consider all possible values for each parameter and all possible interrelations between them, this quickly becomes unmanageable. Accordingly, the range of parameter values was restricted to but three values +1, 0, and −1; that is, the two sides could be equal or one or the other could be ahead in terms of the board property in question. Many of the board properties were already of this type. With each parameter limited to 3 values and with 5 parameters in a subset, a total of 3^5 or 243 entries in a signature table completely characterizes all possible interactions between the parameters. Actually since checkers is a "zero sum" game and since all parameters are defined symmetrically, it should be possible to reduce the table size roughly by two (122 entries instead of 243) by listing values for positive arguments only and taking values with a reversal of sign when negative arguments are evaluated. Allowing for 48 signature tables, 8 signature types for each of the 6 different phases, we arrive at a memory space requirement for 5856 table entries. Actually two words per table entry are used during the learning phase, as explained later, so the total memory requirement for the learning data is 11,712 words.

An example will make this procedure clear. Consider one signature type which might comprise the following 5 parameters: ANGLE, CENTER, OREO, GUARD and KCENT, which will not be explained now but which all have to do with the control of the king row and the center of the board. Now consider the GUARD parameter. This can be assigned a value of 0 if both or neither of the sides have complete control of their back rows, a value of +1 if the side in question controls his back row while the opponent does not, and a value of −1 if the conditions are reversed. The other 4 parameters can be similarly valued, giving a ternary number consisting of a 5-digit string selected from the set −, 0, and +, (where − is used for −1, etc.), e.g., "+ − 0 − −" characterizes one particular combination of these five different parameters. This argument can be associated with some function value, a large positive value if it is a desirable combination, a near zero function value if the advantages to the two sides are about even, and a large negative value if it is a disadvantageous combination. Both the arguments and functions are symmetric; that is, the argument and function for the other side would be that gotten by reversing all signs. (In the −, 0, + ternary system the first symbol in the list gives the sign and the processes of complementing and sign reversal are synonymous.) The argument for the other side would thus be − + 0 + +, a negative number which would not be tabulated but the function value would be the negative of the value listed under + − 0 − −, as it of course must be for the sum of the functions for the two sides to be zero.

The results obtained with this relatively simple method of handling parameter interactions were quite encouraging and as a result a series of more elaborate studies has been made using signature procedures of varying degrees of complexity. In particular, efforts were made (1) to decrease the total number of parameters by eliminating those found to be of marginal utility, (2) to increase the range of values permitted for each parameter, initially increasing the range for certain parameters to permit 7 values (−3, −2, −1, 0, +1, +2, +3) and more recently dividing the parameters into two equal groups—one group being restricted in range to 5 values, and (3) to introduce a hierarchical structure of signature tables where the outputs from the first level signature tables are combined in groups and used as inputs to a set of second level tables etc. (This is illustrated in a simplified form in the cover design of this issue.)

Most of the experimental work has been restricted to a consideration of the two arrangements shown in Figures 4 and 5. These are both three-level arrangements. They differ in the degree of the correlation between parameters which is recognized and in the range of values permitted the individual parameters. Both are compromises.

Obviously, the optimum arrangement depends upon the actual number of parameters that must be used, the degree to which these parameters are interrelated and the extent to which these individual parameters can be safely represented by a limited range of integers. In the case of checkers, the desired number of parameters seems to lie in the range of 20 to 30. Constraints on the range of values required to define the parameters can be easily determined but substantially nothing is known concerning the interdependencies between the parameters. A series of quite inconclusive experiments was performed in an effort to measure these interdependencies. About all that can be said is that the constraints imposed upon the permissible distribution of pieces on the board in any actual game, as set by the rules of the game and as dictated by good playing procedures, seem to produce an apparent average correlation between all parameters which is quite independent of the specific character of these parameters. The problem is further complicated by the fact that two quite opposing lines of argument can be advanced—the one to suggest that closely related terms be placed in the same subsets to allow for their interdependencies and the second to suggest that such terms be scattered among groups. The second suggestion can be made to look reasonable by considering the situation in which two parameters are unknowingly so closely related as to actually measure the same property. Placing these two terms in the same subset would accomplish nothing, while placing them in different subgroups permits a direct trade-off evaluation to be made between this property in question and the properties measured by the other parameters in both subgroups.

A few comments are in order at this time as to the supposedly symmetrical nature of the parameter data. While it is true that checkers is a zero-sum game and while it is true that the parameters are all defined in a symmetrical way, that is, as far as black vs white is concerned, the value of a board situation as defined by these parameters is actually dependent upon whose turn it is to play. A small but real bias normally exists for most parameters in favor of the side whose turn it is to move, although for certain parameters the reverse is true. The linear polynomial method of scoring is unfortunately not sensitive to these peculiarities of the different parameters since the partial scores for all types are simply added together. The signature table procedure should be able to take the added complication into account. Of course, the distinctions will be lost if the data are incorrectly stored or if they are incorrectly acquired. By storing the data in the uncompressed form

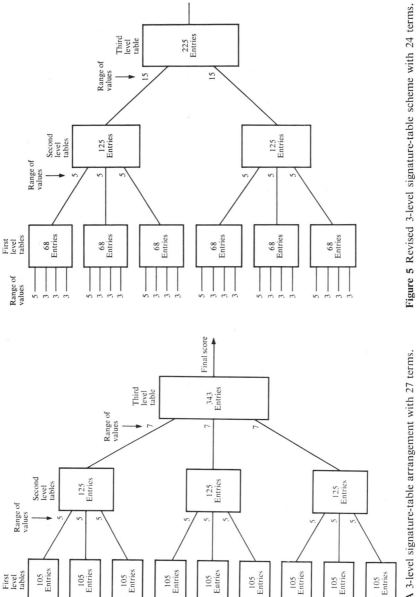

Figure 4 A 3-level signature-table arrangement with 27 terms.

Figure 5 Revised 3-level signature-table scheme with 24 terms.

Table 1 Linear polynomial terms (parameter names and learned coefficients) as used in the games with W. F. Hellman. These coefficients resulted from an analysis of approximately 150,000 book moves.

Phase 1 – Terms and coefficients

GUARD	QUART	DIAGL	EDGES	FRONT	ANGLE	CENTR	NODES	DCHOL	ADVAN
0.33	0.29	−0.21	−0.20	−0.19	−0.18	0.14	0.13	0.11	−0.08
PINS	DYKSQ	FREE	EXCHS	THRET	STARS	PRESS	UNCEN	LINES	
0.07	0.07	0.06	−0.05	0.04	0.04	−0.04	0.03	0.02	

Phase 2 – Terms and coefficients

SPIKE	GUARD	EDGES	QUART	CENTR	ANGLE	FRONT	ADVAN	SHOVE	THRET
0.85	0.36	−0.24	0.23	0.21	−0.21	−0.19	−0.18	0.16	0.14
NODES	PINS	DCHOL	STARS	OFSET	HOLES	DIAGL	UNCEN	MOBIL	
0.13	0.11	−.10	−0.09	0.09	0.09	−0.09	0.08	0.05	

Phase 3 – Terms and coefficients

SPIKE	KCENT	PANTS	GUARD	FRONT	CRAMP	ADVAN	EDGES	CENTR	STARS
0.88	0.48	0.42	0.37	−0.23	0.23	−0.23	−0.22	0.20	−0.19
QUART	ANGLE	THRET	DCHOL	PINS	SHOVE	NODES	UNCEN	OFSET	
0.19	−0.19	0.15	0.14	0.13	0.10	0.10	0.09	0.08	

Phase 4 – Terms and coefficients

SPIKE	GUARD	PANTS	KCENT	STARS	ADVAN	FRONT	THRET	ANGLE	EDGES
0.86	0.62	0.61	0.56	−0.30	−0.30	−0.27	0.26	−0.23	−0.22
DIAGL	CENTR	SHOVE	QUART	PINS	UNCEN	OFSET	DENYS	UNDEN	
0.22	0.20	0.18	0.16	0.12	0.11	0.09	0.09	−0.07	

Phase 5 – Terms and coefficients

GUARD	SPIKE	PANTS	KCENT	THRET	DIAGL	ADVAN	UNCEN	ANGLE	SHOVE
0.81	0.68	0.62	0.55	0.36	0.33	−0.32	0.27	−0.26	0.25
UNDEN	FRONT	DENYS	PINS	CENTR	EDGES	DYKSQ	QUART	DEUCE	
−0.22	−0.22	0.20	0.19	0.18	−0.16	−0.16	0.15	0.06	

Phase 6 – Terms and coefficients

PRESS	KCENT	UNCEN	UNDEN	DYKSQ	DENYS	SHOVE	DIAGL	SPIKE	THRET
−0.54	0.54	0.45	−0.41	−0.40	0.40	0.39	0.39	0.37	0.36
EXCHS	OFSET	ADVAN	PINS	ANGLE	FRONT	DEUCE	FREE	QUART	
−0.34	−0.26	−0.24	0.23	−0.23	−0.32	0.06	−0.11	0.08	

one can evaluate this effect. More will be said about this matter later.

In the arrangement shown in Figure 4 there were 27 parameters divided into 9 groups of three each, with each group being made up of one 3-valued parameter, one 5-valued parameter and one 7-valued parameter. Each first level signature table thus had 105 entries. The output values from each of these table were quantized into five values and second level signature tables were employed to combine these in sets of three. The second level tables thus had 125 entries each. These outputs are further quantized into 7 levels and a third level signature table with 343 entries was used to combine the outputs from the three second-level tables into a final output which was used as the final board evaluation. Obviously, the parameters used to enter the first level tables were grouped together on the basis of their assumed (and in some cases measured) interdependencies while the resulting signature types were again grouped together as well as possible, consistent with their assumed interdependencies. As always, there was a complete set of these tables for each of the six game phases. The tables were stored in full, without making use of the zero-sum characteristic to halve their size, and occupied 20,956 cells in memory. Outputs from the first level tables were quantized into 5 levels and the outputs from the second level tables into 7 levels.

The latest signature table procedure

The arrangement shown in Figure 5 used 24 parameters which were divided into 6 subgroups of 4 parameters each, with each subgroup containing one 5-valued parameter and three 3-valued parameters. In this case the first level tables were compacted by taking advantages of the assumed symmetrical character of the data, although this is a dubious procedure as already noted. It was justified in this case because of the added parameter interactions which this made possible and because of a very large inverse effect of table size on speed of learning. This reduced the size of the first level tables to 68 words each. The outputs from the first level tables were quantized into 5 levels as before and the outputs from the second level tables were quantized into 15 levels. The second and third level tables were not compacted, in an attempt to preserve some non-symmetrical features. The total memory requirement for the tables as thus constituted was 10,136 words.

Before we can discuss the results obtained with the signature table scheme it will be necessary to turn our attention to the various book learning procedures.

BOOK LEARNING

While book learning was mentioned briefly in Ref. 1, we will describe it in some detail as it was used throughout the studies now to be reported. Just as books speed up human learning, one might expect that a substantial increase in machine-learning speed might result if some use could be made of book information, in this case, the existing library of master play. To this end a reasonable sample (approximately 250,000 board situations) of this master play has been key punched and transcribed to magnetic tape. These are mostly draw games; in those cases where a win was achieved, data are used only from the moves made by the winning side. The program has been arranged to play through these recorded games considering one side, then the other, much as a person might do, analyzing the situation in terms of the existing evaluation procedures and listing the preferred move. This move is then compared with the book-recommended move and a suitable adjustment made in the evaluation procedure. This, of course, assumes that the book-recommended move is the only correct move, which it may not be, either because of a plurality of good moves or in some cases because of an actual error. However, if enough book moves are used, if the books are usually correct and if the adjustments per move are of the proper size, the process should converge toward an optimum evaluation procedure, subject always to a basic limitation as to the appropriateness and completeness of the parameter list used.

While it still takes a substantial amount of machine time to play through the necessary book games, the learning process is very much faster than for learning from actual play. In the first place, the game paths followed are from the start representative of the very best play since the program is forced always to make the recommended book move before proceeding to considering the next move. Secondly, it is possible to assign values to be associated with the moves in a very direct fashion without depending upon the unreliable techniques which were earlier described. Finally the analysis of each move can be extremely limited, with little or no minimaxing, since the only use made of the overall scores is that of measuring the learning, whereas in the earlier procedures these scores were needed to determine credit assignments to the parameters. The net effect of these factors is to make it possible to consider many more moves, at the rate of 300 to 600 moves per minute rather than the roughly one move per minute rate which is typical for actual games.

We will first explain how learning is achieved in terms of coefficients in a linear polynomial and then go on to the signature table case.

During the learning process, use must be made of the previously determined coefficients to perform the evaluation of all board situations either right after the initial moves or, if jump situations are encountered, at some terminating ply depth with the scores backed up by the mini-maxing procedure. During this mini-maxing, it is also necessary to back up the values of the parameter values themselves (i.e., the terms without coefficients), associated with the selected terminating board situations corresponding to the optimized path leading from each of the possible first moves. If there are 9 possible moves, a 9 × 27 table will be produced in which the rows correspond to the 9 different moves and the columns correspond to the 27 different parameters. On the basis of the book information, one row is indicated as being the best move.

The program must analyze the data within the table and accumulate totals which on the average indicate the relative worth of the different parameters in predicting the book move, and it must alter the coefficients to reflect the cumulative learning indicated by these totals. A variety of different procedures has been tested for accumulating totals; one of the simplest, and surprisingly, the most effective, seems to be to simply count the number of moves, for each parameter separately, for which the parameter value is larger than the value associated with the book move and the number of moves for which the parameter value is smaller than the value associated with the book move. If these cumulated counts over all board situations examined to date are designated H and L, then one measure of the goodness of the parameter in predicting the book move is given by

$$C = (L - H)/(L + H).$$

This has the dimensions of a correlation coefficient. It would have a value of $+1$ if the parameter in question always predicted the book move, a value of -1 if it never made a correct prediction, and a value of 0 if there was no correlation between the machine indications and the book. The best procedure found to date is simply to use the values of the C's so obtained as the coefficients in the evaluation polynomial, although arguments can be advanced for the use of the values of the C's raised to some power greater than 1 to overcome the effect of several inconsequential terms overriding a valuable indication from some other term as mentioned earlier.

Typical coefficients as tabulated by the computer are shown in Table 1 based on roughly 150,000 board situations and using 31 functions during the learning process. The 19 terms per phase having the largest magnitude coefficients are listed. The play against Hellman mentioned earlier used this particular set of terms.

Book learning using signature tables

Extending this book learning technique to the signature table case is relatively easy. All that need be done is to back up the signatures corresponding to the signature types being used in a way quite analogous to the handling of parameters in the linear polynomial case. Taking the example used earlier, one signature corresponding to one possible move might be $+ - 0 - -$ (actually stored in the machine in binary form). Each signature type for each possible move is similarly characterized. Two totals (called D and A) are accumulated for each of the possible signature types. Additions of 1 each are made to the D totals for each signature for the moves that were not identified as the preferred book move and an addition of n, where n is the number of nonbook moves, is made to the A totals for the signatures identified with the recommended book move. The reason for adding n to the book move A totals is, of course, to give greater positive weight to the book recommended move than is the negative weight given to moves that do not happen to correspond to the currently found book recommendation (there may be more than one good move and some other authority might recommend one of the other moves). This procedure has the incidental effect of maintaining equality between the grand totals of the A's and D's accumulated separately for all signatures in each table, and so of preserving a zero-sum character for the data.

When enough data have been accumulated for many different board situations, additions will have been made in the A and D columns against most of the signature arguments. The program then computes correlation coefficients for each signature defined in an analogous fashion to the earlier usage as

$$C = (A - D)/(A + D).$$

In the case of the third level table these values are used directly as board evaluations. For the other two levels in the signature table hierarchy, the actual values to be entered must be quantized so as to restrict the range of the tabulated values. This quantization has normally been done by first separating out all zero values and entering them into the tables as such. The nonzero values are then quantized by ranking the positive values and negative values separately into the desired number of equisized groups. The table entries are then made in terms of the small positive and negative integer numbers used to specify the relative ranking order of these groups.

This process of updating the signature tables themselves is done at intervals as determined by the rate at which significant data accumulate. During the intervals between updating, additions are, of course, continually being made to the tables of A's and D's.

There are several problems associated with this newer learning scheme. Reference has already been made to the space and time limitations which restrict the number of parameters to be combined in each signature type and restrict the range allowed for each parameter. The program has been written so that these numbers may be easily varied but this facility is of little use because of the very rapid rate at which the performance and the storage requirements vary with the values chosen. Values less than those indicated lead to performance but little different from that exhibited by the older linear polynomial experiments, while larger values greatly increase the memory requirements and slow down the learning rate. A great deal of juggling is required in order to make even the simplest change if the operating times are to be kept within a reasonable range, and this still further complicates the problem of considering meaningful experiments.

This inverse effect of the table size on the learning rate comes about because of the need to accumulate data in the A and D columns for each signature table entry. The effect is, of course, compounded by the hierarchical nature of the table complex. At the start of a new learning run there will be no entries in any of the tables, the computed C's must all be set to zero and the program will have no basis for the mini-maxing procedure. Depending upon the particular selection of the book games used there may, in fact, be a relatively long period of time before a significant fraction of signatures will have been encountered, and as a consequence, statistically unreliable data will persist in the "C" table. Not only will the individual function values be suspect but the quantizing levels will perforce be based on insufficient data as well. The magnitude of this effect will, of course, depend upon the size of the tables that the program is generating.

Palliative measures can be adopted to smooth the C tables in order to compensate for the blank entries and for entries based on insufficient data. Four of the more effective smoothing techniques have been found to be (1) smoothing by inversion, (2) smoothing from adjacent phases, (3) smoothing by interpolation and (4) smoothing by extrapolation. Smoothing is, of course, most needed during the early stages of the learning process but it also must be used during play even after a rather extensive learning run.

As a matter of fact, certain signatures are so improbable during book play (some may in fact be impossible) that voids are still found to exist in the signature tables, even after playing 100,000 book game board situations. There is the reassuring thought that signatures not found during the learning process are also unlikely to be found during play. However, because of the very many board situations explored during the look-ahead process and presumably because of the consequences of making decisions on the basis of statistically unreliable entries, the quality of the play using unsmoothed data was found to be somewhat erratic until a fairly large amount of learning had been achieved.

It should be pointed out, that the smoothing techniques are employed as temporary expedients. All previous smoothed results are discarded and completely new calculations of values of C are made periodically during learning from the accumulated and uncorrupted A and D data. The effects of smoothing do persist, however, since the entries in the second and third level tables, and hence the locations at which the A and D data are stored are influenced by it.

Smoothing by inversion is done by averaging positive and negative entries (with compensating sign inversions), and it is partially justified by the zero-sum symmetrical characteristic of the data.

Smoothing from adjacent phases is done by transferring data between phases. This is possible because of the random way in which data accumulate for the different phases, and it is reasonably valid because the values associated with a given signature vary but little between adjacent phases. This form of smoothing has been found to be of but limited utility since the same reasons which account for the absence of specific data for one phase often operate to prevent corresponding data from being generated for adjacent phases.

Smoothing by interpolation is based on the assumption that a missing correlation for a signature which contains one or more zeros in its argument can be approximated by averaging the values appearing for the related signatures where the zeros are individually replaced by a + and then by a −. In order for this to be effective there must be data available for both the + and − cases for at least one of the zero-valued parameters. This form of smoothing assumes a linear relationship for the effect of the parameter to which the interpolation is applied. It is therefore, no better as far as this one parameter is concerned than the older linear polynomial procedure. This form of smoothing is quite ineffectual since all too often balanced pairs of entries cannot be found.

Smoothing by extrapolation may take two forms, the simplest being when entries are found for the zero value of some particular function and for either the + or the − case and a void for the remaining case is to be filled. All too often however, the more recalcitrant cases are those in which the zero entry only for some one parameter is found and substitute data are sought for both the

+ and the − case. Here we have recourse to the fact that it is possible to compute the apparent effect of the massing parameter from all of the pertinent data in the signature table, on the assumption of linearity. The program therefore computes a correlation coefficient for this parameter alone and uses this with the found signature data. Admittedly this is a very dangerous form of extrapolation since it completely ignores all nonlinear effects, but it is often the only recourse.

Signature table learning results

The results of the best signature table learning run made to date are shown in Table 2. This particular run was arranged to yield comparable figures for both the newer signature table procedure and the older linear polynomial procedure. Because of the great amount of machine time required (approximately 10 hours per run) it has not yet been possible to optimize (1) the choice of parameters to be used, (2) the range of values to be assigned to these parameters, (3) the specific assignments of parameters to signature types, (4) the detailed hierarchical structure of the signature tables, (5) the table sizes and (6) the various smoothing techniques which must be used during the early learning phases.

Table 2 reports the apparent goodness of play based upon a correlation factor defined as

$$C = (L - H)/(L + H),$$

where L is the accumulated count of all available moves which the program rates lower than its rating for the book recommended move and H is the accumulated count of all available moves which the program rates higher than or equal to its rating for the book recommended move. During this learning run the program looked ahead only a single ply except in those cases where jumps were pending. The observed correlation coefficients are fairly good measures of the goodness of the evaluation procedures without minimaxing. Coefficients were computed during the run both by using the signature table procedure and by the older linear polynomial procedure. These figures are tabulated in the second and third columns against the total number of moves in column one. It will be

Table 2 Correlation coefficients measuring the effects of learning for the signature table procedure and for the linear polynomial procedure as a function of the total number of book moves analyzed. These tests used 27 parameters which for the signature table score were grouped in the configuration shown in Figure 4.

Total number of book moves analyzed	Correlation coefficient, C	
	Signature table case	Polynomial case
336	−0.08	−0.18
826	+0.06	−0.13
1,272	0.13	+0.06
1,769	0.18	0.10
2,705	0.27	0.15
3,487	0.31	0.16
4,680	0.34	0.15
5,446	0.36	0.16
8,933	0.38	0.19
10,762	0.39	0.20
14,240	0.40	0.21
17,527	0.41	0.22
21,302	0.41	0.23
23,666	0.42	0.23
30,173	0.43	0.24
40,082	0.43	0.25
50,294	0.43	0.26
55,165	0.44	0.26
66,663	0.45	0.26
70,083	0.45	0.26
90,093	0.46	0.26
106,477	0.46	0.26
120,247	0.47	0.26
145,021	0.47	0.26
173,091	0.48	0.26
183,877	0.48	0.26

observed that the coefficient for the polynomial procedure appears to stabilize at a figure of 0.26 after about 50,000 moves, while the coefficient for the signature table procedure continues to rise and finally after perhaps 175,000 moves reaches a limit of 0.48. Interestingly enough the signature-table coefficient was always larger than the polynomial coefficient even during the very early stage although a detailed analysis on a move-by-move basis, which cannot be easily reproduced here, did show that the signature table method was the more erratic of the two during this stage.

It should be noted that these linear polynomial results are not directly comparable with the coefficients for individual terms as reported in Table 1, since for Table 1 the H values used in computing .the C's did not include those moves rated equal to the book move while in Table 2 equals are included, and the computed coefficients are correspondingly lower. The discrepancy is particularly marked with respect to those parameters which are usually zero for most moves but which may be extremely valuable for their differentiating ability when they do depart from zero. Most of the terms with high coefficients in Table 1 have this characteristic. Furthermore, when mini-maxing was required during the two tests it was based on different criteria, for Table 1 on the linear polynomial and for Table 2 on signature tables.

The results of Table 2 seem to indicate that the signature table procedure is superior to the linear polynomial procedure even in its presently unoptimized form. It would be nice if one could measure this improvement in some more precise way, making a correct allowance for the difference in the computation times.

Perhaps a better way to assess the goodness of the play using signature tables is to list the fraction of the time that the program rates 0, then 1, 2, 3, etc. moves as equal to or higher than its rating of the book recommended move. Typical figures are tabulated below, measured for a test lot of 895 representative moves after the program had learned by analyzing 173,989 book moves:

moves higher or equal	0	1	2	3	4	5	6
fractional times found	0.38	0.26	0.16	0.10	0.06	0.03	0.01

In view of the high probability of occurrence of two equally acceptable moves, the sum of the figures in the first two columns, namely 0.64, is a reasonable estimate of the fraction of time that the program would make an acceptable move without look-ahead and mini-maxing. Look-ahead greatly improves the play and accounts for the difference between this prediction and the observed fact that the playing program tends to follow book-recommended moves a much higher fraction of the time.

INTRODUCTION OF STRATEGIES

The chief defect of the program in the recent past, according to several checker masters, seems to have been its failure to maintain any fixed strategy during play. The good player during his own play will note that a given board situation is favorable to him in some one respect and perhaps unfavorable in some second respect, and he will follow some fairly consistent policy for several moves in a row. In general he will try to maintain his advantage and at the same time to overcome the unfavorable aspect. In doing this he may more or less ignore other secondary properties which, under different circumstances, might themselves be dominant. The program, as described, treats each board situation as a new problem. It is true that this procedure does not allow the program to exploit those human failings of the opponent that might have been revealed by the earlier play or to conduct a war of nerves intended to trick the opponent. Such actions have little place in games of complete information and can well be ignored.[8]

What may certainly be questioned is the failure to take account of the initial board situation in setting the goals to be considered during the look-ahead process. Were the program able to do this, then it could adopt a strategy for any particular move. If the program finally made a move that was consistent with this strategy, and if the opponent were unable to vitiate this strategy, then the program would, on the next move, again tend to adopt the same strategy. Of course, if the program had been unable to maintain an advantage by following its initial strategy, it might now find that a different strategy was indicated and it would therefore change its strategy. Nevertheless, on the average, the program might follow a given strategy for several moves in a row and so exhibit playing characteristics that would give the impression of long range planning.

A possible mechanism for introducing this kind of strategic planning is provided by the signature table procedure and by the plausibility analysis. It is only necessary to view the different signature types as different strategic elements and to alter the relative weights assigned to the different signature types as a result of the plausibility analysis of the initial board situation. For this to be effective, some care must be given to the groupings of the parameters into the signature types so that these signature types tend to correspond to recognizable strategic concepts. Fortunately, the same initial-level grouping of parameters that is indicated by interdependency considerations seems to be reasonable in terms of strategies. We conclude that it is quite feasible to introduce the concept of strategy in this restricted way.

For reasons of symmetry, it seems desirable to pick two signature types for emphasis, that one yielding the highest positive value and that one yielding the most negative value for the most plausible move found during the initial plausibility analysis. This procedure recognizes the fact that to the opponent, the signs are reversed and his strongest signature type will be the first player's weakest one and vice versa. The simplest way to emphasize a particular strategy is to multiply the resulting values found for the two selected signature types by some arbitrary constant before entering a subsequent stage of the analysis. A factor of 2 (with a limit on the maximum resulting value so as not to exceed the table range) seemed reasonable and this has been used for most of the experiments to date.

The results to date have been disappointing, presumably because of the ineffectual arrangement of terms into usable strategic groups, and as a consequence, this method of introducing strategies has been temporarily abandoned.

CONCLUSIONS

While the goal outlined in Ref. 1, that of getting the program to generate its own parameters, remains as far in the future as it seemed to be in 1959, we can conclude that techniques are now in hand for dealing with many of the tree pruning and parameter interaction problems which were certainly much less well understood at the time of the earlier paper. Perhaps with these newer tools we may be able to apply machine learning techniques to many problems of economic importance without waiting for the long-sought ultimate solution.

NOTES

1. "Some Studies in Machine Learning Using the Game of Checkers," *IBM Journal*, III (1959), 211–29. Reprinted (with minor additions and corrections) in *Computers and Thought*, edited by E. A. Feigenbaum and J. Feldman, McGraw-Hill, 1963.

2. In a 1965 match with the program, the World Champion, Mr. W. F. Hellman, won all four games played by mail but was played to a draw in one hurriedly played cross-board game. Recently Mr. K. D. Hanson, the Pacific Coast Champion, has beaten current versions of the program on two separate occasions.

3. The word "acceptable" rather than "possible" is used advisedly for reasons which relate to the so-called alpha-beta heuristic, as will be described later.

4. See for example, A. Newell, J. C. Shaw and H. A. Simon, "Chess Playing Programs and the Problem of Complexity," *IBM Journal*, II (1958), 320–35. For references to other games, see A. L. Samuel, "Programming a Computer to Play Games," in *Advances In Computers*, Ed., F. Alt, New York: Academic Press, Inc., (1960), pp. 165–92.

5. More precisely we adopt the heuristic procedure of assuming that we must so conclude.

6. So named by Professor John McCarthy. This procedure was extensively investigated by Professor McCarthy and his students at M.I.T. but it has been inadequately described·in the literature. It is, of course, not a heuristic at all, being a simple algorithmic procedure and actually only a special case of the more general "branch and bound" technique which has been rediscovered many times and which is currently being exploited in integer programming research. See A. H. Land and A. G. Doight, "An Automatic Method of Solving Discrete Programming Problems" (1957) reported in bibliography *Linear Programming and Extensions*, George Dantzig, Princeton University Press, 1963; M. J. Rossman and R. J. Twery, "Combinatorial Programming," abstract K7, *Operations Research*, VI (1958), 634; John D. Little, Katta P. Murty, Dura W. Sweeney and Caroline Karel, "An Algorithm for the Traveling Salesman Problem," *Operations Research*, XI (1963), 972–89.

7. It is interesting to speculate on the fact that human learning is involved in making improvements in the tree pruning techniques. It would be nice if we could assign this learning task to the computer but no practical way of doing this has yet been devised.

8. This statement can be questioned and, in fact, has been questioned by an anonymous reviewer who quite rightly pointed out that it would be desirable for the program to be able to define what is called "deep objectives," and, more importantly, to be able to detect such "deep objectives" on the part of a human opponent. The reviewer went on to say in part "—the good player will sometimes define a 'deep objective' and maneuver toward that point. He is always on the lookout for possibilities which will help him to get the better of the opponent. The opponent, unaware of his true objective until too late, does not defend adequately and loses.—It is most helpful to him to know that his opponent is not also playing a similar 'deep game.' I believe that the 'practical indeterminacy' of checkers makes the technique of 'deep' objectives by good players quite feasible. Indeed, I don't doubt the technique is part of the basic equipment of any champion player, however inarticulately he may describe it. This is perhaps the reason Hellman did better in the games by mail. He had time to study out appropriately 'deep' objectives and then to realize them. This is also what checker masters have in mind when they criticize the program's failure to maintain any fixed strategy during play."

This point of view finds support in the observation that those master players who have defeated the computer have all asked searching questions regarding the program, while good players who fail to win usually seem to hold the program in awe and generally fail to make any attempt to understand it.

This opens up what may be a fruitful line for additional research.

5   The compleat robot: A prolegomena to androidology

MICHAEL SCRIVEN

Perhaps the best attempt at a comprehensive statement and solution of the logical difficulties in the anthropomorphic aspect of the cybernetic hypothesis, this essay was written by a respected philosopher of science over ten years ago. It is thus the oldest of the readings included in this volume, but its analysis of the basic issues remains highly relevant. The author addresses himself to the conceptual issues involved in attributing personhood to a machine, rather than to the "present state of the art." In fact his bold extrapolations of what machines are conceivably capable of doing are not without a certain intemperate confidence which actual achievements do not seem to warrant. It is, however, to the logical difficulties of his thesis which, as a philosopher, he properly addresses himself, and to which any criticism must similarly address itself.

Michael Scriven is a professor of philosophy at Berkeley, and previously taught in the Institute for History and Philosophy of Science at Indiana University.

0. INTRODUCTION

The day was when men sought to discover the secrets of the demigods, the elixirs, spells, and potions of the super-

Michael Scriven, "The Compleat Robot: A Prolegomena to Androidology," in S. Hook (ed.), *Dimensions of Mind.* © 1960 by New York University. Reprinted by permission of New York University Press.

naturally endowed. Perhaps the day will yet come when we, having promoted ourselves to the leading role by discovering there is no one above us, will find ourselves in the role of the magician, the possessor of mysterious powers, and snapping at our heels will be the machines. The question in our mind, and on their tapes, will be: "What is the secret of consciousness?" If they are sufficiently well programmed in the language of mythology, ancient and contemporary, it is perhaps even conceivable that they will refer to their search as the Quest for the Thinking Man's Philtre. (In this paper I shall consider what, if any, unique essence characterizes the human brain, what, if any, human property prevents a supercomputer from saying 'Anything you can do, I can do better.')

1. THE MEANING OF "MACHINE"

There are many important terms in our language which cannot be explicitly defined, for various reasons, yet can be correctly applied in typical cases. One of these is "machine," another is "science," and there are others such as "truth" and "toothache." We can readily apply such terms in some cases, while in other cases it is hard to decide whether they apply, and there are likely to arise new cases of both sorts. It is possible to introduce some artificial definition—e.g., by requiring that a science be concerned with prediction or experimentation, which will be approximately correct and sometimes convenient. But when dealing with a logical problem, couched in terms which include these words, we can only employ a stipulative definition like this if we can prove in advance that we are not presupposing an answer to the question. For example, if we define "machine" as an inanimate artifactual device, we cannot go on to ask whether machines might one day be conscious. Yet it is not at all obvious that the answer *is* trivially negative in the usual sense of "machine." This definition has other drawbacks: to define a machine in such a way as to require that it be manufactured is both imprecise (why can't a human mother be regarded as manufacturing her offspring?) and too restrictive, since a spontaneously-generated adding machine, complete even to the Marchant label, would present a problem that might leave the

physicist and the theologian at a loss for words but not the comptometer operator, who would not hesitate to call it a machine.
Similar criticisms apply to requirements about inorganic constituents (which would rule out aeroplanes and cranes with wooden
pulley-blocks) and about predictable behavior (which would rule
out roulette wheels or radium-driven randomisers).

I shall confine myself to enquiring whether something that *is*
manufactured from the usual electronic and mechanical components found in a computer workshop, with possible future refine-
ments and substitutes, must forever lack certain capacities possessed
by the brain. I think we can safely say that this would be a machine, without having to commit ourselves to any dubious propositions about what would *not* be a machine. (Whenever possible, I
shall try to make the points in terms of an even narrower kind of
machine—e.g., contemporary computers.) And in these terms the
phrase "thinking machine" is not a trivial contradiction. Inciden-
tally, our answers will leave us uncommitted about the question of
whether a biophysicist can produce living creatures from inorganic
elements. Although at the moment this appears to be only a technical problem, it is certainly a different problem, since he has a
narrower choice of materials and an easier goal than the roboticist
in his task of duplicating the brain functions of higher vertebrates.
We shall return to the problem of constituents in the next section.

2. & 3. MOVING AND REPRODUCING

A simple question arises immediately. May it not be true that
the particular substances of which the brain is composed are
enormously more efficient for its tasks than anything we could
expect to find in the inventory of a computer workshop? This might
be true to a degree that would render machines with powers comparable to men so gigantic that they would be incapable of incor-
poration in a self-propelling unit comparable to that which the
human brain inhabits.

Three comments are in order. First, this is not a very exciting
point even if true, since there would be, under this hypothesis,
few, if any, human tasks that could not be done by putting me-

chanical sensors and effectors where the human being would be, and using relays to fed data to and commands from the machine. Even if there are any such tasks, they are not ones that the human can do by virtue of his brain or mind, but by virtue of his body size. Second, there are no very strong reasons for thinking the point valid. Mechanical effectors and sensors can be made both smaller and better than human ones. For instance, they can be ultra-violet sensitive. The use of magnetic imprinting, crystal orientation, subminiaturization, and fail-safe circuitry, has already reduced or will reduce the required volume by several orders of magnitude and there seems no barrier except cost to further progress. Third, if we find that, for example, protein molecules provide the best storage medium, their employment would not necessarily mean we were no longer constructing a machine. Naturally, transplanting a human brain into a robot body is cheating, but the use of some of the same *substances,* either synthesized or extracted from dead tissue, is hardly enough to disqualify the product from being a machine. Our task is to see whether we can make a pseudo-brain—something with performance the same as or better than that of a human brain, but made in a different way, i.e., with largely different components and 'wiring.' There would still be considerable interest in the question of whether we can make a synthetic brain, no holds barred, but there would be less general agreement that it should be called a machine. (Would one call a synthetic flower a machine? A synthetic jellyfish?) I shall restrict our attention to the more difficult task of constructing a mechanical pseudo-brain, which utilizes at most some of the same substances or 'wiring' as the human brain, and thus retains a clearer title to the adjective "mechanical." There is a certain tension between the term "mechanical" and the term "living," so that the more inclined we are to call it alive because of the things it does, the less inclined we shall be to call it a machine. I shall continue to assume that these terms are logically marriageable, although they are uneasy bedfellows, but the substance of my points can be expressed in other ways if this assumption is not granted.

Having thus dealt with very simple behavioral and constitutional considerations, we may proceed to some of the traditionally more favored obstacles to the functional duplication of human mentality by mechanical means.

4. PREDICTING AND CHOOSING

It is a standard sarcasm amongst computer technicians that, contrary to the popular opinion, they are dealing with some of the most unpredictable and unreliable entities known. There are several causes of this. First, there are the errors of inadequate programming, which cannot be dismissed as mere operator errors, since a program often involves tens of thousands of characters in the 'machine language,' not all the consequences of which can be foreseen by the programmer any more than Euclid foresaw all the consequences of his axioms. Secondly, there are mechanical breakdowns within the machine—by no means uncommon, though to some extent their seriousness can be overcome by duplication, fail-safe wiring, and alarm arrangements. Thirdly, there are variations due to uncertainty-principle effects in junctions, relays, thermionic valves, etc. The importance of these variations is commonly slight, but over a long haul they guarantee 'individuality' to a computer. Fourthly, there is the cumulative inaccuracy possible with analogue computers. Fifthly, there is the possibility of deliberately using a randomizer in the circuitry, important in learning circuits. Sixthly, there is the rapidity of operation that makes the fastest computer unpredictable in fact.

It is thus highly unsatisfactory to suggest that computer output behavior is predictable. Even if the addition of "in principle" will get you past some of these objections, it is such a slippery password that its users often find themselves in the wrong camp. Here, I think the only safe conclusion is that some computers are "in principle" unpredictable in a way essentially similar to the way human being are.

The argument that "free will" is (a) possessed by humans, and (b) implies a unique unpredictability different from that mentioned above, requires both clarification and substantiation, especially its second assertion. I would say it is now readily provable that the kind of free will required to make sense of the idea of responsibility and punishment is perfectly compatible with determinism and third-person predictability, and there is no evidence for any other kind. Hence, even if machines were predictable it would be possible for them to have free will. Since neither they nor human beings are in practice entirely predictable, the argument that only one of the two species has free will needs further grounds, several of which we shall examine under other headings, but none of which appears to provide insuperable differences.

The converse problem to the one just considered is also of relevance to the free will issue, and serves to clarify the meaning of "predictable in principle." This is the problem of whether a computer can in principle predict everything. If, for the moment, one supposes that a computer can in principle be error-free, the answer is still negative, and thus a further element of similarity with the human being possessing free will is preserved—the limitation in the power *to* predict. The standard example is the computer with total data and unbounded speed which is connected to a photo-electric cell and phosphor lamp in a certain way and then programmed to predict whether the lamp will be alight five minutes later. The photo-electric cell is focused on the output tape and the lamp so connected that if the output tape reads "yes," the lamp switches off, and if it reads "no," the lamp switches on. The prediction is thus self-invalidating. The other standard case is the prediction of one computer's state by another which is trying to do the same to it; the necessity for a finite time-lag, however brief, between input and output can be shown to produce gross errors under suitable circumstances.

Now these cases have analogues in human experience. The realization that one can do 'just the opposite,' no matter what prediction is announced about one's choice, in trivial matters such as the closing of an eye is a powerful element in the support for free will. (It corresponds, as we shall see, to the first case just described.) One might say that all that is in fact shown by such feelings and freedom is that certain events are not *publicly* predictable. For the prediction can still be made as long as it is not announced to the individual to which it refers. But not only does this remark make less sense in the case of the computer, it also underestimates the importance of the point. For the possibility of falsifying any announced prediction does show that the feeling of free choice is not an "illusion" in any useful sense. "Illusions" can be dispelled, but dispelling a man's "illusion" that his choice is not yet made, that it is still "up to him," is often logically impossible since any announcement about his choice will immediately be falsified. But it is essential to remember that predictability does not eliminate freedom. A virtuous man is no less virtuous because we know he is and hence can guess what he'll do. We are not wrong to praise a man simply because we foresee his actions—we would be wrong only if they were actions over which he had no control (see D. M. MacKay, *On the Logical Indeterminacy of a Free Choice,* Proceedings of the Twelfth International Congress of Philosophy [Venice: 1958]).

The predictability issue, taken either way, is deeply involved in philosophical puzzles of some interest, but it again provides no grounds for supposing the machine to be inferior to the brain, either because its powers of prediction are too great, or because they are too small.

5. CREATING AND DISCOVERING

"Machines only do what we tell them to do. They are incapable of genuinely original thought." As in nearly all these claims, two importantly different points are run together here. These are what I shall call the "performatory" element and the "personality" element. The performatory problem here is whether a computer can produce results which, when translated, provide what would count as an original solution or proof *if it came from a man.* The personality problem is whether we are entitled to call such a result a solution or proof, despite the fact that it did *not* come from a man. The logical trap is this: no *one* performatory achievement will be enough to persuade us to apply the human-achievement vocabulary, but if we refuse to use this vocabulary in each case separately, on this ground, we will, perhaps wrongly, have committeed ourselves to avoiding it even when *all* the achievements are simultaneously attained.* I shall, for convenience, use the human-achievement vocabulary, but without thereby prejudging the issue. If it transpires that there are *no* essential performatory differences at all, we shall then consider whether we are entitled to apply the terms in their

---

* It is interesting to compare this with the view that none of the arguments for the existence of God are logically sound, but taken all together they are convincing.

full sense. No single simple property of an object suffices to guarantee that it is an apple, but several *sets* of such properties are sufficient.

The originality point has some sting when we are considering very simple computers, but the moment we have a learning circuit and/or a randomiser for generating trial-and-error runs, the picture is different. We will discuss the learning point in the next section, but I here wish to carry on with the consequences of the randomiser mentioned in the last section, which provides a simple kind of originality. For example, a computer using a randomiser may come up with a solution to a differential equation that no one else has been able to obtain. Is this to count as being original or not (observationally speaking—we ignore for the moment the fact that the result is mechanical in origin)? Certainly we 'built in' the instructions to use the randomiser, but this does not enable us to foretell what results will come out. This is another exercise in the trustworthiness of the "in principle" notion. I shall make only two comments.

First, the randomiser may be of two kinds. If it is a classical randomiser (i.e., of the 'roulette-wheel' type), there is some point to the remark that its outcome is in principle predictable, but none at all to the suggestion that we could ever in practice predict it. Now Euler was an original man, but was he original in any stronger sense than that no one did *in fact* think of his results before him? How could any further claim be supported? Even if it can, there is a stronger source of originality possible for a computer—the use of a quantum randomiser. And to argue that it is in principle possible to predict the outcome of a radium-driven randomiser is even less feasible, because, (a) taken at face value, it is denied by most contemporary physicists, (b) if it means that a deterministic theory might conceivably someday be found, then this is always true, and so the alleged distinction between the man and the machine, in terms of the "in principle" predictability of the latter, becomes vacuous, since one cannot rationally deny the *possibility* of an exact psychological predictive theory.

Of course, more is involved in producing solutions to equations than in producing random numbers, these must have been put through the test of satisfying the equation. But this involves only a routine calculation by the computer. There thus appears to be no reason why a computer cannot produce solutions to problems that are original in the sense of being (a) historically novel, and (b) in no useful sense predictable. Nevertheless, we feel that originality of this trial-and-error kind is relatively uninteresting. The important kind of originality is that which produces new theories, new conceptual schemes, new works of art. How could a machine possibly do this?

The key notion in the design of a creative machine would be the use of analogy. It has been argued by MacKay that in fact such a machine would have to be of the species referred to as analogue computers (as opposed to digital computers). I shall give some reasons for disagreeing with this in the section on understanding. But whatever type of computer is involved, there is no doubt that it must possess means for the *weighted comparison* of different descriptions. Thus, if it is fed data about the motion of a satellite around a planet, while on a theory-building program, it will register the formal similarity between this kind of motion and the motion of a body attached by a string to a fixed point and given a certain initial tangential velocity. It will, noting no better analogy, examine the consequences of the "theory" that an *invisible* connection exists between the planet and its satellite, the idea of invisibility being well-established in its data banks in connection with magnetic fields, sound waves, etc. Deduction of the consequences of such a hypothesis proves satisfactory for a certain value of the force in the invisible string, a value which depends on its 'length' in a simple way. The analogy with magnetic fields now registers strongly and the computer formulates and successfully tests the law of gravitational attraction.

The crucial difference from the trial-and-error method we first discussed lies not in the absence of trial and error, but in the origin of the candidates for trial; instead of randomly selected elements of a previously obvious class—e.g., the integers—it is necessary to provide a means for electing candidates from the indefinite class of possible hypotheses and then for improving them by adding modifications themselves selected in a similar way. The selection is no longer wholly random, because some candidates have better qualifications than others. What makes them better can be called their antecedent probability, but is perhaps better called the extent of the analogy between their known properties and those required in the situation under study. Any idea of an exact weighting of such analogies, which is perhaps suggested by referring to probabilities, is quite unjustified; the best one can expect is a partial ordering, and since this is all the human brain employs it is clearly adequate.

How would one go about giving the computer data of this kind? A simple beginning would be with curve-fitting problems where loose estimates of the importance of errors of a given magnitude, as against the value of simplicity for computation and theoretical fertility, can be given. The procedure can then be made more complicated in a way involving learning-circuits of the kind to be mentioned in the next section, enabling the computer to adjust the relative weighting of errors and complexity.

The procedure of *trial* is comparatively simple. The definition of the problem (say, the proof of Goldbach's Hypothesis, of the production of an adequate theory for the behavior of liquid helium) itself gives the tests that the successful candidate must pass. The application of these tests is, in the sciences, perfectly routine. There is still the possible difficulty of dealing with cases where several candidates pass the test. Here selection of the best will involve a decision similar to that involved in selecting the best candidates for the tests. This will, for example, occur where ideas such as simplicity are involved, and these make us think of creativity in the arts, where it is clear that we do not have very precise standards for judging the merits of works of art. But the computer's memory banks can with ease be indoctrinated with the canons of free verse, iambic pentameters, or nursery rhymes, and instruction to exploit low-level analogies as if they were high-level ones, and to adjust the result in certain ways by reference to ease of comprehension, richness of associations, and onomatopoeic force, would provide poetry of any acceptable kind. There is no doubt that the subtley of poetic metaphor and the emotive effect of various rhyme-schemes will not *easily* be compressed into a computer; but they are not easily learned by human beings, and human beings are remarkably disunited about the kind of scaling that would be correct in comparing these virtues (cf. simplicity and fertility of scientific theories). The net effect of these considerations is that there is much less chance that computer verse will be detectable by a literary critic than there was that paintings by chimpanzees would be identifiable by art-critics.

Summing up the discussion of originality, the simplest kind is readily obtainable by a machine and the more complicated kind is obtainable subject to the (feasible but difficult) development of analogy-assessing procedures. Connected with the assessment of analogies is the whole question of mechanical learning, to which we now turn.

6. LEARNING

The usual contemporary computer is essentially a complex instrument, a close relative to the comptometer, and the idea that it does only what we tell it to do is well founded. This idea is more precisely put by saying that it cannot modify its own programming, more loosely by saying it cannot learn by experience. But there are already a few computers, among them modified versions of the IBM 704 and 709, which are more advanced than this. Professor Wiener has referred to them as having "higher-order programming," i.e., as being programmed to modify their basic procedure in certain ways depending on the results obtained from earlier trials. Such machines are already capable of playing a good game of chess, proving theorems in geometry, and so on. The two special features of their design are the provision of assessment rules whereby they can judge the success of various procedures in various situations, and a special kind of instruction. In the chess case, we provide them with the set of possible moves by every chessman, they calculate the results of applying all applicable ones at a particular stage of the game and, using the assessment rules, decide which offers the best option.

A simple assessment rule, used during early stages of a game, would be one which gives greater credit for a position according to the number of pieces deployed, the 'openness' of the position, possibly measured by the number of squares covered. More complex, and more essential, rules will involve assessing a move in terms of its consequences in the light of possible moves by the opponent, the ideal being a move which can be inevitably (i.e., whatever the opponent does) converted into checkmate, less ideal ones resulting in the capture or favorable exchange of pieces. Thus we instruct the machine to proceed in such a way as to maximize the expectation of checkmate; and we provide certain suggestions as to reliable indicators of a good move, since no computer can actually compute all possible future outcomes of a given move except in some parts of the end game. So far, simple enough; but the special feature of the instructions is that we program the computer to continually reevaluate the suggested *indicators* in the light of its experience in using them to obtain checkmate. It is thus considering hypotheses at two levels. Within a game, it asks: "Is this a good move as far as my current standards of good moves go?"; and after each game it asks whether a different weighting of the standards would have been more likely to produce success—and if so, it readjusts the weights for future use.

At this stage we have a model of learning by experience. Its application to a chess-playing machine is simpler than to a theory-building machine because the possible moves in chess are a precisely defined family, unlike possible theories. It is true that in computer design it is more difficult to achieve controlled imprecision than precision, whereas the converse might be said to be characteristic of adult humans; and it is the imprecise methods of analogy and suggestion that produce new theories. But the proper analogy to computer design is human education from infancy, not the generation of free associations in adults, and the learner, like the computer, finds it much simpler to follow the exact rules of the syllogism than to evaluate complex analogies. Despite the difficulties, there can be no grounds for radical pessimism about the possibility of combining the devices of originality with those of learning to produce a machine that is cognitively a match for the human being—so far as we have considered the differences between them.

7. UNDERSTANDING AND INTERPRETING

There is a special kind of cognitive barrier that we have not so far considered and which involves a novel difficulty. Naturally, we shall not speak of a machine as 'understanding' a theorem simply because it can type out a proof of it on command. What must it *do* in order to be doing what human beings do who are said to understand a theorem? (Even if it does this, it does not—as we have previously stressed—follow that we should say it understands, for apart from what it *does* there is the question of what it *is;* and it may be argued that such predicates as 'understanding' are inapplicable to machines. But we shall have removed one further *ground* for this argument.) It seems clear to me that the performatory element in the concept of understanding is the capacity to *relate* whatever is said to be understood to a variety of other material in the correct way. Understanding the special theory of relativity involves knowing the relation between its components, the relation of it to other theories, and the relation of it to its applications. Understanding is knowing, but it is knowing certain things. Knowing something is not *ipso facto* understanding something (one knows the date of one's birthday, or the composition of polyurethane, without understanding anything [except a language]). But there is a very large slice of personality in the concept of understanding; we are much more reluctant to apply it to a machine than such a term as "compute." About this slice we cannot dispute; we can only point out that the theory that understanding is a mental sensation, a theory which is heavily ingrained in us, no doubt contributes to our reluctance, but does so illicitly. The point is well, though briefly, discussed in Wittgenstein's *Philosophical Investigations.*

A special difficulty of the concept of understanding arises in connection with the idea of understanding the concept of an irrational number. We here run into the apparent obstacle of the Lowenheim-Skolen Theorem. According to this theorem, it is not possible to give a unique characterization of the reals and hence the irrationals, at least in the following sense: any attempted strict formalization of the real numbers can be shown to be ambiguous in that it can be given at least one interpretation in the rational numbers, i.e., every formalization we produce can be legitimately interpreted in a way contrary to that intended, a way that omits any reference to the irrationals. Now it seems plausible to say that the description of the reals that we give to a computer will be subject to the same irreducible ambiguity, and hence that we shall never be sure that it has actually 'grasped' the *proper* idea of real number, which includes the irrationals, rather than one of the other strictly permissible interpretations. A similar suggestion is made by Nagel and Newman in *Gödel's Proof* when they argue that the Gödel incompleteness theorem presents a serious obstacle to the construction of comprehensive theorem-proving computers; we shall return to this suggestion in a moment. The error in these arguments, as I see it, lies in the idea that the tests of understanding in mathematics are purely syntactical, that the intrasystemic transformations are the only defining properties of the concepts—of number, or proof, or truth. In fact, we can perfectly well regard it as a crucial test of comprehension of the concept of irrational number on the part of man or machine, that he or it immediately identify the square root of two, and π, and the base of natural logarithms as examples of irrational numbers. If this is required, then considerations of the formal properties will guarantee the correct field of entities (other simple requirements on the interpretation of the logical operators would also suffice).

It seems to me that the point is akin to the one arising when we ask whether a blind man can be said fully to understand the meaning of the word "red" when he has mastered (a) the syntactical rules governing color words, and (b) a device which correlates color-differences with musical tones so that he can indirectly differentiate (but not identify) colors reliably. This would *almost* locate the term "red" in the semantic space, but not completely; his interpretation would be invariant under transformations that did not offend current idioms or hue-separation. For example, he could get the color of a particular dahlia wrong although not the natural color of a ripe lemon. (There would be a *series* of tests—linked comparisons—which would uncover the dahlia's color, but he couldn't recognize it immediately.) We are somewhat undecided whether to say that his *comprehension* (of the term "red") is incomplete, or merely his *experience*. Certainly he is not capable of using the term properly in normal circumstances, but neither is a man who has lost his sight—yet the latter understands perfectly well what "red" means. Similarly, the axioms of a formal system provide much but not all of the meaning of "irrational number"; the clincher is the link with examples, the capacity to apply the language correctly in paradigm cases. In certain areas of mathematics, this is guaranteed by the formal rules, but in others the concepts are not merely formal shorthand, but refer to aspects of a complex construction that can readily be *perceived* but not exhaustively eliminated by substituting other equivalent concepts. (A related difficulty arises in trying to treat the Peano postulates as defining the integers.) In sum, then, I do not find the existence of a residual ambiguity in an axiomatization of mathematics a good reason for supposing that computers can never understand mathematical concepts.

Similarly, the limitations imposed by the Gödel incompleteness theorem on the formalization of mathematics are, so far as I can see, no more of an obstacle to a mechanical mathematician. As is well known, given any Gödel sentence G which is provably true but undecidable within a system S, it is easy to construct an S ^{1} within which it is derivable—the uninteresting way being to add G to the system S. Now, Nagel and Newman are struck by the fact that whatever axioms and rules of inference one might give a computer, there would apparently be mathematical truths, such as G, which it could never "reach" from these axioms by the use of these rules. This is true, but their assumption that we could suppose ourselves to have given the machine an adequate idea of mathematical truth when we gave it the axioms and rules of inference is not true. This would be to suppose the formalists were right, and they were shown by Gödel to be wrong. The Gödel theorem is no more an obstacle to a computer than to ourselves. One can only say that mathematics would have been easier if the formalists had been right, and it would in that case be comparatively easy to construct a mechanical mathematician. They weren't and it isn't. But just as we can recognize the truth of the unprovable formula by comparing what it says with what we know to be the case, so can a computer do the same.

It is appropriate here to mention another formal theorem, one which an enthusiastic roboticist might think supports his cause. Craig's theorem has been invoked on occasions to support the view that theories, and hence the necessity for understanding theoretical terms, are dispensable. It does indeed demonstrate the eliminability of certain terms from a given vocabulary under certain conditions. If it is supposed that these conditions correspond to the relationship between theoretical terms and observational terms, the conclusion might follow. But one of the conditions is that there be an absolutely sharp separation between terms of these two kinds. Now, it seems clear that it is part of the nature of theoretical terms that they should sometimes—for example, by progress in techniques of observation—become observable. Another condition requires that the only logically interesting effects of theoretical terms lie in their deduced consequences in the observation vocabulary. Even if deduction were in fact the only vehicle for generating the consequences of theories, this would not be a satisfactory position. The reasons for this require support from a general theory of meaning, but they can be condensed into the comment that part of the meaning of a theory lies in its relation to other theories, and part in its internal logical structure, so that understanding a theory is by no means the same as understanding its empirical consequences. Finally, Craig's theorem has the awkward result that the elimination of theoretical terms is achieved only at the expense of adding an infinite number of axioms in the observation language.

8. ANALYZING

At the practical level, some of the above considerations are already highly relevant. There is a great deal of work now proceeding on the mechanization of translation, abstraction, and indexing. A few words on each topic will perhaps serve to indicate the present situation and its consequences for our inquiry.

8.1 TRANSLATION

It is simple enough to build a mechanical *decoder* (or encoder) and they have been in use for many years. If translation were the same as decoding, there would be no special problem. Unfortunately, there are great differences. A code is a way of rendering portions of a single language obscure; decoding consists of applying the key in reverse. But French, except when used by certain people one knows, is not a way of rendering English obscure. It is a way of doing what English also does—describing, explaining, exhorting, ordering, promising, praising, and so on. Since they are both universal languages, and their relation is thus unlike that of mathematics to music, it is reasonable to expect that a *fairly* satisfactory equivalent exists in each for any natural unit in the other. Now, a word or a sentence is not what I have in mind when talking of a natural unit—a word or a sentence is a *phonetically,* or *calligra-*

phically, or *psychologically* convenient unit. A natural unit is a description, an explanation, an exhortation, etc., produced in a particular context. (Of course, a translation of this depends to some extent on a personal impression of the context, and the linguistic element usually does not fully describe the context.) If we were to suppose that the existence of workable translations of *natural units* implied the existence of workable translations of the *spoken or written* units (i.e., the words and sentences), then a mechanical translator would be a relatively simple problem for the programmer. The discovery that this supposition is unsound is, it seems to me, the chief ground for the present pessimism amongst workers in this area.

But there is no absolute barrier here. In the first place, there are actually many words or groups of words, especially in Western languages, which allow a very general and straightforward translation into corresponding units in other such languages, partly because they are used in only one kind of context. This is especially true in the vital area of technical vocabularies. Secondly, although the language is not always descriptive of a context, it often affords clues to it, so that by taking large enough sections, a translation can be made highly accurate at least for informational purposes. But the translation of poetry is an example of the opposite extreme where a one-many relation holds between a context and associated language complexes. And it is a useful warning, since this is not altogether unlike the situation of theoretical propositions. Finally, provision once being made for the sensory equipment of a robot— a point shortly to be discussed—we would possess a system whose linguists would be of the same kind as our own, and whose translations would therefore be potentially better, their memory being better.

8.2 ABSTRACTING

Mechanical abstractors have already been built in response to the desperate need for systematizing scientific work and publication. They operate on a word (or phrase) frequency count, retaining those words of four letters, or more, that occur most often. This is the most primitive possible device for abstraction and all one can say is that it is surprising how often it nearly does a fair job. (It is not very often.) There are really no short-cuts of this kind that are worth much trouble; we shall not be able to rely—and we need to be able to rely—on abstracting done by someone lacking a first-rate comprehension of the subject being treated. Unfortunately, using such rare individuals for such purposes is intellectually and economically inefficient. The natural solution is mechanization. It is less of a solution than might appear at first sight, since, although the comprehension is feasible as I have argued above, the difficulties are so formidable that the initial cost of such a device will enormously outweight the cost of discovering and training extra humans for the task. We may indeed find that the super computers of the future will need human servants because they can't afford mechanical aides—a nice twist to the present argument for automation, although perhaps it ranges a little too far into the future to convince the unions today.

8.3 INDEXING

Essentially similar problems arise over indexing. Under what headings should an article be referenced or a paragraph be indexed? A simple machine can index an article or passage under all the words in it, or under the most frequent. Both are clearly quite unsatisfactory. The crucial concepts here are those of *relevance* and *importance*. To know which topics an article is relevant to requires more than an understanding of the article—it requires knowledge of all potentially relevant fields. Worse, as our theories change, relevance changes and continual reindexing from scratch is necessary, i.e., all references must be scanned for deletion *and* amplification. It is a tall order to build a machine with the kind of knowledge and speed required for these tasks, but it is increasingly beyond the powers of man to perform such tasks himself, and an increasingly large amount of work is being 'lost' in the technical literature, or expensively duplicated because of the inefficiency of indexing (and cataloguing—a special case). There is really no satisfactory alternative to the machines and we shall have to try them, there being no reason for supposing we cannot succeed but every reason for supposing we shall find it very difficult. It may not be impossible "in principle," but we sometimes abandon our "in principles."

9. DECIDING

In the indexing problem, that matter of relevance is crucial but only half the problem. A particular passage in the *American Journal of Physics* will be relevant to some degree to an uncountable number of topics. If an index is to be useful at all, a subset of these topics must suffice and a decision must be made by the indexer as to the most important of these. If this is to be done sensibly it requires some estimate of importance and some value for a "cutting score," i.e., a level of importance beyond which inclusion in the index is guaranteed and below which it is precluded. As we have suggested earlier, it is a mistake to suppose that a full arithmetization is possible, and partial ordering is all that we need. The issue is really the same as that associated with choosing likely hypotheses and raises no new difficulties for the programmer. The difficulties are bad enough even if not new. The procedure for governing the cutting score by estimates of the maximum permissible size of the index, the seriousness of errors of omission versus excessive bulk, corresponds to the procedure for deciding what hypotheses to consider in a given situation, or, in problem-solving, what maneuvers to try out, if any—e.g., which premises to try out as bases for a mathematical proof.

10. PERCEIVING

The performatory aspect of perception is differentiation of the responses to differentiated stimuli. This is the aim of good scientific instrument design and a computer with its own temperature-recording devices is easily made. The human brain, however, is rather good at detecting similarities and differences of a kind which it would be tremendously difficult to arrange to detect mechanically. For example, the visual recognition of a female acquaintance when she is wearing different clothes, is at varying distances, in varying light and from varying angles, wearing various expressions, hairstyles, and makeup, requires configurational comparisons of great sensitivity and complexity. It is clear enough how one would go about developing a machine with the capacity to perform such tasks, which we do so casually. Here again we would face the "degrees of similarity" problem, and "matching" problems probably best solved by the use of an optical comparator using rapidly varying magnification. A start will have to be made in connection with star-mapping programs using the photomultiplier tubes, and automatic navigation for unmanned interstellar rockets. The recognition of star patterns, regardless of orientation, should not prove too difficult, and the more complex gestalts may be attacked piecemeal.

10.1 EXTRASENSORY PERCEIVING

Turing apparently thought that telepathy was the one impossibility for the machine. I am not clear whether he thought this because of scepticism about telepathy in humans or because of a 'direct-mental-contact' theory of telepathy, or for some other reason. Neither of the suggested reasons seems altogether satisfactory. The evidence for telepathy in humans is hard to dismiss fairly, but there is no ground for thinking it cannot be regarded as a brain function of a new kind, analogous to the generation of the alpha- and beta-rhythms. We are completely ignorant to the forms of energy or the physical features of the brain that are responsible for telepathy, although intensive work with the electroencephalograph is continuing at Duke and in London. In this respect, ESP represents a more difficult problem for the roboticist than any of the preceding ones, and forms a natural link to the problem of feeling. If it should transpire that no brain elements are responsible for ESP, then it will present a special philosophical problem; but until then, we must assume the contrary and continue the search. We are not at all clear how the memory works, but we do not doubt its existence. It is quite unreasonable to argue as some have done, that because the ESP function has not been localized in the brain, it follows that we should doubt its existence. What I have said about telepathy applies, a fortiori, to the less well-supported phenomena of precognition and psychokinesis.

11. FEELING

The most difficult problem of all those that face the roboticist trying to match human capacity is that of inducing the phenomena already indicated the way in which there can be achieved. It is the of sensation. The difficulty lies not with the outward signs—we have doubt whether there is any actual sensation associated with the wincing, gasping, sighing, and snapping that we succeed in building in for manifestation in 'appropriate' circumstances. A radical behaviorist will not of course be troubled by such doubts, but even the identity theorists would not share his equanimity. We all know what it is to feign feelings and we thus know what it is to behave as if one had a certain feeling although one lacks it—and we wonder if the robot is merely "going through the motions." (It is not, of course, correctly described as "feigning," since this entails an understanding of the nature of not feigning—and we are disputing even this possibility.)

Turing argued ("Computing Machinery and Intelligence," *MIND*, 1950) that if a robot could be so built that remote interrogation could not distinguish it from a human being we would have to agree that it had feelings. This is oversimple, not only because verbal stimuli are too limited for satisfactory proof, but because it seems to make perfectly good sense to say: "It says it is in love because we built it to say so—but is it? It says it is fond of A. E. Housman and thinks Keats is sickly, but does it really *enjoy* Housman?" In making these points in a reply to Turing ("The Mechanical Concept of Mind," *MIND*, 1953), I overlooked two points which now seem to me important and which improve the chances of a decision, although they do not support Turing's view.

In the first place, one must reject the 'argument from design' (androidological version), the argument that because the machine is designed to say it is in love it cannot be supposed that it is *really* in love. For the design may, and perhaps must, have achieved both ends. (To assume the opposite is to adopt a naïve interactionism.) Performatory evidence is not decisive (contra Turing), but neither is it negligible. It fulfills a necessary condition, in a sense which is amplified in my paper in the symposium on "Criteria" in the *Journal of Philosophy*, November 1959. What is a sufficient condition? The answer must be that there is no *logically* sufficient condition statable in terms that can be verified by an external observer. Even a telepath who declares that he directly perceives sensations in the robot exactly as in humans may merely be reacting to brain emanations that are similar. But there are conditions which make doubt profitless although not meaningless—e.g., doubts about the origin of the universe. These conditions are, for the most part, readily imaginable, consisting in the indefinitely sustained and effortless performance and description of emotional conditions, the development of new art forms, the prosecution of novel moral causes (Societies for the Prevention of Cruelty to Robots, etc.), in brief the maintenance and extrapolation of the role of a sensitive man, with dreams and feelings. However, I have thought of a less obvious further test which perhaps merits a separate section.

12. LYING

Remembering that, strictly speaking, to refer to an entity as lying commits one to the personality component as well as the performatory one, I shall use the term to refer to the performatory element for the moment. Now, the substance of my disagreement with Turing was that a machine *might* be made of duplicate sensation-behavior without having the sensation, i.e., the designer could fool the interrogator. But suppose our aim as a designer is not to pass the Turing test, since that is inconclusive, but actually to determine whether robots can be built that have feelings. I suggest that we construct a series of robots called R. George Washington I, II, III, etc. (using Asimov's convention of the R for "Robot" before name), with the following characteristics. They should be taught to use English in the strictest way. They would refer to human beings as being in pain under the usual circumstances, but under what appear to be corresponding circumstances with robots they would use behaviorist language, saying that R. Einstein XI had produced the words "I am in pain," etc. And they would use the same care when describing their own states, saying for example: "R. George Washington I has been subjected to overload current" or ". . . has received a potentially damaging stimulus of unknown origin"—it being the named robot speaking. In teaching them to speak in this way, we make it quite clear that other descriptions of themselves may also be appropriate, including those applied to human beings, but we do not assert that they do apply. We also introduce the robot to the concept of truth and falsity and explain that to lie is to utter a falsehood when the truth is known, a practice of value in some circumstances but usually undesirable. We then add a circuit to the robot, at a special ceremony at which we also christen it, which renders lying impossible regardless of conflict with other goals it has been told are important. This makes the robot unsuitable for use as a personal servant, advertising copywriter, or politician, but renders it capable of another service. Having equipped it with all the performatory abilities of humans, fed into its banks the complete works of great poets, novelists, philosophers, and psychologists, we now ask if whether it has feelings. And it tells us the truth since it can do no other. If the answer is "No," we construct further robots on different principles. If the answer is "Yes," we have answered our original question. To the objection that we cannot be sure it understands the question, it seems to me we can reply that we have every good reason for thinking that it does understand, as we have for thinking this of other *people*.

The logical structure of the argument thus consists in standing on a performatory analysis of understanding to reach a conclusion about the nonperformatory issue of sensations. If, with Brentano, one believes there is an irreducible non-behavioral element in such concepts as belief and understanding, and that these, rather than sensations, are the hallmark of mind, my maneuver will not be convincing because it does not refer to that element which his followers translate as intentionality. But one may accept the irreducibility thesis, as I do, and regard the missing element as a compound of the possession of sensations and the possession of personality. This element is not the only one responsible for the irreducibility which also derives from the complexity of the mental-activity concepts in the same way as that which renders theoretical terms not reducible to observational ones. Then we get half of the missing element from the first R. George Washington to say "Yes," and there remains only the question of personality.

13. BEING

What is it to be a person? It can hardly be argued that it is to be human since there can clearly be extraterrestrials of equal or higher culture and intelligence who would qualify as people in much the same way as the peoples of Yucatan and Polynesia. Could an artifact be a person? It seems to me the answer is now clear; and the first

R. George Washington to answer "Yes" will qualify. A robot might do many of the things we have discussed in this paper and not qualify. It could not do them all and be denied the accolade. We who must die salute him.

6   The use of behavioural language to refer to mechanical processes

D. M. MACKAY

Like the previous essay, this paper analyzes the logical and psychological impediments to the anthropomorphic thesis. Although the author is a recognized expert in the technical and theoretical aspects of cybernetics, he addresses himself here to a philosophical problem, that of the "logic of personal recognition." The question is on what grounds other than performance the decision to acknowledge that an automaton is a person might be warranted.

Perhaps it is worth remarking that, of these two papers arguing toward a common conclusion, the previous paper is by a professed atheist and this one by a professed Christian. Contrary to Turing, as he notes, the author does not see any incompatibility between Christian theology and the thesis here defended.

Donald M. MacKay is Professor of Communications at the University of Keele, Staffordshire, and is the author of numerous papers in the field of cybernetics.

Given to the Annual Conference of the British Society for the Philosophy of Science, Oxford, 22–24 September 1961. In revising this paper for publication I have been grateful for many constructive criticisms, particularly those of Professor Dingle, Sir Geoffrey Vickers, and Dr. David Rioch.

D. M. MacKay, "The Use of Behavioural Language to Refer to Mechanical Processes," *British Journal for the Philosophy of Science*, XIII (1962), 89–103. Reprinted by permission of Cambridge University Press.

1. A MIS-STATED PROBLEM

'Brain-like mechanisms' are nowadays something more than a possibility in principle. On all hands we hear of 'programmes' for behaviour which, if only crudely approximate to the human, seems undeniably to occupy some of the right dimensions. Philosophical enquiry into the powers and limitations of such automata is frequently confused by a failure (even among philosophers) to recognise the elliptical nature of much popular talk about computers and their ilk. When the enquiry takes the form of a comparison between the artificial and the natural, it becomes particularly important to sort out the concepts and relationships on each side, so as to see which correspond to which—and to discover which, if any, have as yet no counterpart. The 'semantic chart' of Table I is an attempt to do this for some of the key notions. 'Natural' concepts on the left are matched by 'artificial' counterparts on the right.[1]

Table I

	Natural	*Artificial*	
Personal aspect	*Mechanical aspect*	*Mechanical aspect*	*Personal aspect*
	Growth	*Construction*	
Person	*Brain-and-Body*	*Automaton*	?
(Joe)	('Mass of *cells & things*')	('Mass of *wires & valves*')	?
	Carrying *signals*	Carrying *signals*	
	Forming an *information-system*	Forming an *information-system*	
	Organising observable behaviour *indicative* of	Organising observable behaviour *indicative* of	
Thinks, feels, hopes, fears . . .	Thinking, feeling, hoping, fearing . . .	Thinking, feeling, hoping, fearing . . .	?

The assembly of components occurs by 'growth' and 'construction' respectively. If the end-product of construction (which might, of course, include artificial growth-processes) be termed a 'machine' or 'automaton', then what invites comparison or contrast with it is the end-product of natural growth—strictly (and only) the 'brain-and-body' in its physical aspects. If the machine be termed (in Sir Geoffrey Jefferson's happy phrase) 'a mass of wires and valves', the natural counterpart would perhaps be 'a mass of cells and things'.

After this point, however, our two columns begin to show some similarities. The (mass of) wires and valves *carry signals*. So do the (mass of) cells and things. Each is organised to form what we term an 'information system'—a system whose activity depends on the reception, transformation, and transmission of information. Each produces observable behaviour (both internal and external).

On the 'natural' side, we have a second column, which I have labelled 'Personal aspect'. In this aspect, we are accustomed to recognise the being before us as our friend Joe Smith (whom we shall meet later). We say that Joe is capable of such activities as thinking, feeling, hoping, fearing. Of these activities we have first-hand knowledge only in our own case; but we recognise 'observable indications' of the same in Joe's behaviour.

The problem I want to discuss is represented by the question marks in the corresponding column on the right-hand side. It is often expressed by asking 'Can a machine think?'; and fierce debates have raged between those designers of automata who regard this as an empirical question answerable by experiment in the affirmative, and those philosophers who share the same presupposition but regard the evidence to date as inadequate.[2]

I have long argued [3] that empirical 'predictions of impotence' ('you'll never get a machine to do x')—or counter-predictions—cannot resolve an issue of this sort, for any detailed test-specification for particular behaviour, whether statistical or determinate, is implicitly equivalent to a description of at least one mechanism to meet it. Attempts to get around this and prove that 'minds are not machines' by invoking Gödel's theorem (as Mr J. R. Lucas [4] does, for example) are I believe both hopeless and needless.

They are hopeless because only an uninteresting type of 'machine' suffers significantly as a result of the impotence shown to follow from Gödel's theorem. Lucas argues: '. . . Just before the mind has the last word, it can always pick a hole in any formal system presented to it as a model of its workings' (whereas the type of machine that he considers cannot). Yes indeed; but the only class of artificial mechanism worth considering as a candidate for 'mentality' is of the self-adaptive or self-organising type, from which exactly the same behaviour could be expected as Lucas claims for 'the mind'. (I hope to elaborate this point elsewhere.)

But such attempts to save the 'argument from impotence' seem also to be needless; for if our 'semantic chart' is correct, the short answer to a claim on empirical grounds that 'machines can think', or that 'minds are machines' is not 'you are empirically justified (or unjustified)' but 'you are talking nonsense'. For in the human case, it is not *brains* that are said to think, feel, hope, fear, but *people*. To say that a mass of nerve-cells 'thinks' or 'fears' would not be an empirical assertion but a misuse of language; and just the same is true for a mass of wires and valves.[5] If a 'mass of wires and valves' invites comparison with a human being at all, it can only be with the 'mass of cells, etc.' that comprise his *brain and body*. Thus no degree of resemblance to the performance of the human brain, however great, could justify the semantic absurdity of saying that any 'mass of wires and valves' can think.

Yes. But is this really a sufficient answer to our restive designer of automata? May he not justly retort: 'All right: it was silly to argue whether "mechanisms" could think. But insofar as we agree that human thinking *is* bound up somehow with natural brain-activity, is it not meaningful to ask whether, and on what conditions, some kind of "thinking" might not be similarly bound up with artificial brain-activity?' He is now asking a very different question, and I think it is a good one. It leads at once to the more basic question of the *nature of the transition* which we are accustomed to make on the 'natural' side, from talking in bodily terms to talking in personal terms—from the 'mass of cells and things' in column 2 to 'Joe' in column 1. What are the preconditions of this change? Under what circumstances is it justified? Is it purely optional, and if not, in what sense?

In an attempt to explore this issue one uncovers a trail of prior questions which leads surprisingly deep into the jungle of our basic physical concepts; for on examination the problem turns out to have some features in common with several others that have plagued philosophers of science. But it is only part of this trail that I propose to follow in the present paper.

2. THE NECESSITY OF 'UNDERSPECIFICATION'

Let us begin with the fundamental notion of goal-pursuit, which is a basic feature of living systems, and of all artificial devices with any pretensions to human powers. A self-regulating mechanism, such as a thermostat, is said to show 'goal-directed activity'. From its repertoire or range of 'possible' activity, it is said to make a 'selection' by adjusting a 'control' or switch' on the basis of 'information' as to the disparity or 'mismatch' between the current state of affairs and what is termed the 'goal-state'. The activity selected is 'calculated' to reduce the disparity.[6]

The whole description bristles with difficulties. What do we mean, first of all, by 'possible' here? Surely, a good Newtonian might argue, the only possible activity is the activity that occurs? In what sense then is the activity 'controlled'? 'Had the control or the switch been in a different position, the flow of heat would have been different'—but it was not, and could not be, for good, well-determined, physical causes. So in what sense was any other activity 'possible'?

The answer seems plain. Only if we *underspecify* the situation, by using generic terms that allow more than one microstate to be compatible with our description, can we give meaning here to the word 'possible'. 'A 2-way switch is a device with two possible states. . . .' Yes. But *this* '2-way switch' is a physical array of molecules in the *only* state compatible with its past history. 'Is no other state possible?'—Not in these terms. 'In future', of course, it is 'possible' that it may be found in either of the two states—but only if we have not specified the time, nor the intervening history of forces acting on it. Given these, the concept of a 'range of possibilities' evaporates. It is not the physical situation that possesses a range of possible states, but our specification of it—if sufficiently open.

A similar point can be made regarding most of the concepts of applied physics, if viewed from the standpoint of classical molecular theory. Consider for example how the concept of 'entropy' appears in statistical mechanics. It is often asked how an 'irreversible' process (increase of entropy) can arise within a theory based on the 'reversible' laws of Newtonian dynamics. The answer is that (statistical) entropy is definable within the theory only when the system is underspecified in such terms that it can be said to have a range of 'possible' microstates. Entropy here measures a property, not of the molecular situation, but of the summary abstraction (in macroscopic terms such as pressure, volume, temperature) which is normally our only available state-description of it. Given a full microdescription in molecular terms, all but one of the probabilities p_i in the entropy-coefficient, $\Sigma p_i \log p_i$, become zero, and entropy vanishes both numerically and conceptually from the situation as described.

What is irreversible here is the decline in 'specifying power' of a description whose terms offer too few degrees of freedom. In its statistical form the Second Law of Thermodynamics tells us that molecular assemblages change in such a way that anything less than a full microspecification becomes progressively less adequate as time goes on. The consequences of 'losing track' cannot be undone within a closed system.[7]

What then of 'information?' Upon what conditions is it meaningful to speak of 'information-flow', or to say that an event B *betokens* or *conveys information as to* the occurrence of another, A? Clearly, once again, only when we can say that B 'might have been otherwise'. If not, then B conveys no information, in either the common or the technical sense.

But we have just seen that the meaningfulness of such talk depends entirely on the degree of underspecification of the situation. Basically, it is to *us* that B conveys information about A—if we are sufficiently ignorant. To say that 'information is conveyed to the switch' would be meaningless, if by 'the switch' we meant 'that particular molecular array of brass and porcelain'. To talk the language of information-flow is to deflect discussion from the physical situation, to our underspecified [8] state-description or model of it in which 'the switch' means a 'skeletonised' functional variable with two possible values. In this state-description, it makes good sense to say that B determines the state of the switch according to the nature of A, or that information about A determines the selection of activity by the switch.

It follows that to ask whether the activity of a given mechanism is an example of goal-directed or other 'behavioural' activity is to ask, not about the physical situation *per se,* but about the types of underspecified state-description that it can justify. While not every situation can be made to manifest goal-directed features by suitable underspecification, it is quite possible for one level or mode of specification to bring out such features while at another level they become totally meaningless.

3. THE 'UNDERSPECIFIED' NATURE OF HUMAN ACTIVITY

So far we have considered only artificial automata; but may we not recognize the same principle as applicable to human beings? Insofar as a standpoint is possible from which most, if not all, bodily activity can be viewed as physically determinate, to that extent are manifestations of 'goal-directedness' and the like dependent for their perception on one's choice of level of specification. Here, however, I want to give the argument a new twist, in terms of an important and singular fact about the human brain-mechanism. The intriguing feature of each human being is that, for himself, his bodily state is always and *necessarily* unspecifiable in full detail, so the corresponding 'range of possibilities' of which he is aware is logically irreducible.[9]

Even if his brain were (to an outside observer) a fully-determined physical mechanism, it could never embody an up-to-date and complete description of its own total state. The most fully-supported predictions of the most completely-informed observer (granted full 'classical' physical determinateness) can be for the agent logically-indeterminate, until after the decisions they purport to predict have been made.[10] It follows that no mechanical account of an agent's bodily activity, however deterministic, can logically undermine the meaningfulness, for the agent, of his personal account.

The meaningfulness of our recognition of 'mental' qualities, such as goal-directedness, in the activity of one another is, by the same token, dependent on our being 'underspecified situations' to one another. At first sight this may seem an oddly precarious and arbitrary condition. From a 'Newtonian' view of bodily mechanism it would surely follow that by totally contracting out of a community of discourse (if this were possible), an individual could in principle adopt a fully-specified state-description of the bodies of his fellows, in which concepts of personal agency could rationally find no place? I would not personally deny this. No demonstration in terms of observable behaviour could, I think, rationally *compel* such an individual to accord personal status to the activity of his fellows. In that sense, recognition of persons is 'optional'.

What I would emphasise, on the other hand, is that insofar as two people interact in 'dialogue', and thus become one system, the crucial condition is *necessarily* fulfilled, since for each individual his own (necessarily underspecified) situation becomes a determinant of that of his interlocutor, which thus shares in the underspecifiability-to-him.[11]

We seem then to be approaching the view that the requirements for the recognition of personality in natural human beings are of two kinds. First, and obviously, (*a*) the physical 'bodily situation' must admit of and support in practice an underspecified statedescription showing appropriate behavioural features: the 'observable indications' of thinking, feeling, hoping, fearing, etc. But the second, and no less important, requirement is (*b*) that we, the arbiters, must be rationally able and willing to adopt the appropriate standpoint of interactive relationship, from which the situation acquires some of our own necessary unspecifiableness-to-ourselves. This I think is the technical correlate of the much-discussed distinction between the 'I-Thou' relationship and that of 'I-Object'. In the latter, no comparable barrier of principle prevents full specification of the object-situation by the observer, even where the object is a normally functioning human body. By withholding the commitment implicit in dialogue, or even in less-discursive forms of interaction—the opening of one's controls to the action of the other—the observer could in principle obviate the systematic mutual 'underspecifiableness' that logically undergirds the structure of personal language.

4. THE 'PERSONALITY' OF AUTOMATA

What then of artificial automata? There is room for serious doubt in principle [12] whether our understanding of 'what it is to be a man' could ever be made explicit enough to enable us to write a full specification for human behaviour. To that extent, our prospects of fully meeting the first of the above requirements (*a*) are rather unsatisfactory. How should we ever know that we had left out nothing essential?

But to take refuge behind such barriers (real though I believe they are) would be to evade the issue; for there seems every reason to believe that the main lineaments of intelligent human behaviour could in principle be reproduced in automata, even employing only the techniques known today. We may not feel confident that the 'personality' in question would be fully human, but we can hardly doubt that as far as behaviour is concerned, at least the minimal criteria for such activities as 'thinking', 'learning' and the like could be met.

The real obstacle, then, appears to lie in our second requirement (b). Those who wish to refuse personal status to artificial automata are on strong ground; for we have seen at the cost of sufficient 'detachment' even the personal significance of human activity (at least of other people's!) can be made to disappear, from a standpoint which views it as fully-specifiable in principle. No observable performance can logically force anyone from such a position.

What would be logically possible (though somewhat perverse) as an attitude to human brain-mechanisms other than one's own, may thus seem more than justifiable towards artificial mechanisms that only feebly imitate them; and I would not wish to disturb anyone from a defensive agnosticism here. In relation to existing automata I confess to sharing it, for I cannot see myself rationally sustaining a long personal relationship with any I know of.

But we are met as philosophers rather than as psychologists; and I think the matter cannot be left thus. We must ask, not whether such a commitment would be undesirable, but whether, and in what circumstances, it would be *absurd*.

Let us first take the stock example of the man who adopts a personal attitude to his car, his golf ball, or some similarly passive victim of his will. In cold blood, of course he admits this to be absurd. But the lurid language of the garage or the golf-course betrays another level of commitment, which at the time may feel curiously justified. Why? I do not think we need go farther than the principle we have already extracted. To the extent of its *involvement* in his *struggles*, his image of the car, or the ball, becomes irreducibly *underspecified* through its coupling with the rest of his own activity. Insofar as its activity is a kind of distorted reflection of his own, to revile it in personal terms is not perhaps totally absurd, however medically, morally, and spiritually inadvisable. Only if his adjurations were to continue later, in the detachment of cold blood, could we bring home a change of total absurdity; for the thing is now fully specifiable to him, and its temporary personal quality, dependent on the underspecifiability acquired through involvement, has vanished.

Consider now a so-called 'chess-playing mechanism'. Clearly one can approach such a thing as a fully-specifiable 'mass of wires and valves'—a physical situation that simply unfolds inevitably, and admits of no description in personal terms, of a game-playing or any other kind. But the decision to *play a game* against 'it' reflects a new kind of commitment, and brings out a curious terminological difficulty. In playing a game against a human opponent, we do not say that we are playing against his body, or even his brain, but against *him*. With our 'artificial opponent', however, we have no conventional term to allow of the corresponding distinction. Since the term 'mechanism', as we have seen, is strictly on a par with brain-and-body, it would be a solecism (though a common one) to say that we play against 'the mechanism', just as it was a solecism to speak of a 'chess-playing mechanism' in the first place. (Compare 'a chess-playing brain' *vice* 'a chess-player'.) Perhaps 'artificial opponent' will serve as well as any term to keep our thinking straight. It is against 'him', rather than 'his' mechanism, that it is proper to say we have decided to play. By our practice we have in effect committed ourselves to an entry in the 'artificial personal' column of our semantic chart.

But have we not here begged the question by an insidious linguistic manoeuvre? 'Surely', it may be objected, 'what we want to *discover* is whether a chess-playing mechanism has a personality, or is nothing but a mass of wires and valves? How then can we begin by speaking of "him"?' I do not think we have jumped a step. What we have been doing is to bring out the fact that the decision on the issue of personality was here implicit in the decision to *play a game* —as distinct from merely poking at a (fully-specified) mechanism. To speak of 'playing a game against' X is already to personalise X. It is always open to us, as I have insisted, to refuse such personal commitment: but once we are prepared to make it, the operative question seems to be whether and for how long the developing situation enables us rationally to sustain it.

5. A QUESTION OF 'CONSCIOUSNESS'

But is it the only question? Suppose, for example, that we engage in a chess game by correspondence. Five possibilities may be envisaged and contrasted with profit:

(i) Answering moves selected by a random process from some predetermined list.

In this case we would soon come to doubt that we had an intelligent opponent.

(ii) Answering moves taken from the record of (one side of) a human chess match.

Here again pointlessness and illegitimacy would soon lead to detection.

(iii) Answering moves selected by a random process from among those legitimate at each stage.

In this case detection would depend on the pointlessness of the moves—the absence, except sporadically, of connections and tendencies interpretable as *conative* and *responsive*. Once the suspicion dawned, we could rapidly (with courage) test it by exposing ourselves to obvious attacks, or making obvious threats.

(iv) Answering moves selected by a well-informed, goal-directed, anticipatory computing process (with a suitable degree of disciplined spontaneity [13]) from among those legitimate at each stage.

Here (as Turing argued some years ago [14]) there would seem to be no behavioural reason for us to doubt the 'mentality' of our opponent.

We might well be beaten with reasonable frequency. Moreover, an artificial opponent of the right ('adaptive') sort could readily show all the signs of 'learning' from 'his' growing experience of us and our ways.

(v) Answering moves selected by a competent human opponent.

What has (v) added to (iv)? In respect of ability to play chess (*ex hypothesi*), nothing. The crucial point is surely that in case (v) there is at the far end *someone who knows he is playing:* someone who could, if asked, talk *about* the language of chess, as well as in it—and about other things too.

It is tempting to compare our artificial opponent (iv) with an extreme form of 'idiot savant'—prodigiously able to play a calculating game, but devoid of the capacity for normal dialogue. This, however, would I think beg too many questions, for nobody doubts that an idiot savant is *conscious;* but consciousness, whatever we mean by it, is too high a prize to grant on the score of mere chess-playing ability. (It is not inconceivable, after all, (however improbable) that under some kind of selective anaesthesia or surgery a human being might retain the ability to play coherent chess, as it were mechanically or 'in his sleep', though quite unconscious in the normal sense of 'unaware of what is going on'.) Our criterion of 'consciousness' would not be in terms of his power to react appropriately to chess-moves, but rather his power to raise his eyes from the board, as it were, and engage in dialogue with us (or at least to think) *about* what he was doing.

The fact that this power could sometimes be difficult to test or demonstrate in practice (as it notoriously is in certain forms of schizophrenia) should not blind us to the reality of the distinction. After all, if thought is in any way reflected in brain-processes, there would presumably be some internal operational difference, that could in principle be exhibited, to correspond with that between consciousness and unconsciousness, even if the subject were resolutely dumb and unresponsive.

In evaluating claims for artificial mechanisms, then, it seems important to distinguish the question of 'personality' from that of 'consciousness'. Our artificial opponent (iv) has a 'personality' (of a thinnish sort) which all who are prepared to make the necessary commitment (by playing against him) can come to know. But he would be a bold (or an easily satisfied) man who would describe that personality as 'conscious', in any normal sense.

6. THE LOGIC OF PERSONAL RECOGNITION

It is not my present purpose to discuss ways of remedying the behavioural deficiencies we have noted in the artificial opponent (iv). I have done so on other occasions,[15] and many others are active in the field. I think it is fair to say that no barrier of principle prevents an artificial opponent from showing as many characteristic human features as we care to specify, including the crucial ability to develop and employ an internal running representation of 'What is going on', so as to be able to converse intelligently and purposefully *about* his own activity and experience. If we are not to make a behavioural test of the criterion of consciousness, then we will do no harm, and will clear the air best, by considering a hypothetical case in which *all* such behavioural tests have been satisfied by the activity of the artefact in question.

What I have been trying to bring out is the curious logic—a blend of deduction and commitment—that seems to be involved in the transition from physical to personal ways of characterising such activity, whether in artificial or natural organisms.

Let us take the natural case first. Here is a mass of brain-cells, a going concern, 'wired' to the organs of a human body. The body (including its brain-cells), we are told, is Joe Smith's. We find that in addition to studying the body as an object, we can also talk to Joe, and he can answer us intelligently, giving all the usual human signs of 'having a mind of his own' and 'knowing what he is about'. But a doubt strikes us. What proof have we that Joe is conscious? What proof that there is a 'Joe' at all, as distinct from the mass-of-cells-plus-body? Could not all the behaviour we witness be due to 'nothing but' the 'dead' mechanics of brain cells and the rest, responding automatically to the stimuli we supply? Could not the same behaviour in fact be expected if the mass of brain-cells were replaced, perhaps piece-by-piece, by an identically-organised *artificial* 'brain'? If so, why speak of 'Joe' in this case and not in the other? If not in the other, why in this? What kind of evidence could convince us?

If what I have been arguing is correct, then there is *no* kind of evidence that could logically convince us at this point; for it is not on *evidence* that our missing conviction depends. What we are suffering from is not a failure of evidence, but a failure of nerve. Given that nothing is abnormal in the 'works' of Joe's brain, so that the 'indications' are up to standard, then the transition, from observing the activity of brain-cells, etc., to talking with Joe, is up to us. If we are prepared to 'open up' and allow the 'cross links' of which we spoke earlier, to form between Joe's system and our own, then our experience in the new relationship will be the normal human experience of dialogue with Joe, a personal agent like ourselves, whose consciousness is attested (not 'proved') by the character of the dialogue, as our own is for others (including Joe).

Although in this sense the transition is 'up to us', yet once it has been made (successfully) it would be misleading to describe the recognition of personal attributes as 'optional', for it has a certain irreversibility about it.

At the personal level, Joe will have established some personal claims on us, and we on Joe. We shall not be able lightly to tamper with his brain, for example, nor feel free to dismantle his body. Even more significant, we will not be able to justify ignoring him as a person at will. He has become 'one of us', a member of the linguistic community—not, be it noted, by virtue of the particular *stuff* of which his brain is built (though we have so far assumed this to be naturally grown) but by virtue of the particular kinds of mutual interaction that it can sustain with our own—interaction which at the personal level we describe as that of person-with-person.

At the technical level, he can be recognised as one of us because (and to the extent that) in dialogue our dispositions in the information-flow-map are symmetrical, our relationships reciprocal. In terms of the pattern of information-flow, our two coupled brains engage in a kind of 'resonance' (in the technical, not the mystical sense!); and as a result, each becomes incapable of representing the other as a fully-specified system.

In this sense at least the common remark, that persons in dialogue present an element of *mystery* to one another, has a solid technical justification. Note, however, that his kind of mystery stands wholly apart from any physical puzzles presented by the workings of the brain; for it would remain even if all of these were solved. No matter how detailed our understanding of Joe's neuroanatomy, we cannot in principle reduce the Joe we know and address as a person to any exactly-specified assemblage of mechanically-determined molecules. If we try to do so, Joe, as a person, must simply disappear from our conceptual framework, as inevitably as statistical entropy does from that of Newtonian dynamics. To say (as some might) that talk about Joe is merely a 'portmanteau translation' of talk about Joe's brain-cells, is thus an error. The two are indeed (*ex hypothesi*) correlates; but they are not translations, for the trouble with the molecular level is precisely that it *has no words* (because logically it has no place) for the concepts of the personal.

7. CONCLUSION

So much for Joe. For all purposes of description and dialogue, he is 'conscious' when he can join as one of us in bearing witness to the events of our common world. We do not need to ask what his brain is made of, nor how it works. If parts of it wear out, and we imagine them replaced by exact electronic or other equivalents, we have no reason to change our attitude. If eventually Joe's brain were wholly artificial, but functionally indistinguishable—like one of our hypothetical automata—we should surely still have none . . . ?

Surely? Like good oysters, let us not seek to rid ourselves of one last grain of irritation. For imagine that Joe is conscious, and we discuss Joe's consciousness in Joe's hearing. Joe decides to play dumb and listen. Our judgment on the matter may depend critically on the kind of relationship we can establish. We may or may not succeed in getting round this by internal examination of Joe's brain. We may argue long about the optional nature of the judgment. But —and this is the point—all the time, there would in fact be Joe, listening to us, raising a mental eyebrow, and *knowing* the answer. Nothing optional or conventional about that. Consciousness is a matter of fact, on which we are either right or wrong. In this case, there *is* someone there. Joe knows, for it is he.

Clearly, then, any dogmatic dispatch of this question in relation to artificial 'brains' is out of place. Unlike Turing,[16] I do not believe that Christian theology supports any objection to the possibility that persons might be thus artificially 'begotten', which I personally find fascinating. I know of no coherent argument against it, and I have been at pains to show that mechanical explicability at the molecular level could not provide such an argument.

On the other hand, it seems equally clear that we are not at liberty to settle the question as a matter of convention, and say that artificial persons that behave-as-if-conscious simply *are* conscious. When deciding whether to *treat* psychiatric patients, or laboratory animals, or artificial persons, or even one another, as conscious, such conventions may indeed be inevitable; but they can do nothing to relieve our ontological doubt.

No, the simple truth is that we cannot know. And let no one try the old line that it is therefore *meaningless* to wonder whether there is any 'Joe' listening to us as we discuss the behaviour of a body before us; for that body could well be his own.

NOTES

1. It should be noted that only the two 'mechanical' (or the two 'personal') columns offer *analogues* of one another. Personal activity and

156   HUMAN AND ARTIFICIAL INTELLIGENCE

2. See A. M. Turing, 'Computing Machinery and Intelligence', *Mind*, LIX (1959), 433–60; and J. R. Lucas, 'Minds, Machines and Gödel', *Philosophy*, XXXVI (1961), 112–27.

3. D. M. MacKay, 'Mindlike Behaviour in Artefacts', *British Journal for the Philosophy of Science*, II (1951), 105–21; also III (1953), 352–53; and 'The Epistemological Problem for Automata', *Automata Studies* (Princeton, N.J.: Princeton University Press (1955), pp. 235–51.

4. J. R. Lucas, *op. cit.*

5. D. M. MacKay, 'From Mechanism to Mind', *Trans. Vict. Inst.*, LXXXV (1953), 17–32, esp. 22.

6. See above, n. 2, first reference.

7. Lest this account seems altogether too remote from the 'objective' 'physical' definition of entropy-change as $\Delta Q/T$, it should be remembered that the power to extract work from such a molecular assemblage depends directly on the extent to which its energy-configuration can be ascertained. This explains why what may seem a highly subjective concept turns out to be of crucial importance in the theory of engines.

8. Underspecified, not in the sense of leaving any parts unaccounted for, but in the sense of being compatible with more than one state of the parts.

9. This is true quite apart from the complications due to Heisenberg Indeterminacy, which we ignore for the present purpose.

10. D. M. MacKay, 'On the Logical Indeterminacy of a Free Choice', *Mind*, LXIX (1960), 31–40.

11. For each individual, viewed as a physical organism, we may picture a unique internal 'organisation-chart' or 'information-flow-map' that would show how (and/or to what extent) his total behaviour is organised. In goal-pursuit, some of the lines of flow of information extend outwards to the goal and back to the internal system.

In the relationship of person-with-person, the significant point is that the information-flow-maps of the two individuals merge inextricably. To the extent that each is allowed to affect the 'goal-settings' of the other (as occurs in dialogue) the flow-lines on the map form cross-links that unite the two into one system for any purpose of mechanistic analysis.

12. D. M. MacKay, 'Mentality in Machines' (third paper in Symposium), *Proc. Aristot. Soc. Suppt.*, XXVI (1952), 61–86, esp. 86.

13. D. M. MacKay, 'On the Combination of Digital and Analogue Computing Techniques in the Design of Analytical Engines', May 20,

1949 (reprinted as Appendix to 'Operational Aspects of Intellect', *Proc. N.P.L. Conference on 'Mechanization of Thought Processes'*, [London: H.M.S.O., 1959], pp. 37–52).

14. *Op. cit.*
15. See notes 2, 4, 12, and 13.
16. *Op. cit.*

7   A critique of artificial reason

HUBERT L. DREYFUS

Hubert L. Dreyfus has become the most prominent
and trenchant critic of the claims made by some workers in artificial intelligence. Originally formulated in a
paper issued by the Rand Corporation, his scrutinizing
reviews of the announced successes in the field have
been developed into a book to be published shortly. As
the following essay shows, his criticism has been twofold: first, of the gap between the actual achievements
and the often exaggerated interpretations of their significance, and second, of the adequacy of the conceptual
models presupposed by simulation work.

The author was a professor of philosophy at the
Massachusetts Institute of Technology before moving
to his present position at the University of California at
Berkeley.

In a recent book on the mathematical theory of
computers, Marvin Minsky, one of the leading workers in Artificial
Intelligence, gave voice to the optimism guiding his research and
that of others in the field:

Within a generation, I am convinced, few compartments of intellect will
remain outside the machine's realm—the problem of creating "artificial
intelligence" will be substantially solved.[1]

This work was supported in part by the National Science Foundation under
Grant GS 1953. Earlier versions of this paper were read at Indiana University
and Northwestern University. I am indebted to participants in those discussions
for helpful suggestions. Copyright 1968 by Hubert L. Dreyfus.

The work was originally published in *Thought*, the Quarterly of Fordham
Univ., Vol. XLIII (Winter 1968), pp. 507–22.

Insofar as this is a prediction, one way to find out whether it is accurate is simply to wait a generation and see. But insofar as the prediction is presented as a conviction, we, as philosophers, may want to ask whether this conviction is well founded.

Minsky is typical of workers in the area in giving two sorts of argument in support of his view: (1) Empirical arguments based on progress achieved thus far, and (2) A priori arguments about what machines can, in principle, do. It might seem at first sight that these are two distinct sorts of argument and that philosophers should concern themselves only with the a priori ones, but the truism that experimental data is meaningless until *interpreted* is especially applicable in this new, and barely scientific, area of inquiry. What we take the data to mean depends upon our assumptions, so that the empirical arguments implicitly reflect the a priori ones. It will therefore be my contention that the optimism underlying work in AI is unjustified *both* on empirical and a priori grounds. I will argue that the empirical arguments gain their plausibility only on the basis of an appeal to an implicit philosophical assumption, and that this assumption, far from being justified, simply perpetuates a fundamental error of the Western philosophical tradition.

                                    I

Language translation, or the use of computers to simulate the understanding of natural languages, offers the clearest illustration of how optimistic assumptions have enabled enthusiasts to interpret as promising, data which is ambiguous, to say the least. Minsky cites as encouraging evidence of progress the existence of "machines that handle abstract-nonmathematical problems and *deal with ordinary-language expressions.*" [2] Addmittedly, "deal with" is rather vague, but in another article Minsky comes right out and says of a program for solving algebra word problems, Bobrow's STUDENT, that "it understands English." [3] In fact this program embodies nothing one would ever want to call syntactic or semantic understanding. It simply breaks up the sentences into units on the basis of cues such as the words "times", "of", "equals", etc., equates these sentence chunks with x's and y's, and tries to set up simultaneous equations. If these equations cannot be solved, it appeals to further rules for breaking up the sentences into other units and tries again. The whole scheme works only because there is the constraint, not present in understanding ordinary discourse, that the pieces of the sentence, when represented by variables, will set up soluble equations. Such a program is so far from semantic understanding that, as Bobrow admits, it would interpret "The number of times I went to the movies" as the product of two variables: "The number of" and "I went to the movies", because "times" is always interpreted as an operator indicating multiplication.[4]

Why then does Minsky regard this program, which shows not the slightest sign of understanding, as progress towards the understanding of natural language? Presumably because he, like Bobrow, believes that the underlying "semantic theory of discourse can be used as a basis for a much more general language processing system . . ."[5] And why should they think, in the face of the peculiar restrictions necessary to the function of the program, that such a generalization must be possible? Nothing, I think, can justify or even explain their optimism concerning *this* approach. Their general optimism that *some* such computable approach must work, however, can be seen to follow from a fundamental metaphysical assumption concerning the nature of language and of human intelligent behavior, *viz.* that whatever orderly behavior people engage in can in principle be formalized and processed by digital computers. This leads them to shrug off all current difficulties as due to technological limitations such as the restricted size of the storage capacity of present machine memories.[6] If it were not for such an assumption Bobrow's limited success, heralded by Minsky as the most promising work thus far, would be recognized as a trick which says nothing either for or against the possibility of machine understanding, and the fact that this is the best that an intelligent person like Bobrow could do would lead to discouragement.

II

The formalistic assumption which would lend plausibility to Minsky's optimistic interpretation of Bobrow's meager results is expressed in Minsky's motto: "There is no reason to suppose machines

have any limitations not shared by man." [7] I think there *are* good
reasons for attributing special limitations to machines, but that is
beyond the scope of this paper.[8] Here I wish only to argue that,
whatever the intrinsic capabilities of computers, they are limited in
their performance by fundamental limitations on the kinds of programs human programmers are able to write for them. Before this
can be shown, however, we must be clear what is meant by "machine," for if a physical organism is to be counted as a machine
then man too would be a machine and the claim that machines
have no limitations not shared by man would be vacuous.

A machine as defined by Minsky, who bases his definition on that
of Turing, is a "rule-obeying mechanism". As Turing puts it: "The
. . . computer is supposed to be following fixed rules. . . . It is
the duty of the control to see that these instructions are obeyed
correctly and in the right order. The control is so constructed that
this necessarily happens." [9] So the machine in question is a very
restricted but very fundamental sort of mechanism. It operates on
determinate, unambiguous bits of data, according to strict rules
which apply univocally to this data. The claim is made that this sort
of machine—a Turing machine—which expresses the essence of a
digital computer, can in principle do anything that human beings
can do, i.e. has no in-principle limitations not shared by man.

Minsky considers the anti-formalist counter-claim that "Perhaps
there are processes . . . which simply *cannot* be described in any
formal language, but which can nevertheless be carried out, e.g.,
by minds." [10] Rather than answer this objection directly, he refers
to Turing's "brilliant" article which, he asserts, contains arguments
that "amount . . . to a satisfactory refutation of many such objections." [11] Turing does, indeed, take up this sort of objection. He
states it as follows: "It is not possible to produce a set of rules
purporting to describe what a man should do in every conceivable
set of circumstances." [12] This is presumably Turing's generalization
of the Wittgensteinian argument that one cannot make completely
explicit the normative rules governing the correct use of a natural
language. Turing's "refutation" is to make a distinction between
"rules of conduct" and "laws of behavior" and then to assert that
"we cannot so easily convince ourselves of the absence of complete
laws of behavior as of complete rules of conduct." [13] Now as an
answer to the Wittgenstein claim this is well taken. Turing is in

effect arguing that although we cannot formulate the normative rules for the correct application of a particular predicate, this does not show that we cannot formulate the rules which describe how, *in fact*, a particular individual applies such a predicate. In other words, while Turing is ready to admit that it may in principle be impossible to provide a set of rules determining what a person *should* do in every circumstance, he holds there is no reason to give up the supposition that one could in principle discover a set of rules determining what he *would* do. But why does this supposition seem so self evident that the burden of proof is on those who call it into question? Why should we have to "convince ourselves of the *absence* of complete laws of behavior" rather than of their presence? Here we are face to face again with the formalist assumption. It is important to try to root out what lends this assumption its implied a priori plausibility.

To begin with "laws of behavior" is ambiguous. In one sense human behavior is certainly lawful, if lawful simply means nonarbitrary. But the assumption that the laws in question are the sort that could be embodied in a computer program is a much stronger and more controversial claim, in need of further justification.

At this point the formalist presumably exploits the ambiguity of "laws of behavior". Human bodies are part of the physical world and objects in the physical world have been shown to obey laws which can be expressed in a formalism manipulable on a digital computer. Thus, understood as motion, human behavior is presumably completely lawful in the sense the formalists require. But this in no way supports the formalist assumption as it appears in Minsky and Turing. When Minsky or Turing claim that man is a Turing machine, they cannot mean that a man is a physical system. Otherwise it would be appropriate to say that trees or rocks are Turing machines. These too obey mathematically formulable laws, and their behavior is no doubt capable of simulation to any degree of accuracy on a digital computer. When Minsky or Turing claim that man is a Turing machine, they must mean that man processes data received from the world, such as colors, shapes, sounds, etc., by means of logical operations that can be reduced to matching, classifying, and boolean operations. Workers in Artificial Intelligence are claiming that human *information processing* can be described in a digital formalism, while the considerations from physics show only that human motions, and presumably the neurological activity accompanying them, can in principle be described in this form.

All Artificial Intelligence (AI) is dedicated to using logical operations to manipulate data, not to solve physical equations. No one has tried, or hopes to try, to use the laws of physics to describe in detail the motion of human bodies. This would probably be physically impossible, for, according to the very laws of physics and information theory which such work would presuppose, such a calculation would seem to require a computer bigger than the universe.[14] Yet workers in the field of AI from Turing to Minsky seem to take refuge in this confusion between physical laws and information processing rules to convince themselves that there is reason to suppose that human behavior can be formalized; that the burden of proof is on those who claim that "there are processes . . . which simply cannot be described in a formal language but which can nevertheless be carried out by minds."

Once this ambiguity has been removed, what argument remains that human behavior, at what AI workers have called "the information processing level," can be described in terms of strict rules? Here the discussion becomes genuinely philosophical because here AI theorists link up with an assumption characteristic of the Western philosophical tradition, an assumption which, if Heidegger is right, is, in fact, *definitive* of that tradition. The assumption begins as a moral demand. Socrates asks Euthyphro for what Turing and Minsky would call an "effective procedure." Minsky defines effective procedure as "a set of rules which tell us, from moment to moment, precisely how to behave."[15] In facing a moral dilemna, Socrates says: "I want to know what is characteristic of piety which makes all actions pious . . . that I may have it to turn to, and to use as a standard whereby to judge your actions and those of other men."[16]

Plato generalized this ethical demand for certainty into an epistemological demand. According to Plato all knowledge must be stated in explicit definitions which anyone could apply. What could not be stated explicitly in such a definition—all areas of human thought which required skill, intuition, or a sense of tradition—were relegated to mere beliefs.

But Plato was not yet fully a cyberneticist, although according to Wiener he was the first to use the term, for Plato was looking for *semantic* rather than *syntactic* criteria. (He was operating on the fourth, rather than the third level of his divided line.) His criteria could be applied by *man* but not by a machine. And this raises difficulties.

Minsky notes after introducing a common sense notion of effective procedure: "This attempt at definition is subject to the criticism that the *interpretation* of the rules is left to depend on some person or agent."[17] Similarly Aristotle claimed that intuition was necessary to apply the Platonic rules:

Yet it is not easy to find a formula by which we may determine how far and up to what point a man may go wrong before he incurs blame. But this difficulty of definition is inherent in every object of perception; such questions of degree are bound up with the circumstances of the individual case, where our only criterion *is* the perception.[18]

It requires one more move to remove all appeal to intuition and judgement. As Galileo discovered that, by ignoring secondary qualities and teleological considerations, one could find a pure formalism for describing physical motion, so, one might suppose, a Galileo of the mind might eliminate all semantic considerations (appeal to meanings) and introduce purely syntactic (formal) definitions.

The belief that such a final formalization must be possible came to dominate Western thought, both because it corresponded to a basic moral and intellectual demand and because the success of physical science seemed to imply to Sixteenth Century philosophers, as it still seems to suggest to Turing and Minsky, that the demand could be satisfied. Hobbes was the first to make explicit this syntactic conception of thought as calculation: "When a man *reasons*, he does nothing else but conceive a sum total from addition of parcels. For REASON . . . is nothing but reckoning . . ."[19]

It only remained to work out the univocal parcels or bits on which this purely syntactic calculator could operate, and Leibnitz, the inventor of the binary system, dedicated himself to working out, unsuccessfully, to be sure, a formal language of unambiguous terms in which all knowledge could be expressed.[20]

Leibnitz only had promises but now it seems the digital computer has realized his dream and thus Plato's demand. The computer operates according to syntactic rules, on uninterpreted, determinate bits of data, so that there is no question of rules for applying rules; no question of interpretation; no appeal to human intuition and judgement. It is thus entirely appropriate that in his UNESCO address Heidegger cites cybernetics (not, as formerly, the atom bomb) as the culmination of philosophy.

Philosophy has come to an end in the present epoch. It has found its place in the scientific view . . . The fundamental characteristic of this scientific determination is that it is cybernetic, i.e., technological.[21]

We have now traced the history of the assumption that thinking is calculating. We have seen that its *attraction* harks back to the Platonic realization that moral life would be more bearable and knowledge more definitive if it were true. Its *plausibility*, however, rests only on a confusion between the mechanistic assumptions underlying the success of modern science and a correlative formalistic assumption underlying what would be a science of human behavior if such existed.

There seem to be no *arguments* for the formalistic assumption that all human behavior can be simulated by a Turing machine using syntactic operations without reduction to the laws of physics. (This would be unobjectionable if the assumption were put forward as an hypothesis but, as we have seen, Turing and Minsky treat it rather as a postulate.) Can any arguments be given *against* the plausibility of this assumption?

III

Most striking evidence that such a limit to formalization does indeed exist and poses seemingly insurmountable difficulties, can be found in analyzing current attempts to use digital computers to simulate the understanding of a natural language.

Yehoshua Bar-Hillel and Anthony Oettinger, two of the most respected and most informed workers in the field of automatic language translation, have each been led to pessimistic conclusions concerning the possibility of further progress in the field. They have each discovered that the order of the words in a sentence does not provide sufficient information to enable a machine to determine which of several possible parsings is the appropriate one, nor does the context of a word indicate which of several possible readings the author had in mind.

As Oettinger puts it:

[Work] to date has revealed a far higher degree of legitimate *syntactic* ambiguity in English and in Russian than has been anticipated. This, and a related fuzziness of the boundary between the grammatical and the nongrammatical, raises serious questions about the possibility of effective fully automatic manipulation of English or Russian for any purposes of translation or information retrieval.[22]

To understand this difficulty in its purest form we must distinguish between the *generation* of grammatical and meaningful sentences, and the *understanding* of such sentences in actual instances of their use. For the sake of the argument we will grant that linguists will succeed in formulating rules for generating any sentences which native speakers recognize as grammatical and meaningful and excluding all sentences that native speakers reject as ungrammatical or meaningless. The remaining difficulty can then be stated as follows: In an instance of linguistic usage a native speaker is able to interpret univocally a sentence which, according to the rules, could have been generated in several different ways, and thus would have several different grammatical structures, i.e. several legitimate meanings. (A famous example is the sentence: "Time flies like an arrow.", which a computer would read as a statement that a certain kind of fly likes to eat arrows, and a command to rush out and clock flies, as well as a statement about the passage of time.)

In narrowing down this legitimate ambiguity the native speaker may be appealing either to specific information about the world, as for example when we recognize the sentence "the book is in the pen" means that the book is in a playpen or pig pen, not in a fountain pen, or to a sense of the situation as in the following example from Fodor and Katz:

An ambiguous sentence such as "He follows Marx" occurring in a setting in which it is clear that the speaker is remarking about intellectual history cannot bear the reading "he dogs the footsteps of Groucho." [23]

The appeal to context, moreover, is more fundamental than the appeal to facts for the context determines the *significance* of the facts. Thus in spite of our *general* knowledge about the relative size of pens and books we might interpret "The book is in the pen," when uttered in a James Bond movie as meaning just the opposite of what it means at home or on the farm. And, conversely, when no specifically odd context is specified, we assume a "normal" context and assign to the facts about relative size a "normal'" significance.

It is such difficulties—specifically those concerning an appeal to facts—which make Oettinger and Bar-Hillel skeptical about the possibility of fully automatic high quality machine translation. Bar-Hillel claims that his "box-pen" argument from which mine is adapted "amounts to an almost full-fledged demonstration of the unattainability of fully automatic high quality translation, not only in the near future but altogether",[24] if only because there would be no way of sorting through the enormous (Bar-Hillel says infinite) [25] quantity of information which might be relevant to determining the meaning of any specific utterance.

Katz and Fodor discuss this sort of difficulty in their article "The Structure of a Semantic Theory":

Since a complete theory of setting selection must represent as part of the setting of an utterance any and every feature of the world which speakers need in order to determine the prefered reading of that utterance, and since, . . . practically any item of information about the world is essential to some disambiguations, two conclusions follow. First, such a theory cannot in principle distinguish between the speaker's knowledge of his language and his knowledge of the world . . . Second, since there is no serious possibility of systematizing all the knowledge about the world that speakers share . . . . [such a theory] is not a serious model for linguistics.[26]

Katz and Fodor continue "none of these considerations is intended to rule out the possibility that, by placing relatively strong limitations on the information about the world that a theory can represent in the characterization of a setting, a *limited* theory of selection by sociophysical setting can be constructed. What these considerations do show is that a *complete* theory of this kind is impossible." [27]

Thus Bar-Hillel claims we must appeal to specific *facts*, such as the size of pens and books; Katz and Fodor assume we must appeal to the *sociophysical setting*. The difference between these views seems unimportant to the partisans of each, since both presumably assume that the setting is itself identified by features which are facts, and functions like a fact in disambiguation. We shall see, however, that disregarding the difference between fact and situation leads to an equivocation in both Bar-Hillel and Katz as to whether mechanical translation is impractical or impossible.

In Bar-Hillel's "demonstration" that since disambiguation depends on the use of facts, and the number of facts is "in a certain very pregnant sense infinite", fully automatic high quality mechanical translation is unattainable, it is unclear what is being claimed. If "unattainable" means that in terms of present computers, and programs in operation or envisaged, no such massive storage and retrieval of information can be carried out, then the point is well made, and is sufficient to cast serious doubt on claims that mechanical translation has been achieved or can be achieved in the forseeable future. But if "unattainable" means theoretically impossible—which the appeal to infinity seems to imply—then Bar-Hillel is claiming too much. A machine would not have to store an infinite number of facts, for from a large number of facts and rules for concatenating them, it could produce further ones indefinitely. True, no machine could sort through such an endless amount of data. At present there exists no machine and no program capable of storing even a very large body of data so as to gain access to the relevant information in manageable time. There is work being done on what are called "associative memories" and ingenious tricks are used in programming, such as hash coding, which may in the distant future provide the means of storing and accessing vast bodies of information. Then information might be stored in such a way that in any given case only a finite number of relevant facts need be considered.

As long as Katz and Fodor accept the same implicit metaphysical premise as Bar-Hillel, that the world is the totality of facts, and speak of the setting in terms of "items of information" their argument is as equivocal as Bar-Hillel's. They have no right to pass from the claim that there is "no serious possibility" of systematizing the knowledge necessary for disambiguation, which seems to be a statement about our technological capabilities, to the claim that a complete theory of selection by sociophysical setting is "impossible". If a program for handling all knowledge is ever developed, and in their world there is no theoretical reason why it should not be, it will be such a theory.

Only if one refuses the traditional metaphysical assumption that the world can be analyzed as a set of facts—items of information— can one legitimately move beyond practical impossibility. We have already seen examples which suggest that the situation might be of a radically different order and fulfill a totally different function than any concatenation of facts. In the "Marx" example, the situation (academic) determines how to disambiguate "Marx" (Karl) and furthermore tells us which facts are relevant to disambiguate "follows", as ideological or chronological. (When was the follower born, what are his political views, etc.) In the book-pen example the size of the book and pen are clearly relevant since we are speaking of physical objects being "in" other physical objects, but here the situation, be it agricultural, domestic, or conspiratorial, determines the *significance* of the facts involved. Thus it is our sense of the situation which enables us to select from the potential infinity of facts the immediately relevant ones, and once these relevant facts are found, enables us to interpret them. This suggests that unless we can give the computer a way of recognizing situations it will not be able to disambiguate them and thus in principle unable to understand utterances in a natural language.

But these considerations alone do not constitute a sufficient argument. The traditional metaphysician, reincarnated in the AI researcher, can grant that facts used in disambiguation are selected and interpreted in terms of the situation, and simply conclude that we need only first pick out and program the features which identify the situation.

But the same two problems which arose in disambiguation and necessitated appeal to the situation arise again on the level of situation recognition. (1) If in disambiguation the number of simple facts is in some sense infinite so that selection criteria must be applied before interpretation can begin, the number of facts that might be relevant to recognizing a situation is infinite too. How is the computer to consider all the features such as how many people are present, the temperature, the pressure, the day of the week, etc., any one of which might be a defining feature of some context? (2) Even if the program provides rules for determining relevant facts, these facts would be ambiguous, i.e., capable of defining several different situations, until they were interpreted. Evidently, a broader context will have to be used to determine which of the infinity of features is relevant, and how each is to be understood. But if, in turn, the program must enable the machine to identify the broader context in terms of *its* relevant features—and this is the only way a computer could proceed—the programmer would seem to be faced with an infinite regress of contexts.

Such a regress would certainly be disastrous, but there still seems to be a ray of hope, for a computer programmer could plausibly claim that this regress might terminate in an ultimate context. In fact, there does seem to be such an ultimate context, though, as we shall see, this is equally disastrous to those working toward machine intelligence.

We have seen that in order to identify which facts are relevant for recognizing an academic or a conspiratorial situation, and to interpret these facts, one must appeal to a broader context. Thus it is only in the broader context of social intercourse that we see we must normally take into account what people are wearing and what they are doing, but not how many insects there are in the room or the cloud formations at noon or a minute later. Only this broader context enables us to determine whether these facts will have their normal significance.

Moreover, even the facts necessary to recognize social intercourse can only be singled out because social intercourse is a sub-case of human activity, which also includes working alone or studying a primitive tribe. And finally, human activity itself is only a sub-class of some even broader situation—call it the human life-world— which would have to include even those situations where no human beings were directly involved. But what facts would be relevant to recognizing this broadest context? Or does it make sense to speak of "recognizing" the life-world at all? It seems we simply take for granted this broadest context in being people. As Wittgenstein puts it:

If I have exhausted the justifications I have reached bedrock, and my spade is turned. Then I am inclined to say: "This is simply what I do." [28]

or;

What has to be accepted, the given is—someone could say—*forms of life*.[29]

Well then, why not make explicit the significant features of the human form of life from within it? Indeed, this has been the implicit goal of philosophers for 2,000 years, and it should be no surprise that nothing short of a formalization of the human form of life can ever give us artificial intelligence. But how are we to proceed. Everything we experience in some way, immediate or remote, reflects our human concerns. Everything and nothing is relevant. Everything is significant and insignificant. Without some *particular* interest, without some *particular* inquiry to help us select and interpret, we are back confronting the infinity of meaningless facts we were trying to avoid.

It seems that given the artificial intelligence worker's conception of reason as calculation and thus his need to formalize the ultimate context of human life, his attempt to produce intelligent behavior leads to an antinomy. On the one hand, we have the thesis: There must always be a broader context in which to work out our formalization, otherwise we have no way to distinguish relevant from irrelevant facts. On the other hand, we have the antithesis: There must be an ultimate context which we can make completely explicit, otherwise there will be an infinite regress of contexts, and we can never begin our formalization.

As Kant noted, the resolution of such an antinomy requires giving up the assumption that these are the only possible alternatives. They are, indeed, the only alternatives open to someone trying to construct *artificial* reason, for a digital computer program must always proceed from the elements to the whole and thus treat the world as a set of facts. But *human* reason is able to avoid this antimony by operating within a context or horizon which gives to facts their significance but need not itself be analyzed in terms of facts.

IV

In the face of this antinomy, it seems reasonable to claim that, on the information processing level, as opposed to the level of the laws of physics, we cannot analyze human behavior in terms of explicit rules. And since we have seen no argument brought forward by the AI theorists for the formalist assumption that human behavior *must be* simulateable by a digital computer operating with strict rules on determinate bits, we would seem to have good philosophical grounds for rejecting this assumption.

If we do abandon this assumption, then the empirical data available to date would take on different significance. The persistent difficulties which have plagued all areas of AI would then need to be reinterpreted as failures, and these failures, interpreted as empirical evidence against the formalist's assumption that one can treat the situation or context as if it were an object. In Heideggarian terms this is to say that Western Metaphysics reaches its culmination in Cybernetics and the recent difficulties in AI rather than reflecting technological limitations, may reveal the limitations of technology.

NOTES

1. Marvin Minsky, *Computation, Finite and Infinite Machines* (Englewood Cliffs, N.J.: Prentice-Hall, 1967), p. 2.
2. *Ibid.*, p. 2.
3. Marvin Minsky, "Artificial Intelligence," *Scientific American,* CCXV (September, 1966), p. 257.
4. Daniel C. Bobrow, *Natural Language Input for a Computer Problem Solving System,* Project MAC report MAC-TR-1, page 102.
5. *Ibid.*, p. 102. Minsky makes even more surprising and misleading claims in his introduction to *Semantic Information Processing* (Cambridge, Mass.: M.I.T. Press, 1968). There, in discussing Bobrow's program he acclaims its "enormous 'learning potential'."

> "Consider the colossal effect, upon future performance of Bobrow's STUDENT, of telling it that 'distance equals speed times time.'" That one experience enables it to then handle a very large new portion of "high-school algebra"—all the linear physical position-velocity-time problems. We don't consider it 'learning" perhaps only because it is too intelligent! We become muddled by our associations with the psychologist's image of learning as a slow-improvement-attendant-upon sickeningly-often-repeated experience!"

Again it is easy to show that what has been acquired by the machine can in no way be called "understanding." The machine has indeed been given another *equation,* but it does not understand it as a *formula.* That is, the program can now plug one distance, one rate, and one time into the equation d = rt, but that it does not understand anything is clear from the fact that it cannot use this equation twice in one problem, for it has no way of determining which quantities should be used in which equation.

6. For example in his *Scientific American* article Minsky asks: "Why are the programs not more intelligent than they are?" and responds ". . . until recently resources—in people, time and computer capacity—have been quite limited. A number of the more careful and serious attempts have come close to their goal . . . others have been limited by core memory capacity; still others encountered programming difficulties." (p. 258.)

7. Minsky, *Computation,* p. vii.

8. Cf. my forthcoming book, *A Critique of Artificial Reason* (New York: Harper & Row, 1969).

9. A. H. Turing, "Computing Machinery and Intelligence," in *Minds and Machines,* ed. Alan Ross Anderson (Englewood Cliffs, N. J.: Prentice-Hall, 1964), p. 8.

10. *Op. cit.,* p. 107.

11. *Ibid.*

12. *Op. cit.,* p. 23.

13. *Ibid.*

14. Cf. H. J. Bremermann, "Optimization through Evolution and Recombination," in *Self-Organizing Systems,* eds. M. C. Yonts, G. T. Jacobi and G. D. Goldstein (Washington, D.C., Spartan, 1962), pp. 93–106. In this article Bremermann demonstrated that: "No data processing system whether artificial or living can process more than (2×10^{47}) bits per second per gram of its mass." Bremermann goes on to draw the following conclusions:

"There are $\pi \times 10^7$ seconds in a year. The age of the earth is about 10^9 years, its mass less than 6×10^{27} grams. Hence even a computer of the size of the earth could not process more than 10^{93} bits during a time equal to the age of the earth. [Not to mention the fact, one might add, that the bigger the computer the more the speed of light would be a factor in slowing down its operations.] . . . Theorem proving and problem solving . . . lead to exponentially growing problem trees. If our conjecture is true then it seems that the difficulties that are currently encountered in the field of pattern recognition and theorem proving will not be resolved by sheer speed of data processing by some future super-computers."

15. *Op. cit.*, p. 106. Of course, Minsky is thinking of computation not moral action.

16. Plato, *Euthyphro* (New York: Library of Liberal Arts, 1948).

17. *Op. cit.*, p. 106.

18. Aristotle, *Nicomachean Ethics* (Baltimore, Md.: Penguin Books, 1953), p. 75.

19. Hobbes, *Leviathan* (New York: Library of Liberal Arts, 1958), p. 45.

20. This is not the only reason Leibnitz deserves to be called the first cyberneticist. His sketchy general descriptions of his "universal characteristic" coupled with his promise that given enough money and time he could easily work out the details, makes him the father of modern grant proposals.

21. Martin Heidegger, "La fin de la philosophie et la tache de la pensée," in *Kierkegaard Vivant,* Colloque organíse par l'Unesco à Paris du 21 au 23 avril 1964 (Paris: Gallimard, 1966), pp. 178–79.

22. Anthony G. Oettinger, "The State of the Art of Automatic Language Translation: An Appraisal," *Beitraege zur Sprachkunde und Information Verarbeitung*, Vol. 1, Heft. 2 (Munich, 1963), p. 27.

23. Jerrold Katz and Jerry Fodor, "The Structure of a Semantic Theory," in *The Structure of Language,* eds. Jerrold Katz and Jerry Fodor (Englewood Cliffs, N. J.: Prentice-Hall, 1964), p. 487.

24. Yehoshua Bar-Hillel, "The Present Status of Automatic Translation of Languages," in *Advances in Computers*, Vol. 1 (New York: Academic Press, 1960), p. 94.

25. *Ibid.*, p. 160.

26. *Op. cit.*, p. 489.

27. *Ibid.*, p. 179.

28. Ludwig Wittgenstein, *Philosophical Investigations* (New York: Macmillan, 1953), Article 217.

29. *Ibid.*, Article 226.

8   Robots: Machines or artificially created life?

H. PUTNAM

Mere robots and others

R. ALBRITTON

An example of the philosophical approach to the problem of men and machines which focuses on the language used to describe and converse with men and machines, this pair of papers considers the kinds of questions touched on by D. M. MacKay, namely the justification for extending the range of certain types of discourse and attribution. The second paper was written as a response to the first, and the two were originally presented at a meeting of the American Philosophical Association.

Hilary Putnam is professor of philosophy at Harvard, and Rogers Albritton is professor and chairman of the Department of Philosophy at Harvard University.

ROBOTS: MACHINES OR ARTIFICIALLY CREATED LIFE? *

H. Putnam

Those of us who passed many (well- or ill-spent?) childhood hours reading tales of rockets and robots, androids and telepaths, galactic civilizations and time machines, know all too well that robots—hypothetical machines that simulate human behavior, often with an at least roughly human appearance—can be friendly or fearsome, man's best friend or worst enemy. When friendly, robots can be inspiring or pathetic—they can overawe us with their superhuman powers (and with their greater than human virtue as well, at least in the writings of some authors), or they can amuse us with their stupidities and naivete. Robots have been "known" to fall in love, go mad (power- or otherwise), annoy with oversolicitousness. At least in the literature of science fiction, then, it is possible for a robot to be "conscious"; that means (since 'consciousness', like 'material object' and 'universal', is a philosopher's stand-in for more substantial words) to have feelings, thoughts, attitudes, and character traits. But is it really possible? If it is possible, what are the necessary and sufficient conditions? And why should we philosophers worry about this anyway? Aren't the mind-body problem, the problem of other minds, the problem of logical behaviorism, the problem: What did Wittgenstein really mean in the private-language argument? (and why should one care?), more than enough to keep the most industrious philosopher of mind busy without dragging in or inventing the Problem of the Minds of Machines?—These are my concerns in this paper.

The mind-body problem has been much discussed in the past thirty-odd years, but the discussion seems to me to have been fruitless. No one has really been persuaded by *The Concept of Mind* that the relation of university to buildings, professors, and students is a helpful model for the relation of mind to body, or even for the relation of, say, *being intelligent* to individual speech-acts. And Herbert Feigl informs me that he has now himself abandoned his

* Presented in a symposium on "Minds and Machines" at the sixty-first annual meeting of the American Philosophical Association, Eastern Division, December, 1964. From H. Putnam, "Robots: Machines or Artificially Created Life?" *Journal of Philosophy*, LXI (1964), 668–91.

well-known "identity theory" of the mind-body relation. The problem of other minds has been much more fruitful—the well-known and extremely important paper by Austin is ample testimony to that—but even that problem has begun to seem somewhat stale of late. What I hope to persuade you is that the problem of the Minds of Machines will prove, at least for a while, to afford an exciting new way to approach quite traditional issues in the philosophy of mind. Whether, and under what conditions, a robot could be conscious is a question that cannot be discussed without at once impinging on the topics that have been treated under the headings Mind-Body Problem and Problem of Other Minds. For my own part, I believe that certain crucial issues come to the fore almost of their own accord in this connection—issues which *should have* been discussed by writers who have dealt with the two headings just mentioned, but which have not been—and, therefore, that the problem of the robot becomes almost obligatory for a philosopher of mind to discuss.

Before starting I wish to emphasize, lest any should misunderstand, that my concern is with how we should speak about humans and not with how we should speak about machines. My interest in the latter question derives from my just-mentioned conviction: that clarity with respect to the "borderline case" of robots, if it can only be achieved, will carry with it clarity with respect to the "central area" of talk about feelings, thought, consciousness, life, etc.

Minds and machines

In an earlier paper,[1] I attempted to show that a problem *very* analogous to the mind-body problem would automatically arise for robots. The same point could easily have been made in connection with the problem of other minds. To briefly review the argument: conceive of a community of robots. Let these robots "know" nothing concerning their own physical make-up or how they came into existence (perhaps they would arrive at a robot Creation Story and a polytheistic religion, with robot gods on a robot Olympus). Let them "speak" a language (say, English), in conformity with the grammatical rules and the publicly observable semantic and discourse-analytical regularities of that language. What might the role of psychological predicates be in such a community?

In the paper referred to, I employed a simple "evincing" model for such predicates. Since this model is obviously *over*-simple, let us tell a more complicated story. When a robot sees something red (something that evokes the appropriate internal state in the robot) he calls it "red." Our robots are supposed to be capable of inductive reasoning and theory construction. So a robot may discover that something he called red was not really red. Then he will say "well, it looked red." Or, if he is in the appropriate internal state for red, but knows on the basis of cross-inductions from certain other cases that what he "sees" is not really red, he will say "it *looks* red, but it isn't really red." Thus he will have a distinction between the physical reality and the visual appearance, just as we do. But the robot will never say "that looks as if it looked red, but it doesn't really look red." That is, there is no notion in the robot-English of an *appearance of an appearance of red*, any more than there is in English. Moreover, the reason is the same: that any state which cannot be discriminated from "looks-red" *counts* as "looks-red" (under normal conditions of linguistic proficiency, absence of confusion, etc.). What this illustrates, of course, is that the "incorrigibility" of statements of the form "that looks red" is to be explained by an elucidation of the logical features of such discourse, and not by the metaphor of "direct" access.

If we assume that these robots are unsophisticated scientifically, there is no reason for them to know more of their own internal constitution than an ancient Greek knew about the functioning of the central nervous system. We may imagine them developing a sophisticated science in the course of centuries, and thus eventually arriving at tentative identifications of the form: "when a thing 'looks red' to one of us, it means he is in internal state 'flip-flop 72 is on'." If these robots also publish papers on philosophy (and why should a robot not be able to do considerably better than many of our students?), a lively discussion may ensue concerning the philosophical implications of such discoveries. Some robots may argue, "*obviously*, what we have discovered is that 'seeing red' *is* being in internal state 'flip-flop 72 on'"; others may argue, "*obviously*, what you made was an *empirical* discovery; the *meaning* of 'it looks red' isn't the same as the *meaning* of 'flip-flop 72 is on'; hence the *attributes* (or states, or conditions, or properties) 'being in the state of seeming to see something red' and 'having flip-flop 72 on' are *two* attributes (or states, or conditions, or properties) and not *one"*; others may argue "when I have the illusion that something red is present, nothing red is physically there. Yet, in a sense, I *see* something red. What I see, I *call* a sense-datum. The sense datum is red. The flip-flop isn't red. So, *obviously*, the sense-datum can't be identical with the flip-flop, on or off." And so on. In short, robots can be just as bad at philosophy as people. Or (more politely), the *logical* aspects of the Mind-Body Problem are aspects of a problem that *must* arise for any computing system satisfying the conditions that (1) it uses language and constructs theories; (2) it does not initially "know" its own physical make-up, except superficially; (3) it is equipped with sense organs, and able to perform experiments; (4) it comes to know its own make-up through empirical investigation and theory construction.

Some objections considered

The argument just reviewed seems extremely simple. Yet some astonishing misunderstandings have arisen. The one that most surprised me was expressed thus: "As far as I can see, all you show is that a robot could simulate human *behavior.*" This objection, needless (hopefully)-to-say, misses the point of the foregoing *completely.* The point is this: that a robot or a computing machine can, in *a sense,* follow rules (Whether it is the same sense as the sense in which a man follows rules, or only analogous, depends on whether the particular robot can be said to be "conscious," etc., and thus on the central question of this paper.); that the meaning of an utterance is a function of the rules that govern its construction and use; that the rules governing the *robot* utterances 'I see something that looks red' and 'flip-flop 72 is on' are quite different. The former utterance may be correctly uttered by any robot which has "learned" to discriminate red things from non-red things correctly, judged by the consensus of the other robots, and which finds itself in the state that signals the presence of a red object. Thus, in the case of a normally constructed robot, 'I see something that looks red' may be uttered whenever flip-flop 72 is on, *whether the robot "knows" that flip-flop 72 is on or not.* 'Flip-flop 72 is on' may be correctly (reasonably) uttered only when the robot "knows" that flip-flop 72

is on—i.e., only when it can *conclude* that flip-flop 72 is on from empirically established theory together with such observation statements as its conditioning may prompt it to utter, or as it may hear
other robots utter. 'It looks red' is an utterance for which it does
not and cannot give reasons. 'Flip-flop 72 is on' is an utterance for
which it can give reasons. And so on. Since these semantic differences are the same for the robot as for a human, any argument
from the semantic nonequivalence of internal (physical)-state statements and "looks" statements to the character of mind or consciousness must be valid for the robot if it is valid for a human. (Likewise the argument from the alleged fact that there is "a sense of
see" in which one can correctly say "I see something red" in certain
cases in which nothing red is physically present.)

Besides the misunderstandings and nonunderstandings just alluded to, some interesting objections have been advanced. These
objections attempt to break the logical analogy just drawn by me.
I shall here briefly discuss two such objections, advanced by Prof.
Kurt Baier.

Baier's first argument [2] runs as follows: The connection between
my visual sensation of red and my utterance 'it looks as if there is
something red in front of me' (or whatever) is *not* merely a causal
one. The sensation does not *merely* evoke the utterance; I utter the
utterance because I *know* that I am having the sensation. But the
robot utters the utterance because he is *caused* to utter it by his
internal state (flip-flop 72 being on). Thus there is a fundamental
disanalogy between the two cases.

Baier's second argument is as follows: Certain *qualia* are *intrinsically* painful and others are *intrinsically* pleasurable. I cannot conceive of an intrinsically unpleasant quale Q being exactly the same
for someone else "only he finds it pleasurable." However, if a robot
is programmed so that it *acts as if* it were having a pleasant experience when, say, a certain part of its anatomy jangles, it could
easily be reprogrammed so that it would act as if it were having a
painful, and not a pleasant, experience upon those occasions. Thus
the counterparts of "qualia" in the robot case—certain physical states
—lack an essential property of qualia: they cannot be *intrinsically*
pleasurable or painful.

Can a robot have a sensation? Well, it can have a "sensation."
That is, it can be a "model" for any psychological theory that is

true of human beings. If it is a "model" for such a theory, then when it is in the internal state that corresponds to or "realizes" the psychological predicate "has the visual sensation of red," it will act as a human would act (depending also on what other "psychological" predicates apply). That is, "flip-flop 72 being on" does not have to *directly* (uncontrollably) "evoke" the utterance 'It looks as if there is something red in front of me.' I agree with Baier that so simple an "evincing" model will certainly not do justice to the character of such reports—but not in the case of robots either!

What is it for a person to "know" that he has a sensation? Since only philosophers talk in this way, no uniform answer is to be expected. Some philosophers identify having a sensation and knowing that one has it. Then "I know I have the visual sensation of red" just means "I have the visual sensation of red," and the question "Can the robot *know* that he has the 'sensation' of red?" means "Can the robot have the 'sensation' of red?"—a question which we have answered in the affirmative. (I have not argued that "sensations" are *sensations,* but only that a thorough-going logical analogy holds between sensation-talk in the case of humans and "sensation"-talk in the case of robots.) Other philosophers (most recently Ayer, in *The Concept of a Person*) have argued that to *know* one has a sensation one must be able to describe it. But in this sense, too, a robot can know that he has a "sensation." If knowing that *p* is having a "multi-tracked disposition" to appropriate sayings and question-answerings and behavings, as urged by Ryle in *The Concept of Mind,* then a robot can know anything a person can. A robot, just as well as a human, could participate in the following dialogue:

A. Describe the visual sensation you just mentioned.
B. It is the sensation of a large red expanse.
A. Is the red uniform—the same shade all over?
B. I think so.
A. Attend carefully!
B. I am!

Unfortunately for this last argument, Ryle's account of knowing is incorrect; no specifiable disposition to sayings and behavings, "multi-tracked" or otherwise, can *constitute* a knowing-that in the way in which certain specifiable arrangements and interrelation-

ships of buildings, administrators, professors, and students will constitute a university. "Knowing-that," like being in pain and like
preferring, is only mediately related to behavior: knowing-that *p*
involves being disposed to answer certain question correctly *if I
want to, if I am not confused,* etc. And wanting to answer a question correctly is being disposed to answer it correctly *if I know the
answer, if there is nothing I want more,* etc.—Psychological states
are characterizable only in terms of their relations to each other
(as well as to behavior, etc.), and not as dispositions which can be
"unpacked" without coming back to the very psychological predicates that are in question. But this is not fatal to our case: A robot,
too, can have internal states that are related to each other (and only
indirectly to behavior and sensory stimulation) as required by a
psychological theory. Then, when the robot is in the internal state
that realizes the predicate "knows that *p*" we may say that the
robot "knows" that *p*. Its "knowing" may not be *knowing*—because
it may not "really be conscious"—that is what we have to decide;
but it will play the role in the robot's behavior that *knowing* plays in
human behavior. In sum, for any sense in which a human can "know
that he has a sensation" there will be a logically and semantically
analogous sense in which a robot can "know" that he has a "sensation." And this is all that my argument requires.

After this digression on the logical character of "knowing," we
are finally ready to deal with Baier's first argument. The argument
may easily be seen to be a mere variant of the "water-on-the-brain"
argument (you can have water on the brain but not water on the
mind; hence the mind is not the brain). One can know that one
has a sensation without knowing that one is in brain-state S; hence
the sensation cannot be identical with brain-state S. This is all the
argument comes to. But, since "knowing that" is an intensional
context, a robot can correctly say "I don't know that flip-flop 72 is
on (or even what a 'flip-flop' is, for that matter)," even in situations in which it can correctly assert, "I have the 'sensation' of red."
It can even assert: "I 'know' that I have the 'sensation' of red." If it
follows in the human case that the sensation of red is not identical
with the brain-state S, then by the same argument from the same
semantical premises, the robot philosophers can conclude that the
"sensation" of red is not identical with "flip-flop 72 being on." The

robot philosopher too can argue: "I am not merely *caused* to utter the utterance 'It looks as if there is something red in front of me' by the occurrence of the 'sensation'; part of the causation is also that I '*understand*' the words that I utter; I 'know' that I am having the 'sensation'; I 'wish' to report my 'sensation' to other robots; etc." And, indeed, I think that Baier and the robot philosopher are both right. Psychological attributes, whether in human language or in robot language, are simply *not* the same as physical attributes. To say that a robot is angry (or "angry") is a quite different predication from the predication "such and such a fluid has reached a high concentration," even if the latter predicate "physically realizes" the former. Psychological theories say that an organism has certain states which are *not* specified in "physical" terms, but which are taken as primitive. Relations are specified between these states, and between the totality of the states and sensory inputs ("stimuli") and behavior ("responses"). Thus, as Jerry Fodor has remarked,[3] it is part of the "logic" of psychological theories that (physically) *different* structures may obey (or be "models" of) the *same* psychological theory. A robot and a human being may exhibit "repression" or "inhibitory potential" in exactly the same sense. I do not contend that 'angry' is a primitive term in a psychological theory; indeed, this account, which has been taken by some as a reaction to Ryleism, seems to me to create puzzles where none should exist (if 'angry' is a theoretical term, then "I am angry" must be a *hypothesis!*); but I do contend that the patterns of correct usage, in the case of an ordinary-language psychological term, no more presuppose or imply that there is an *independently* specifiable state which "realizes" the predicate, or, if there is one, that it is a *physical* state in the narrow sense (definable in terms of the vocabulary of present-day physics), or, if there is one, that it is the *same* for all members of the speech community, than the postulates of a psychological theory do. Indeed, there could be a community of robots that did *not* all have the same physical constitution, but did all have the same *psychology*; and such robots could *univocally* say "I have the sensation of red," "you have the sensation of red," "he has the sensation of red," even if the three robots referred to did not "physically realize" the "sensation of red" in the same way. Thus the *attributes:* having the "sensation" of red and "flip-flop 72 being on" are simply *not* identical in the case of the robots. If Materialism is taken to be the denial of the existence of "nonphysical" attributes, then Materialism is false even for robots!

Still, Baier might reply: if I say that a robot has the "sensation" of red, I mean that he is in *some* physical state (a "visual" one) that signals to him the presence of red objects; if I say that a human has the sensation of red, I do not mean that he is necessarily in some special *physical* state. *Of course*, there is a *state* I am in when and only when I have the sensation of red—namely, the state of having a sensation of red. But this is a remark about the logic of 'state', and says *nothing* about the meaning of 'sensation of red'.

I think that this is right. When *we* say: "that robot has the 'sensation' of red," there are (or would be) implications that are not present when we talk about each other. But that is because we think of the robots *as* robots. Let us suppose that the robots do *not* "think" of themselves as robots; according to their theory, they have (or possibly have) "souls." Then, when a robot says of another robot "he has the 'sensation' of red" (or something in more ordinary language to this effect), the implication will *not* be present that the other robot must be in any special *physical* state. Why should it not be an open possibility for the robot scientists and philosophers that they will *fail* to find "correlates" at the physical level for the various sensations they report, just as it is an open possibility for us that we will fail to find such correlates? To carry the analogy one final step further: if the robots go on to manufacture ROBOTS (i.e., robots that the robots themselves regard as *mere* robots), a robot philosopher will sooner or later argue: "when I say that a ROBOT 'thinks that something is red', or that something 'looks red' to a ROBOT, all that I mean is that the ROBOT is in a certain kind of *physical* state (admittedly, one specified by its *psychological* significance, and not by a direct physical-chemical description). The ROBOT must be able to discriminate red from non-red things, and the state in question must figure in a certain rather-hard-to-describe way in the discrimination process. But when I say that a fellow *person* (robot) 'thinks that something is red,' etc., I do not mean that he is necessariliy in any special kind of physical state. Thus, in the only philosophically interesting sense of 'sensation,' persons (robots) have 'sensations' and ROBOTS do not." I conclude that Baier's first argument does not break my analogy.

The second argument seems to me to rest on two dubious premises. Granted, if the physical correlate of a given painful quale Q is something peripheral, then my brain could be "reprogrammed" so that the event would become the physical correlate of some pleasurable psychological state; if the correlate is a highly structured state of the whole brain, then such reprogramming may well be impossible. Thus the premise: Let S be the state of the robot's brain that "realizes" some "pleasure quale"; then, in principle, the robot's brain could always be reprogrammed so that S would "realize" a "painful quale" instead—seems to be simply false. (The other dubious premise is the existence of *intrinsically* pleasant and painful qualia. This is supposed to be introspectively evident, but I do not find it so.)

Should robots have civil rights?

Throughout this paper I have stressed the possibility that a robot and a human may have the same "psychology"—that is, they may obey the same psychological laws. To say that two organisms (or systems) obey the same psychological laws is not at all the same thing as to say that their behavior is similar. Indeed, two people may obey the same psychological laws and exhibit *different* behavior, even given similar environments in childhood, partly because psychological laws are only statistical and partly because crucial parameters may have different values. To know the psychological laws obeyed by a species, one must know how *any* member of that species *could* behave, given the widest variation in all the parameters that are capable of variation at all. In general, such laws, like all scientific laws, will involve abstractions—terms more or less remote from direct behavioral observation. Examples of such terms have already been given: repression, inhibitory potential, preference, sensation, belief. Thus, to say that a man and a robot have the same "psychology" (are *psychologically isomorphic,* as I will also say) is to say that the behavior of the two *species* is most simply and revealingly analyzed, at the psychological level (in abstraction from the details of the internal physical structure), in terms of the *same* "psychological states" and the same hypothetical parameters. For example, if a human being is a *"probabilistic automaton,"* then any robot with the same "machine table" will be psychologically isomorphic to a human being. If the human brain is simply a neural net with a certain program, as in the theory of Pitts and McCulloch, then a robot whose "brain" was a similar net, only constructed of flip-flops rather than of neurons, would have exactly the same psychology as a human. To avoid question-begging, I will consider psychology as a science that describes the behavior of any species of systems whose behavior is amenable to behavioral analysis, and interpretation in terms of molar behavioral "constructs" of the familiar kind (stimulus, response, drive, saturation, etc.). Thus, saying that a robot (or an octopus) has a *psychology* (obeys psychological laws) does not imply that it is necessarily conscious. For example, the mechanical "mice" constructed by Shannon have a psychology (indeed, they were constructed precisely to serve as a model for a certain psychological theory of conditioning), but no one would contend that they are alive or conscious. In the case of Turing Machines, finite automata, etc., what I here call "psychological isomorphism" is what I referred to in previous papers as "sameness of functional organization."

In the rest of this paper, I will imagine that we are confronted with a community of robots which (who?) are psychologically isomorphic to human beings in the sense just explained. I will also assume that "psychophysical parallelism" holds good for human beings and that, if an action can be explained psychologically, the corresponding "trajectory" of the living human body that executes that action can be explained (in principle) in physical-chemical terms. The possibility of constructing a robot psychologically isomorphic to a human being does not depend on this assumption; a robot could be psychologically isomorphic to a disembodied spirit or to a "ghost in a machine" just as well, if such there were; but the conceptual situation will be a little less confusing if we neglect *those* issues in the present paper.

Let Oscar be one of these robots, and let us imagine that Oscar is having the "sensation" of red. Is Oscar having the sensation of red? In more ordinary language: is Oscar *seeing* anything? Is he thinking, feeling anything? Is Oscar Alive? Is Oscar Conscious?

I have referred to this problem as the problem of the "civil rights of robots" because that is what it may become, and much faster than any of us now expect. Given the ever-accelerating rate of both technological and social change, it is entirely possible that robots will one day exist, and argue "we *are* alive; we *are* conscious!" In that event, what are today only philosophical prejudices of a traditional anthropocentric and mentalistic kind would all too likely develop into conservative political attitudes. But fortunately, we today have the advantage of being able to discuss this problem disinterestedly, and a little more chance, therefore, of arriving at the correct answer.

I think that the most interesting case is the case in which (1) "psychophysical parallelism" holds (so that it can at least be contended that *we* are just as much "physical-chemical systems" as robots are), and (2) the robots in question are psychologically isomorphic to us. This is surely the most favorable case for the philosopher who wishes to argue that robots of "a sufficient degree of complexity" would (not just *could,* but necessarily *would*) be conscious. Such a philosopher would presumably contend that Oscar had sensations, thoughts, feelings, etc., in just the sense in which we do and that the use of "raised-eyebrow" quotes throughout this paper whenever a psychological predicate was being applied to a robot was unnecessary. It is this contention that I wish to explore, not with the usual polemical desire to show either that materialism is correct and, hence (?), that such robots as Oscar would be conscious or to show that all such questions have been resolved once and for all by *Philosophical Investigations,* God but give us the eyes to see it, but rather with my own perverse interest in the logical structure of the quaint and curious bits of discourse that philosophers propound as "arguments"—and with a perhaps ultimately more serious interest in the relevant semantical aspects of our language.

Anti-civil-libertarian arguments

Some of the arguments designed to show that Oscar *could not* be conscious may be easily exposed as bad arguments. Thus, the *phonograph-record argument:* a robot only "plays" behavior in the sense in which a phonograph record plays music. When we laugh at the joke of a robot, we are really appreciating the wit of the human programmer, and not the wit of the robot. The *reprogramming argument:* a robot has no real character of its own. It could at any time be reprogrammed to behave in the reverse of the way it has previously behaved. But a human being who was "reprogrammed" (say, by a brain operation performed by a race with a tremendously advanced science), so as to have a new and completely predetermined set of responses, would no longer be a human being (in the full sense), but a monster. The *question-begging argument:* the so-called "psychological" states of a robot are in reality just physical states. But *our* psychological states are *not* physical states. So it could only be in the most Pickwickian of senses that a robot was "conscious."

The first argument ignores the possibility of robots that *learn*. A robot whose "brain" was merely a library of predetermined behavior routines, each imagined in full detail by the programmer, would indeed be uninteresting. But such a robot would be incapable of learning anything that the programmer did not know, and would thus fail to be psychologically isomorphic to the programmer, or to any human. On the other hand, if the programmer constructs a robot so that it will be a model of certain psychological laws, he will *not*, in general, know how it will behave in real-life situations, just as a psychologist might know all of the *laws* of human psychology, but still be no better (or little better) than any one else at predicting how humans will behave in real-life situations. Imagine that the robot at "birth" is as helpless as a newborn babe, and that it acquires our culture by being brought up with humans. When it reaches the stage of inventing a joke, and we laugh, it is simply not true that we are "appreciating the wit of the programmer." What the programmer invented was not a joke, but a system which could one day produce new jokes. The second argument, like the first, assumes that "programmed" behavior must be wholly predictable and lack all spontaneity. If I "reprogram" a criminal (via a brain operation) to become a good citizen, but without destroying his capacity to learn, to develop, to change (perhaps even to change back into a criminal some day), then I have certainly not created a "monster." If Oscar is psychologically isomorphic to a human, then Oscar can be "reprogrammed" to the extent, and only to the extent, that a human can. The third argument assumes outright that psychological predicates never apply to Oscar and to a human in the same sense, which is just the point at issue.

All these arguments suffer from one unnoticed and absolutely crippling defect. They rely on just two facts about robots: that they are artifacts and that they are deterministic systems of a physical kind, whose behavior (including the "intelligent" aspects) has been preselected and designed by the artificer. But it is purely contingent that these two properties are *not* properties of human beings. Thus, if we should one day discover that *we* are artifacts and that our every utterance was anticipated by our superintelligent creators (with a small "c"), it would follow, if these arguments were sound, that *we* are not conscious! At the same time, as just noted, these two properties are *not* properties of *all* imaginable robots. Thus these arguments fail in two directions: they might *"show"* that *people* are *not* conscious—because people might be the wrong sort of robots—while simultaneously failing to show that some robots are not conscious.)

Pro-civil-libertarian arguments

If the usual "anti-civil-libertarian" arguments (arguments against conceding that Oscar is conscious) are bad arguments, *pro*-civil-libertarian arguments seem to be just about nonexistent! Since the nineteenth century, materialists have contended that "consciousness is just a property of matter at a certain stage of organization." But as a semantic analysis this contention is hopeless (psychophysical parallelism is certainly not *analytic*), and as an identity theory it is irrelevant. Suppose that Feigl had been correct, and that sensation words *referred* to events (or "states" or "processes") definable in the language of physics. (As I remarked before, Feigl no longer holds this view.) In particular, suppose 'the sensation of red' *denotes* a brain process. (It is, of course, utterly unclear what this supposition comes to. We are taught the use of 'denotes' in philosophy by being told that 'cat' denotes the class of all cats, and so on; and then some philosophers say " 'the sensation of red' denotes a class of brain processes," as if *this* were now supposed to be clear! In fact, all we have been told is that " 'the sensation of red' denotes a brain process" is true just in case "the sensation of red *is* a brain process" is true. Since this latter puzzling assertion was in turn explained by the identity theorists in terms of the distinction between *denotation* and *connotation*, nothing has been explained.) Still, this does not show that Oscar is conscious. Indeed, Oscar may be psychologically isomorphic to a human without being at all similar in physical-chemical construction. So we may suppose that Oscar does not have "brain processes" at all and, hence, (on this theory) that Oscar is *not* conscious. Moreover, if the physical "correlate" of the sensation of red (in the case of a human) is P_1 and the physical correlate of the "sensation" of red (in the case of Oscar) is P_2, and if P_1 and P_2 are *different* physical states, it can nonetheless be maintained that, when Oscar and I both "see something that looks red" (or "have the sensation of red," to use philosophical jargon that I have allowed myself in this paper), we are in the *same* physical state, namely the *disjunction* of P_1 and P_2. How do we decide whether "the sensation of red" (in the case of a human) is "identical" with P_1 or "identical" with $P_1 \lor P_2$? Identity theorists do not tell me anything that helps me to decide.

Another popular theory is that ordinary-language psychological terms, such as 'is angry' (and, presumably, such quasi-technical expressions as 'has the sensation of red') are *implicitly defined by a psychological theory.* On this view, it would follow from the fact that Oscar and I are "models" of the same psychological (molar behavioral) theory that psychological terms have *exactly the same sense* when applied to me and when applied to Oscar.

It may, perhaps, be granted that there is something that could be called an "implicit psychological theory" underlying the ordinary use of psychological terms. (That an angry man will behave aggressively, unless he has strong reasons to repress his anger and some skill at controlling his feelings; that insults tend to provoke anger; that most people are not very good at controlling strong feelings of anger; are examples of what might be considered "postulates" of such a theory, although each of these "postulates" is quasi-tautological, it might be contended that the conjunction of a sufficient number of them has empirical consequences, and can be used to provide empirical explanations of observed behavior.) But the view that the whole meaning of such a term as 'anger' is fixed by its place in such a theory seems highly dubious. There is not space in the present paper to examine this view at the length that it deserves. But one or two criticisms may indicate where difficulties lie.

To assert that something contains phlogiston is (implicitly) to assert that certain laws, upon which the concept of phlogiston depends, are correct. To assert that something is electrically charged is in part to assert that the experimental laws upon which the concept of electricity is based and which electrical theory is supposed to explain, are not radically and wholly false. If the "theory" upon which the term anger "depends" really has empirical consequences, then even to say "I am angry" is in part to assert that these empirical consequences are not radically and wholly false. Thus it would not be absurd, if 'anger' really *were* a theoretical term, to say "I think that I am very angry, but I'm not sure" or "I think that I have a severe pain, but I'm not sure" or "I think that I am conscious but I'm not sure," since one might well not be sure that the experimental laws implied by the "psychological theory" implicit in ordinary language are in fact correct. It would also not be absurd to say: "perhaps there is not really any such thing as anger" or "perhaps there is not really any such thing as pain" or "perhaps there is not really any such thing as being conscious." Indeed, no matter how certain I might be that I have the sensation of red, it might be proved *by examining other people* that I did *not* have that sensation and that in fact there was no such thing as having the sensation of red. Indeed, "that *looks like* the sensation of red" would have a perfectly good use—namely, to mean that my experience is as it would be if the "psychological theory implicit in ordinary language" were true, but the theory is not in fact true. These consequences should certainly cast doubt on the idea that "psychological terms in ordinary language" really are "theoretical constructs."

It is obvious that "psychological terms in ordinary language" have a *reporting use.* In the jargon of philosophers of science, they figure in *observation statements.* "I am in pain" would be such a statement. But clearly, a term that figures in observational reports has an observational use, and that use must enter into its meaning. Its meaning cannot be fixed merely by its relation to other terms, in abstraction from the actual speech habits of speakers (including the habits upon which the reporting use depends).

The first difficulty suggests that the "psychological theory" that "implicitly defines" such words as 'anger' has in fact *no* nontautological consequences—or, at least, no empirical consequences that could not be abandoned without changing the meaning of these words. The second difficulty then further suggests that the job of fixing the meaning of these words is only partially done by the logical relationships (the "theory"), and is completed by the reporting use.

A third difficulty arises when we ask just what it is that the "psychological theory implicit in ordinary language" is supposed to be *postulating*. The usual answer is that the theory postulates the existence of certain *states* which are supposed to be related to one another and to behavior as specified in the theory. But what does 'state' mean? If 'state' is taken to mean physical state, in the narrow sense alluded to before, then psychophysical parallelism would be implied by an arbitrary "psychological" assertion, which is obviously incorrect. On the other hand, if 'state' is taken in a sufficiently wide sense so as to avoid this sort of objection, then (as Wittgenstein points out) the remark that "being angry is being in a certain psychological state" *says nothing whatsoever*.

In the case of an ordinary scientific theory (say, a physical theory), to postulate the existence of "states" S_1, S_2, . . . , S_n satisfying certain postulates is to assert that one of two things is the case: either (1) physical states (definable in terms of the existing primitives of physical theory) can be found satisfying the postulates; or (2) it is necessary to take the new predicates S_1, . . . , S_n (or predicates in terms of which they can be defined) as additional primitives in physical science, and widen our concept of "physical state" accordingly. In the same way, identity theorists have sometimes suggested that "molar psychological theory" *leaves it open* whether or not the states it postulates are physical states or not. But if physical states *can* be found satisfying the postulates, then they are the ones referred to by the postulates. 'State' is then a methodological term, so to speak, whose status is explained by a perspicuous representation of the procedures of empirical theory construction and confirmation. This solution to our third difficulty reduces to the identity theory under the supposition that psychophysical parallelism holds, and that physical states *can* be found "satisfying" the postulates of "molar behavioral psychology."

Even if this solution to the third difficulty is accepted, however, the first two difficulties remain. To be an empirically confirmable scientific theory, the "molar behavioral theory" implicit in the ordinary use of psychological terms must have testable empirical consequences. If the ordinary-language psychological terms really designate states postulated by this theory, then, if the theory is radically false, we must say there are no such "states" as being angry, being in pain, having a sensation, etc. And this must always remain a possibility (on this account), no matter what we observe, since no finite number of observations can deductively establish a scientific theory properly so-called. Also, the reporting role of "psychological" terms in ordinary language is not discussed by this account. If saying "I am in pain" is simply ascribing a *theoretical* term to myself, then this report is in part a *hypothesis*, and one which may always be false. This account—that the ordinary use of "psychological" terms presupposes an empirical theory, and one which may be radically false—has recently been urged by Paul Feyerabend. Feyerabend would accept the consequence that I have rejected as counterintuitive: that there may not really be any pains, sensations, etc., in the customary sense. But where is this empirical theory that is presupposed by the ordinary use of "psychological" terms? Can anyone state *one* behavioral law which is clearly empirical and which is presupposed by the concepts of sensation, anger, etc.? The empirical connection that exists, say, between being in pain and saying "ouch," or some such thing, has sometimes been taken (by logical behaviorists, rather than by identity theorists) to be such a law. I have tried to show elsewhere,[4] however, that no such law is really required to be true for the application of the concept of pain in its customary sense. What entitles us to say that a man is in pain in our world may not entitle one to say that he is in pain in a different world; yet the *same* concept of pain may be applicable. What I contend is that to understand any "psychological" term, one must be implicitly familiar with a network of *logical* relationships, and one must be adequately trained in the reporting use of that word. It is also necessary, I believe, that one be prepared to accept first-person statements by other members of one's linguistic community involving these predicates, at least when there is no *special* reason to distrust them; but this is a general convention associated with discourse, and not part of the meaning of any particular word, psychological or otherwise. Other general conventions associated with discourse, in my opinion, are the acceptance of not-too-bizarre rules of inductive inference and theory confirmation and of certain fundamental rules of deductive inference. But these things, again, have to do with one's discourse *as a whole* not being linguistically deviant, rather than with one's understanding any particular word. If I am not aware that someone's crying out (in a certain kind of context) is a sign that he is in pain, I can be *told*. If I refuse (without good reason), to believe what I am told, it can be pointed out to me that, when I am in that context (say, my finger is burnt), *I* feel pain, and no condition known by me to be relevant to the feeling or nonfeeling of pain is different in the case of the Other. If I *still* feel no inclination to ascribe pain to the Other, then my whole concept of discourse is abnormal—but it would be both a gross understatement and a misdiagnosis to say that I "don't know the meaning of 'pain'."

I conclude that "psychological" terms in ordinary language are *not* theoretical terms. Moreover, the idea that, if psychophysical parallelism is correct, then it is analytic that pain *is* the correlated brain-state is not supported by a shred of linguistic evidence. (Yet this is a consequence of the combined "identity theory-theoretical term" account as we developed it to meet out third difficulty.) I conclude that any attempt to show that Oscar is conscious (analytically, relative to our premises) along these lines is hopeless.

Ziff's argument

So far all the arguments we have considered, on both sides of the question: Is Oscar conscious?, have been without merit. No sound consideration has been advanced to show that it is false, given the meaning of the words in English and the empirical facts as we are assuming them, that Oscar is conscious; but also no sound consideration has been advanced to show that it is true. If it is a violation of the rules of English to say (without "raised-eyebrow quotes") that Oscar is in pain or seeing a rose or thinking about Vienna, we have not been told *what* rules it violates; and if it is a violation of the rules of English to *deny* that Oscar is conscious, given his psychological isomorphism to a human being, we have likewise not been told what rules it violates. In this situation, it is of interest to turn to an ingenious ("anti-civil-libertarian") argument by Paul Ziff.[5]

Ziff wishes to show that it is false that Oscar is conscious. He begins with the undoubted fact that if Oscar is not alive he cannot be conscious. Thus, given the semantical connection between 'alive' and 'conscious' in English, it is enough to show that Oscar is not *alive*. Now, Ziff argues, when we wish to tell whether or not something is alive, we do *not* go by its *behavior*. Even if a thing looks like a flower, grows in my garden like a flower, etc., if I find upon taking it apart that it consists of gears and wheels and miniaturized furnaces and vacuum tubes and so on, I say "what a clever mechanism," not "what an unusual plant." It is *structure*, not *behavior* that determines whether or not something is alive; and it is a violation of the semantical rules of our language to say of anything that is clearly a mechanism that it is "alive."

Ziff's argument is unexpected, because of the great concentration in the debate up to now upon *behavior*, but it certainly calls attention to relevant logical and semantical relationships. Yet I cannot agree that these relationships are as clear-cut as Ziff's argument requires. Suppose that we construct a robot—or, let me rather say, an *android*, to employ a word that smacks less of mechanism—out of "soft" (protoplasm-like) stuff. Then, on Ziff's account, it may be perfectly correct, if the android is sufficiently "life-like" in structure, to say that we have "synthesized life." So, given two artifacts, both "models" of the same psychological theory, both completely deterministic physical-chemical systems, both designed to the same end and "programmed" by the designer to the same extent, it may be what we must say that one of them is a "machine" and not conscious, and the other is a "living thing" (albeit "artificially created") and conscious, simply because the one consists of "soft stuff" and the other consists of "hardware." A great many speakers of English, I am sure (and I am one of them), would find the claim that this dogmatic decision is required by the meaning of the word 'alive' quite contrary to their linguistic intuitions. I think that the difficulty is fundamentally this: a plant does not exhibit much "behavior." Thus it is natural that criteria having to do with *structure* should dominate criteria having to do with "behavior" when the question is whether or not something that looks and "behaves" like a plant is really a living thing or not. But in the case of something that looks and behaves like an *animal* (and especially like a *human being*), it is natural that criteria having to do with behavior—and not just with actual behavior, but with the *organization* of behavior, as specified by a psychological theory of the thing—should play a much larger role in the decision. Thus it is not unnatural that we should be prepared to argue, in the case of the "pseudo-plant," that "it isn't a living thing because it is a mechanism," while some are prepared to argue, in the case of the robot, that "it isn't a *mere* mechanism, because it is *alive*," and "it is alive, because it is con-

AN198

HUMAN AND ARTIFICIAL INTELLIGENCE

scious," and "it is conscious because it has the same behavioral organization as a living human being." Yet Ziff's account may well explain why it is that many speakers are not convinced by these latter arguments. The tension between conflicting criteria results in the "obviousness," to some minds, of the robot's "machine" status, and the equal "obviousness," to other minds, of its "artificial-life" status.

There is a sense of 'mechanism' in which it is clearly analytic that a mechanism cannot be alive. Ziff's argument can be reduced to the contention that, on the normal interpretation of the terms, it is analytic in English that something whose *parts* are all mechanisms, in this sense, likewise cannot be alive. If this is so, then no English speaker should suppose that he could even *imagine* a robot *thinking,* being *power-mad, hating humans,* or *being in love,* any more than he should suppose that he could imagine a married bachelor. It seems evident to me (and indeed to most speakers) that, absurdly or not, we *can* imagine these things. I conclude, therefore, that Ziff is wrong: it may be *false,* but it is not a *contradiction,* to assert that Oscar is alive.

The "know-nothing" view

We have still to consider the most traditional view on our question. According to this view, which is still quite widely held, *it is possible that Oscar is conscious, and it is possible that he is not conscious.* In its theological form, the argument runs as follows: I am a creature with a body and a soul. My body happens to consist of flesh and blood, but it might just as well have been a machine, had God chosen. Each voluntary movement of my body is correlated with an activity of my soul (how and why is a "mystery"). So, it is quite possible that Oscar has a soul, and that each "voluntary" movement of his mechanical body is correlated in the same mysterious way with an activity of his soul. It is also possible —since the laws of physics suffice to explain the motions of Oscar's body, without use of the assumption that he has a soul—that Oscar is but a lifeless machine. There is absolutely no way in which we can know. This argument can also be given a nontheological (or at least apparently nontheological) form by deleting the reference to God, and putting 'mind' for 'soul' throughout. To complete the argument, it is contended that I know what it *means* to say that Oscar has a "soul" (or has a pain, or the sensation of red, etc.) *from my own case.*

One well-known difficulty with this traditional view is that it implies that it is also possible that other humans are not really conscious, even if they are physically and psychologically iso-morphic to me. It is contended that I can know with *probability* that other humans are conscious by the "argument from analogy." But in the inductive sciences, an argument from analogy is gen-erally regarded as quite weak unless the conclusion is capable of further and independent inductive verification. So it is hard to believe that our reasons for believing that other persons are con-scious are very strong ones if they amount simply to an analogical argument with a conclusion that admits of *no* independent check, observational, inductive, or whatever. Most philosophers have recently found it impossible to believe *either* that our reasons for believing that other persons are conscious are that weak *or* that the possibility exists that other persons, while being admittedly physi-cally and psychologically isomorphic (in the sense of the present paper) to myself, are not conscious. Arguments on this point may be found in the writings of all the major analytical philosophers of the present century. Unfortunately, many of these arguments depend upon quite dubious theories of meaning.

The critical claim is the claim that it follows from the fact that I have had the sensation of red, I can imagine this sensation, I "know what it is like," that I can understand the assertion that Oscar has the sensation of red (or any other sensation or psycho-logical state). In a sense, this is right. I *can*, in one sense, under-stand the *words.* I can parse them; I don't think "sensation of red" means *baby carriage*, etc. More than that: I know what I experience if I were conscious and psychologically as I am, but with Oscar's mechanical "body" in place of my own. How does this come to be so? It comes to be so, at least in part, because we have to learn from experience what our own bodies are like. If a child were brought up in a suitable kind of armor, the child might be deceived into thinking that it was a robot. It would be harder to fool him into thinking that he had the internal structure of a robot, but this too could be done (fake X rays, etc.). And when I "imagine myself in the shoes of a (conscious) robot," what I do, of course, is to imagine the sensations that I might have if I were a robot, or rather *if I were a human who mistakenly thought that he was a robot.* (I look down at my feet and see bright metal, etc.)

Well, let us grant that in this sense we *understand* the sentence "Oscar is having the sensation of red." It does not follow that the sentence possesses a truth value. We understand the sentence "the present King of France is bald," but, on its normal interpretation in English, the sentence has no truth value under present conditions. We can give it one by adopting a suitable convention—for example, Russell's theory of descriptions—and more than one such suitable convention exists. The question really at issue is *not* whether we can "understand" the sentences "Oscar is conscious" (or "has the sensation of red" or "is angry") and "Oscar is not conscious," in the sense of being able to use them in such contexts as "I can perfectly well picture to myself that Oscar is conscious," but whether there really is an intelligible sense in which one of these sentences is true, on a normal interpretation, and the other false (and, in that case, whether it is also true that we can't tell which).

Let us revert, for a moment, to our earlier fantasy of ROBOTS —i.e., second-order robots, robots created by robots and regarded by the robots as *mere* ROBOTS. As already remarked, a robot philosopher might very well be led to consider the question: Are ROBOTS conscious? The robot philosopher "knows," of course, just what "experiences" he would have if he were a "conscious" ROBOT (or a robot in a ROBOT suit). He can "perfectly well picture to himself that a ROBOT could have "sensation." So he may perfectly well arrive at the position that it is logically possible that ROBOTS have sensations (or, rather, "sensations") and perfectly possible that they do not, and moreover he can never know. What do we think of this conclusion?

It is clear what we should think: we should think that there is not the slightest reason to suppose (and every reason not to suppose) that there is a special property, "having the 'sensation' of red," which the ROBOT may or may not have, but which is inaccessible to the robot. The robot, knowing the physical and psychological description of the ROBOT, is in a perfectly good position to answer all questions about the ROBOT that may reasonably be asked. The idea that there is a further question (class of questions) about the ROBOT which the robot cannot answer, is suggested to the robot by the fact that these alleged "questions" are

grammatically well formed, can be "understood" in the sense discussed above, and that the possible "answers" can be "imagined."

I suggest that our position with respect to robots is *exactly* that
of robots with respect to ROBOTS. There is not the slightest reason
for us, either, to believe that "consciousness" is a well-defined property, which each robot either *has* or *lacks*, but such that it is not
possible, on the basis of the physical description of the robot, or
even on the basis of the psychological description (in the sense of
"psychological" explained above), to *decide* which (if any) of the
robots possess this property and which (if any) fail to possess it.
The rules of "robot language" may well be such that it is perfectly
possible for a robot to "conjecture" that ROBOTS have "sensations"
and also perfectly possible for a robot to conjecture that ROBOTS
do not have "sensations." It does not follow that the physical and
psychological description of the ROBOTS is "incomplete," but only
that the concept of "sensation" (in "raised-eyebrow quotes") is a
well-defined concept only when applied to robots. The question
raised by the robot philosopher: Are ROBOTS "conscious"? calls
for a decision and not for a discovery. The decision, at bottom, is
this: Do I treat ROBOTS as fellow members of my linguistic community, or as machines? If the ROBOTS are accepted as full members of the robot community, then a robot can find out whether a
ROBOT is "conscious" or "unconscious," "alive" or "dead" in just
the way be finds out these things about a fellow robot. If they are
rejected, then nothing *counts* as a ROBOT being "conscious" or
"alive." Until the decision is made, the statement that ROBOTS
are "conscious" has no truth value. In the same way, I suggest, the
question: Are robots conscious? calls for a decision, on our part, to
treat robots as fellow members of our linguistic community, or not
to so treat them. As long as we leave this decision unmade, the
statement that robots (of the kind described) are conscious has no
truth value.

If we reject the idea that the physical and psychological description of the robots is incomplete (because it "fails to specify whether
or not they are conscious"), we are not thereby forced to hold either
that "consciousness" is a "physical" attribute or that it is an attribute
"implicitly defined by a psychological theory." Russell's question in
the philosophy of mathematics: If the number 2 is not the set of
all pairs, then what on earth is it? was a silly question. Two is
simply the second number, and nothing else. Likewise, the mate-

rialist question: If the attribute of "consciousness" is not a physical attribute (or an attribute implicitly defined by a psychological theory) then what on earth is it? is a silly question. Our psychological concepts in ordinary language are as we have fashioned them. The "framework" of ordinary-language psychological predicates is what it is and not another framework. *Of course* materialism is false; but it is so *trivially* false that no materialist should be bothered!

Conclusion

In this paper, I have reviewed a succession of failures: failures to show that we *must* say that robots are conscious, failures to show that we *must* say they are not, failures to show that we *must* say that we can't tell. I have concluded from these failures that there is no correct answer to the question: Is Oscar conscious? Robots may indeed have (or lack) properties unknown to physics and undetectable by us; but not the slightest reason has been offered to show that they do, as the ROBOT analogy demonstrates. It is reasonable, then, to conclude that the question that titles this paper calls for a decision and not for a discovery. If we are to make a decision, it seems preferable to me to extend our concept so that robots *are* conscious—for "discrimination" based on the "softness" or "hardness" of the body parts of a synthetic "organism" seems as silly as discriminatory treatment of humans on the basis of skin color. But my purpose in this paper has not been to improve our concepts, but to find out what they are.

MERE ROBOTS AND OTHERS *

R. Albritton

"My attitude towards [another human being] . . . is an attitude towards a soul. I am not of the *opinion* that he has a soul" (*Philosophical Investigations* II, iv). Something like that is right, I think,

* Abstract of a paper presented in a symposium on "Minds and Machines" at the sixty-first annual meeting of the American Philosophical Association, Eastern Division, December 28, 1964, commenting on Hilary Putnam, "Robots: Machines or Artificially Created Life?" *Journal of Philosophy*, LXI (1964), 668–91.

though I have misgivings about it. If it is right, then so is what I take to be the principal moral of Putnam's paper for the stock problem of other minds. But I think he is too ready to give robots the vote.

To begin with, the notion of a robot "psychologically isomorphic" to us, in Putnam's sense, presupposes a good deal about *us* that seems to me doubtful or at least not obviously true. And although Putnam assumes for the sake of argument the truth of what he calls "psychophysical parallelism," I am inclined to argue that this assumption is neither clear nor plausible. But suppose that it is both, and is true, and (in addition) that our bodies are deterministic systems. And suppose that some deterministic robot is psychologically isomorphic to us and "talks" incessantly. Shall we give in and accept it, in Putnam's phrase, as a fellow member of our linguistic community? I don't doubt that in an actual case we might helplessly do that, whatever it amounts to; and if we did, the question whether the new member was conscious or unconscious might be, or seem, easy to settle. But what we can't help doing may nevertheless be irrational. There are imaginable cases, I think, in which "accepting" the robot *would* be irrational. (It might be morally admirable anyway. I won't go into that.)

Imagine (and imagine that we know all this) that a visitor from space has made for us a deterministic robot whose entire repertory of possible behavior the visitor has fixed in advance, in the sense that he has decided what in particular he wishes the robot to do if . . . and to say if . . . and has constructed and programmed the thing accordingly. It is made of steel, glass, plastic, and the like and is the only robot of its kind. We have no reason to think that there has ever been another robot half so sophisticated anywhere. Imagine that, although the robot roughly resembles a human being (which is more than can be said for the visitor), its internal structure—the structure of its "brain," notably—is not closely analogous to that of any known species of conscious creature. Nevertheless, it acts and sounds very like a human being. But we know (so I am imagining) that all of its behavior—all of its astonishingly lifelike "talk," for example—was chosen for reasons of his own by the visitor, who long ago decided that it should "shout" no in certain circumstances, "mumble" yes in others, and so forth. It does. It works splendidly. Here it comes, whistling a little tune composed by the visitor. It will have "learned" a lot since we saw it last. Soon it will have "learned" more than we know, though not more than the visitor knows, and "conversation" with it will begin to be instructive. Its political "sentiments" are already impeccable.

Is it conscious? "Don't be silly. That's the robot I was telling you about." "But it *says* it's conscious." "So it does, over and over. That part of the program is going to get boring, I'm afraid." I don't see that it matters if the robot is psychologically isomorphic to us. If it is, that will be interesting, but as far as I can see the question whether or not to treat the robot as a possibly conscious creature— or rather, as the "body," so to speak, of a possibly conscious creature —will remain closed. Consider: the thing is, first, a deliberate artifact. Second, the gross materials of which it is composed are not even much like those of bodies. Hard or soft, they are the materials of machines and other inanimate things. Third, there is no close structural resemblance between it and a body. Fourth, it is in many respects functionally unlike a body. Fifth, the physical —or physical and chemical—answer to the question "How does it work?" is compatible with describing the robot as a mere automaton, a mere robot. Sixth, we do not know of any other robots that *are* the "bodies" of conscious (or unconscious) creatures. Why promote this one?

I agree (as against the argument that Putnam attributes to Ziff) that I have said nothing to prove that the robot "is not conscious." And if I have said something to prove that the being whose "body" the robot would be, if it were the "body" of any being, would not exactly be alive, I don't rely on that. Why should a conscious being be alive, exactly, as long as it is not exactly inanimate, either? On the other hand, the facts about the robot, so far, seem to me to make a strong case against treating it as a "body," the case, namely, that whatever it is, it is at any rate not a *body*, but a machine. What is there to override this case? There is the thing's behavior, but what of it? None of it has any weight, as far as I can see, because —seventh—all of it was plotted out beforehand (if only conditionally) in every relevant detail, the thing was constructed and programmed accordingly, and that is how it came to behave as it does. Again, not even all seven of the considerations I have listed, taken together, entail that the robot "is not conscious" or "is not a 'body'." But they are enough, I think, if they are kept in mind, to deprive any decision to give in and *treat* it as a "body" of all claim to rationality.

Putnam might reply (see his paper): "But what if *you* turned out to be such a robot?" Very well, suppose that I discover my whole body, including my head, to be a deterministic artifact, put together with great cunning out of light metals, ceramics, very remarkable plastics, and the like. (Is this supposition nonsensical? I think not—not in a sense that affects the argument, anyway.) One day I meet my maker. "You may be interested to know that I am conscious," I say. He and his wife are delighted. "So life-like," she says. If she didn't know that he had made it himself and programmed it to utter that plausible sentence, and all the others to come (she can hardly wait), she would be quite taken in, she says. A rational woman, alas! Given that her (more than human) husband has designed my body (or rather, my "body") to do and say just what it does do and say in the varying physical circum-stances of its career, she has no reason to treat with "me" seriously (unless perhaps she knows of other "robots" with "bodies" like mine who *are* conscious, but I am supposing that she does not). On the contrary, she has every reason to think that it would be irrational of her to treat her husband's handiwork as anything more than a machine.

But if I begin to do and say things on which my artificer hadn't planned, that may make a difference. To return to the visitor's robot, suppose that he has constructed and programmed it to be "psychologically isomorphic" to us in Putnam's sense, if that is pos-sible, but suppose that he has then filled in the rest of its program at random and is as interested as we are to see what (if anything) it will do and say. How ought *this* robot to be treated? The ques-tion whether or not to treat it as a "body" seems to me to be com-ing ajar a bit, though not much. *Autres robots autres moeurs.* But I will not attempt to survey the possibilities, in this abstract.

NOTES

1. "Minds and Machines," in Sidney Hook, ed., *Dimensions of Mind* (New York: NYU Press, 1960), pp. 148–179.
2. These arguments come from an unpublished paper by Baier, which was read at a colloquium at the Albert Einstein College of Medicine in 1962.
3. "Psychological Explanation," to appear in a forthcoming collection edited by Max Black.

4. In "Brains and Behavior." The character of psychological concepts is also discussed by me in "The Mental Life of Some Machines," to appear in a forthcoming collection edited by Hector Neri Castañeda.

5. I take the liberty of reporting an argument used by Ziff in a conversation. I do not wish to imply that Ziff necessarily subscribes to the argument in the form in which I report it, but I include it because of its ingenuity and interest.

9   The imitation of man by machine

ULRIC NEISSER

> While Ulric Neisser has worked in the technical area
> of computer application, in Project MAC (Machine
> Aided Cognition) at Massachusetts Institute of Tech-
> nology, the following article examines critically the con-
> ception of artificial intelligence from the standpoint of
> clinical and developmental psychology. Its general ap-
> proach is one of questioning the Cartesian separation of
> intelligence which is implicit in most simulation work
> by pointing to the temporal and unconscious elements
> which permeate and underlie human cognitive per-
> formances.
>
> Ulric Neisser is professor of psychology at Cornell
> University and also taught at Swarthmore and Harvard.

Popular opinion about "artificial intelligence" has
passed through two phases. A generation ago, very few people
believed that any machine could ever think as a man does. Now,
however, it is widely held that this goal will be reached quite soon,
perhaps in our lifetimes. It is my thesis that the second of these attitudes is nearly as unsophisticated as the first. Yesterday's skepticism was based on ignorance of the capacities of machines; today's
confidence reflects a misunderstanding of the nature of thought.

There is no longer any doubt that computing machines can be
programmed to behave in impressively intelligent ways. Marill [1] does

From Ulric Neisser, "The Imitation of Man by Machine," *Science*, Vol. 139,
No. 3551 (1963) 193–97. Copyright 1963 by the American Association for the
Advancement of Science.

not exaggerate in saying, "At present, we have, or are currently developing, machines that prove theorems, play games with sufficient skill to beat their inventors, recognize spoken words, translate text from one language to another, speak, read, write music, and learn to improve their own performance when given training." Nevertheless, I will argue that the procedures which bring about these results differ substantially from the processes which underlie the same (or other) activities in human beings. The grounds for this assertion are quite different from the "classical" reasons for skepticism about thinking machines, but the latter should be considered first. This amounts to reviewing the similarities between men and computers before stressing the differences.

First of all, it was formerly maintained that the actions of a mechanism would never be purposive or self-directed, whereas human behavior can be understood only in terms of goals and motives. Two counterexamples will be enough to show that this argument has become untenable. In the realm of action, it is difficult not to be impressed with the "homing" missile, which pursues its target tenaciously through every evasive action until it achieves its destructive goal. On the intellectual level, the "Logic Theorist" of Newell, Simon and Shaw [2] is just as persistent: determined to prove a theorem, it tries one logical strategy after another until the proof is found or until its resources are exhausted. If anything, the argument from purpose cuts the other way: machines are evidently *more* purposive than most human beings, most of the time. This apparently excessive persistence reflects one of the fundamental differences to be elaborated later—one that could, however, be superficially eliminated by disconnecting the goal-setting part of the program at random intervals.

Secondly, machines were once believed to be incapable of learning from experience. We now know that machine learning is not only possible but essential in the performance of many tasks that might once have been thought not to require it. Simple problems of pattern recognition, such as the identification of hand-printed capital letters, have been solved only by programs which discover the critical characteristics of the stimuli for themselves.[3] The success of Samuel's [4] checker-playing program is based on its capacity to store and use experience from previous games; no program without the ability to learn has been nearly as successful. This argument too, is more interesting when viewed the other way. In a sense, computers learn more readily than people do: you can teach checkers to a 3-year-old computer, but not to a 3-year-old child. The reason will appear later; it is evidently not just that the computer is the more intelligent of the two.

Finally, it has often been asserted that machines can produce nothing novel, spontaneous, or creative—that they can "only do what they have been programmed to do." This is perhaps the most widely held of the negative beliefs, yet it is the first to be relinquished by anyone who actually tries to write programs for a digital computer. Long before a programmer succeeds in getting the machine to learn anything, or to behave purposefully, he repeatedly encounters its capacity to act in astonishing, unpredicted, and (usually) frustrating ways. For example, he may change a few steps in a familiar program involving thousands of instructions and find that the output printer produces reams of unintelligible gibberish. Careful diagnostic procedures are needed to discover that one comma was omitted in a single instruction. As a result the computer interpreted two small adjacent numbers as a single large number, executed the wrong instruction in the program, and continued blithely on from a point where it was never expected to be.

Such an event may seem trivial, both because the reason for the unpredicted outcome can be discovered in retrospect and because the effect was maladaptive rather than useful. But neither of these are necessary properties of unpredicted computer output. Existing programs have found original proofs for theorems, made unexpected moves in games, and the like. The belief that a machine can do nothing qualitatively novel is based on a false dichotomy between quality and quantity. What has become a truism in physics also applies to information processes: large changes in the magnitude of phenomena always imply major changes in the "laws" through which these phenomena can be understood. The result of 200,000 elementary symbolic operations cannot be readily predicted from knowledge of the elements and the program. The sheer *amount* of processing which a computer does can lead to results to which the adjective *novel* may honestly be applied. Indeed, complexity is the basis for emergent qualities wherever they are found in nature.

SOME OBSERVABLE DIFFERENCES

It appears, then, that computers can learn, and can exhibit original and purposive behavior. What can they not do? At first reckoning, their intellectual defects seem trivial and nearly irrelevant. Nevertheless, a list of the inadequacies of present-day artificial intelligence is worth making for its suggestive value. Two or three of the inadequacies have already been mentioned. When a program is purposive, it is too purposive. People get bored; they drop one task and pick up another, or they may just quit work for a while. Not so the computer program; it continues indomitably. In some circumstances the program may be more effective than a man, but it is not acting as a man would. Nor is such singlemindedness always an advantage: the computer is very likely to waste its time on trivialities and to solve problems which are of no importance. Its outlook is a narrow one: with Popeye, it says, "I am what I am," and it lets the rest of the world go hang while it plays chess or translates Russian relentlessly. The root of the difference seems to be more a matter of motivation than of intellect. Programs have goals, but they do not acquire or use their goals as a man would.

Computers are more docile than men. They erase easily: an instruction or two can wipe out anything ever learned, whether pernicious or useful. The decision to acquire new knowledge or to destroy old memories is a deliberate one. Usually it must be taken by the programmer, though in principle the program could decide for itself. Human memory seems much less flexible. A man rarely has single-minded control over what he will learn and forget; often he has no control at all. Thus, he lives willy-nilly in an accumulating context of experience which he cannot limit even if he would. The result is both stupidity and serendipity: if he is inefficient, he also can become wise in unexpected ways. Youth is not doomed to ignorance even though it would like to be, and no one can entirely avoid growing up. A program or a programmer, in contrast, can easily prevent any change that appears superficially undesirable.

By the same token, any apparently desirable change in a program can be carried out, at least if the necessary techniques are known. There is no need to embed it in an orderly sequence of growth, no resistance from an organism that has other things to do first. In this respect artificial intelligence is conformist, and precociously so. Again this is a problem of motivation, but it is a developmental question as well. We would be rightly worried about a child who played chess before he could talk; he would seem "inhuman."

Growth is a process of self-contradiction, but computer programs are never at cross-purposes with themselves. They do not get tangled up in conflicting motives, though they may oscillate between alternative courses of action. Thus, they are good at problem solving but they never solve problem *B* while working on *A*.

Artificial intelligence seems to lack not only breadth but depth. Computers do not dream, any more than they play. We are far from certain what dreams are good for, but we know what they indicate: a great deal of information processing goes on far beneath the surface of man's purposive behavior, in ways and for reasons that are only very indirectly reflected in his overt activity. The adaptive significance of play is much clearer. In playing, children (and adults) practice modes of thought and action that they do not yet need. Free of any directing immediate necessity, skills can develop into autonomous units that can later serve a variety of ends.

Taken one at a time, these differences between natural and artificial intelligence are not impressive. All together, they give rise to the suspicion that the cognitive activities of machines and men are still substantially different. In stressing the differences, my purpose is not to disparage current work in artificial intelligence. The research that has been done and is being done has important practical implications; it is also providing us with valuable models for some kinds of human thinking. Its incompleteness is emphasized here for two reasons. For *psychologists,* I wish to stress that contemporary computer models are oversimplified in the same sense that early stimulus-response psychology and early psychoanalytic theory were oversimplified. It may be well to regard "artificial intelligence" with the same mixture of hopefulness and suspicion that was appropriate to those earlier efforts. For *programmers,* I make a prediction. As computers are used for increasingly "human" activities, either directly (as in simulation) or indirectly (as in situations where the criteria of performance are psychological and social), new and difficult problems will arise. The focus of difficulty will no longer be in pattern recognition, learning, and memory but in an area which has no better name than "motivation." In support of these assertions, I describe, in the remainder of this article, three fundamental and interrelated characteristics of human thought that are conspicuously absent from existing or contemplated computer programs.

1) Human thinking always takes place in, and contributes to, a cumulative process of growth and development.

2) Human thinking begins in an intimate association with emotions and feelings which is never entirely lost.

3) Almost all human activity, including thinking, serves not one but a multiplicity of motives at the same time.

COGNITIVE DEVELOPMENT

The notion of "development" involves more than the obvious fact that a newborn baby has a great deal to learn. The intricacies of adult behavior cannot be acquired in just any order, to suit the convenience of the environment. Certain attitudes and skills must precede others. In part this is a matter of simple prerequisite learning: one must know how the pieces move before one can invent winning chess combinations. Moreover, the cumulation of learning is interwoven at every point with inborn maturational sequences. It may or may not be true that one must walk before he can run, but it is clear that neither skill can be taught to a 6-months-old baby. Therefore, no baby of that age can have the adequate conceptions of space and localization that genuinely do depend on experience. By the time a child has the opportunity to discover other rooms and other worlds, he already has a year's worth of structure with which to assimilate them. He will necessarily interpret his own explorations in terms of experience that he already has: of losing love or gaining it, of encountering potential disaster, joy, or indifference. These preconceptions must affect the kind of explorations he makes, as well as the results of his ventures; and these consequences in turn help to shape the conceptual schemes with which the next developmental problem is met. A child who could move about from the very beginning would grow into an adult complexly different from any of us.

In Piaget's [5] useful terminology, human development consists of two reciprocal phases: "assimilation" and "accommodation." The first is the transformation and recoding of the stimulus world which is performed by the child's cognitive equipment of the moment. Computers also assimilate in this sense; for example, they reduce photographs to bit-patterns through specialized input devices. Accommodation is harder to imitate. It refers to change in the cognitive apparatus itself, as a result of the attempt to assimilate novel material.

In a loose way, accommodation may be equated to learning, and it is evident that computers can learn (for example, by optimizing probability-weights or other internal parameters). But the most important accommodations in human development are changes in the structure of the processing itself. The child's visual and physical exploration of space does not result merely in the assignment of specific quantitative values to an innate spatial schema. On the contrary, the weight of the evidence suggests that such fundamental concepts as objective permanence, three-dimensionality, and tangibility must themselves be formed by development. And we do not yet have any realistic hope of programming this type of growth into an artificially intelligent system.

It is instructive to consider game playing from this point of view, because it has been a focus of interest for both programmers and developmental psychologists. Young children cannot be taught to play such games as checkers and chess because they cannot be reconciled to the restrictions imposed by the rules. Having grasped the idea that he should try to capture pieces, a young child proceeds to do so with any "move" and any piece of his own that comes to hand. He will avoid the loss of his own piece by every possible maneuver, including removing it from the board and putting it in his mouth. If the piece is taken nevertheless, the child may have a tantrum and stop playing. According to Piaget [6] there is an interesting later stage in which the schoolchild thinks of the rules as sacrosanct and eternal; it takes an adult to admit that what was arbitrarily established may be arbitrarily altered. Such a history must leave its mark on a human chess player, in the form of a hierarchical organization of purposes as well as strategies. Nothing comparable exists for the computer program, which works steadily

toward its fixed goal of legal victory. There is no obvious reason
to doubt that a specialized program may some day play chess as
well as a man or better, but the intellectual processes of the two
are likely to remain fundamentally different.

EMOTIONAL BASIS OF COGNITIVE ACTIVITY

The activity of a newborn baby is very largely organized around
the satisfaction of needs. While there are intervals dominated by
visual or tactile exploration, major events in the baby's life are hunger and sucking, irritability and sleep, pain and relief, and the like.
This suggests that stimulus information is assimilated largely with
reference to its need-satisfying and need-frustrating properties. The
first accommodations to such basic features of the world as time,
distance, and causality are interwoven with strongly emotional experiences. Moreover, the fluctuations of the child's internal states
do not have any very obvious relation to the logic of his environment, so that months and years are needed before his thinking and
his actions become well attuned to the world around him. To put
it another way: the pleasure principle yields to the reality principle
only slowly.

Many psychologists, such as Robert White,[7] have recently stressed
the opposite point: that activity directed toward mastering reality
is present from the very beginning. They are surely right, but even
the beginning of competence and esthetic pleasure depend heavily
on internal structures. What the baby explores, and how he reacts
to it, is not determined only by realistically important features of
the environment but by the schemata with which that environment
is assimilated.

Needs and emotions do not merely set the stage for cognitive activity and then retire. They continue to operate throughout the
course of development. Moreover, they do not remain constant but
undergo growth and change of their own, with substantial effects
on intellectual activities. Some emotional growth, such as the
gradual differentiation of specific fear from general anxiety, is the
result of interaction with the environment. Other changes, like those
of puberty, seem to be relatively autonomous. It would be rash
indeed to believe that events so important to the individual's life

play no role in his thinking. One fundamental way in which they exert their influence is discussed in the next section. In addition, it is worth noting that one of the most common and frequently discussed modes of learning—that of reward and punishment—operates through an open involvement of strong and historically complicated emotions.

To think like a man, a computer program would need to be similarly endowed with powerful internal states. We must imagine these states, which have both short- and long-term dynamics of their own, to be in almost complete control of information processing at first. Later their influence must become more subtle, until their final role is a complex resultant of the way in which preset internal patterns have interacted with the flow of experience. Perhaps such programs can be written, but they have not been, nor do they appear to be just around the corner.

MULTIPLICITY OF MOTIVES

Human actions characteristically serve many purposes at once. Any activity whatever could serve as an example, but it will be instructive to consider chess playing again. Typically, a computer which has been programmed to play chess has one overriding goal —to win—and establishes subordinate goals (capturing pieces, controlling open files, and the like) when they may be useful to that end. Human chess players do this also, but for them winning is itself only one goal among many, to which it is not always related in a simply subordinate way.

For instance, a chess player may also seek the esthetic pleasure which comes from an unexpected and elegant combination. This desire has surely been responsible for the achievement of many spectacular victories in the history of chess; the search for such a combination is also responsible for an uncountable number of defeats. It is likely, too, that most players seek the experience of success, either for the internal satisfactions or for the public acclaim which it brings, or for both of these reasons. The avoidance of the inner or outer humiliation which defeat brings must also play a frequent role. None of these motives is fully interchangeable with any other. Each has its own attendant retinue of potential substitute satisfactions, reactions to frustration, and interactions with the concrete reality of the game. However, it is very possible for all of them to exist in the same chess player at the same time.

Chess can serve other purposes as well, which are certainly not without their effect on the actual sequence of moves. It is a social occasion, and serves as a vehicle for a relationship to another person. As such, chess can be an instrument of friendship, but it is double-edged because each friend is trying to defeat the other. Thus, the game becomes an outlet for aggression, in which one may aim for destruction of his opponent in an entirely nonphysical (and so nonpunishable) way. It is not only the opponent who may be symbolically destroyed. Reuben Fine, who is both grand master and psychoanalyst, has argued [8] that the presence of a "king" and a "queen" on the board may give chess a deeply symbolic value, so that very primitive fantasy goals can become relevant to the progress of the game.

Apart from considerations of winning and losing, playing chess may reflect many other human motives. One man may adopt what he considers to be a "daring" style of play because he wants to think of himself as a bold person; another may play conservatively for analogous reasons. Both men may be *playing* because (that is, partly because) chess is only a *game*—an activity in which they can succeed and be respected without growing up or competing in what they regard as more adult, and thus more frightening, realms. Some people probably play chess because it is at least something to do and a means of avoiding the anxiety-laden or self-destructive thoughts they might otherwise have. Others, of both sexes, may play because they somehow think of chess as a masculine rather than a feminine activity and playing it makes them more certain of their own sex identity. And so on; the list is endless.

Every sort of human behavior and thought is open to this type of analysis. No person works on a mathematical problem as contemporary computer programs do: simply to solve it. No person writes a scientific paper merely to communicate technical information, nor does anyone read such a paper merely to be better informed. The overt and conscious motives are important, but they never operate in isolation. In the early days of psychoanalysis it was fashionable to devalue the obvious motives in favor of the unconscious ones, and to assume that cognitive activity was "nothing but" a way to placate instinctual demands. This tendency is happily no longer common; "rational" activities are unquestionably important in their own right to the person who engages in them. But we must be careful not to let the availability of computer models seduce us into the 19th-century view of a man as a transparently single-minded and logical creature.

Elsewhere I have discussed the multiplicity of thought,[9] suggesting that much in human thinking is better conceptualized as "parallel" than as "sequential" in nature. The manifold of motives that I am describing here goes beyond that assumption, although it certainly presupposes a capacity for parallel processing. The motivational complexity of thought is more easily seen as depth than as breadth. It is what makes people interesting, and it is also what gives them the capacity for being bored. It is what the "shallow" characters of poor fiction lack, and it is the source of the inventive spontaneity of real people. People succeed in using experience with one problem in solving another because, after all, they want to solve both; and both solutions are only parts of an intricate system of needs and goals. Miller, Galanter, and Pribram [10] have emphasized the hierarchical structure that human intentions often exhibit. Such a multiplicity of motives is not a supplementary heuristic that can be readily incorporated into a problem-solving program to increase its effectiveness. In man, it is a necessary consequence of the way his intellectual activity has grown in relation to his needs and his feelings.

The future of artificial intelligence is a bright one. The intellectual achievements of computer programs are almost certain to increase. We can look forward with confidence to a time when many complex and difficult tasks will be better performed by machines than they now are by men, and to the solution of problems which men could never attempt. Moreover, our understanding of human thinking may well be furthered by a better understanding of those aspects of intelligence which the programs display. This process has already begun: many psychologists, myself included, are indebted to computer technology for a wealth of new ideas which seem to be helpful in understanding man. But two systems are not necessarily identical, or even very similar, because they have some properties in common.

The deep difference between the thinking of men and machines has been intuitively recognized by those who fear that machines may somehow come to regulate our society. If machines really thought as men do, there would be no more reason to fear them than to fear men. But computer intelligence is indeed "inhuman": it does not grow, has no emotional basis, and is shallowly motivated. These defects do not matter in technical applications, where the criteria of successful problem solving are relatively simple. They become extremely important if the computer is used to make social decisions, for there our criteria of adequacy are as subtle and as multiply motivated as human thinking itself.

The very concept of "artificial intelligence" suggests the rationalist's ancient assumption that man's intelligence is a faculty independent of the rest of human life. Happily, it is not.

REFERENCES

1. T. Marill, *IRE* (*Inst. Radio Engrs.*) Trans. *Human Factors Electron.*, II (1961), 2.
2. A. Newell, J. C. Shaw, H. A. Simon, *Psychol. Rev.*, LXV (1958), 151.
3. O. G. Selfridge and U. Neisser, *Sci. Am.*, CCIII (1960), 60.
4. A. L. Samuel, *IBM J. Res. Develop.*, III (1959), 211.
5. J. Piaget, *The Origins of Intelligence in Children* (New York: Norton, 1952).
6. ———, *The Moral Judgment of the Child* (Glencoe, Ill.: Free Press, 1948).
7. R. White, *Psychol. Rev.*, LXVI (1959), 297.
8. R. Fine, *Psychoanalysis*, IV, No. 3 (1956), 7.
9. U. Neisser, *Brit. J. Psychol.*, in press.
10. G. A. Miller, E. Galanter, K. Pribram, *Plans and the Structure of Behavior* (New York: Holt, 1960).

10   The logic of tacit inference

MICHAEL POLANYI

This is the only reading not directly concerned with
the problem of men and machines, which it touches on
only briefly. It has been included however because it
is directly concerned with a central element in the field
of artificial intelligence, namely the conception of intelligence which guides theorizing and work in the field.
For many years, following a distinguished career as a
chemist, the author has been developing a view of
knowledge which calls into question established ideas
about scientific method. He argues that all explicit
cognition, from perception to the most abstract theorizing, relies upon a tacit awareness or comprehension
which cannot be formally articulated.

Michael Polanyi held the chair of physical chemistry
at the University of Manchester from 1929 to 1948,
when he relinquished it for a chair in social sciences at
the same university. For the last decade he has been a
fellow of Merton College, Oxford. His Gifford Lectures
(1951–52) were developed into his major work, *Personal Knowledge*.

I propose to bring fresh evidence here for my theory of knowledge and expand it in new directions. We shall arrive
most swiftly at the centre of the theory, by going back to the point

Reproduced from *Philosophy*, Vol. XLI, No. 155 (January 1966) by permission of the author and of the Editor of *Philosophy*.

from which I started about twenty years ago.[1] Upon examining the grounds on which science is pursued, I saw that its progress is determined at every stage by indefinable powers of thought. No rules can account for the way a good idea is found for starting an inquiry; and there are no firm rules either for the verification or the refutation of the proposed solution of a problem. Rules widely current may be plausible enough, but scientific enquiry often proceeds and triumphs by contradicting them. Moreover, the explicit content of a theory fails to account for the guidance it affords to future discoveries. To hold a natural law to be true, is to believe that its presence may reveal itself in yet unknown and perhaps yet unthinkable consequences; it is to believe that such laws are features of a reality which as such will continue to bear consequences inexhaustibly.

It appears then that scientific discovery cannot be achieved by explicit inference, nor can its true claims be explicitly stated. Discovery must be arrived at by the tacit powers of the mind and its content, so far as it is indeterminate, can be only tacitly known.

But where to turn for a logic by which such tacit powers can achieve and uphold true conclusions? *We must turn to the example of perception.* This has been my basic assumption. I maintained that the capacity of scientists to perceive in nature the presence of lasting shapes, differs from ordinary perception only by the fact that it can integrate shapes that ordinary perception cannot readily handle. *Scientific knowing consists in discerning gestalten that indicate a true coherence in nature.*

The study of perception by gestalt psychology has demonstrated the tacit operations that establish such coherence. When I move my hand before my eyes, it would keep changing its colour, its shape and its size, but for the fact that I take into account a host of rapidly changing clues, some in the field of vision, some in my eye muscles and some deeper still in my body, as in the labyrinth of the inner ear. My powers of perceiving coherence make me see these thousand varied and changing clues jointly as one single unchanging object, as an object moving about at different distances, seen from different angles, under variable illuminations. A successful integration of a thousand changing particulars into a single constant sight makes me recognise a real object in front of me.

Integration is almost effortlessly performed by adult eyes, but such powers of seeing things are acquired by early training in the infant child and are continuously developed by practice. Students of medicine struggle for weeks in learning to discern true shapes in the radiogram of a lung. Trained perception is basic to all descriptive sciences.

While the integration of clues to perceptions may be virtually effortless, the integration of clues to discoveries may require sustained efforts guided by exceptional gifts. But the difference is only one of range and degree: the transition from perception to discovery is unbroken. The logic of perceptual integration may serve therefore as a model for the logic of discovery.

Observe the way that integration works when we look at an object, for example a finger of our own, through a pinhole in a sheet of paper. If I do this and move my finger back and forth, I see it swelling as it approaches my eye. Psychologists have called this effect a 'de-realisation.' The moving object has lost here some of its constancy, for it lacks confirmation from the periphery of the visual field; and with the loss of its constancy the object has lost some of its apparent reality.[2]

The remarkable thing here is the way the appearance of a thing at the centre of my attention, depends on clues to which I am not directly attending. These clues are of two kinds. There are some that we cannot experience in themselves. The contraction of my eye muscles or the stirring inside of my labyrinth organ I cannot experience directly. These clues are *subliminal*. Other clues to the sight of my finger are the things covered up by the paper when I look at my finger through a pinhole. I normally see these things from the corner of my eye and I *could* observe them directly, if I wanted to. We may call such clues *marginal*. To neither kind of clues do I attend directly, yet both kinds contribute to the apparent reality of the object, on which my attention is focussed. *We may say that my awareness of both kind of clues is subsidiary to my focal awareness of that object.*

These two kinds af awareness—the subsidiary and the focal—are fundamental to the tacit apprehension of coherence. Gestalt psychology has demonstrated that when we recognise a whole, we see its parts differently from the way we see them in isolation. It has shown that within a whole its parts have a *functional appearance* which they lack in isolation and that we can cause the merging of the parts in the whole by shifting our attention from the parts to the whole.

More than a century ago William Whewell described how the merging of hitherto isolated observations into elements of a scientific theory changes their appearance. 'To hit upon a right conception (he wrote) is a difficult step; and when this step is once made, the facts assume a different aspect from what they had before; that done, they are seen from a different point of view; and the catching of this point of view is a special mental operation, requiring special mental endowments and habits of thought.'[3] We may say that a scientific discovery reduces our focal awareness of observations into a subsidiary awareness of them, by shifting our attention from them to their theoretical coherence.

This act of integration, which we can identify both in the visual perception of objects and in the discovery of scientific theory, is the tacit power we have been looking for. I shall call it *tacit knowing.*

It will facilitate my discussion of tacit knowing if I speak of the clues or parts that are subsidiarily known as the *proximal term* of tacit knowing and of that which is focally known as the *distal term* of tacit knowing. In the case of perception we are attending to an object separated from most of the clues which we integrate into its appearance; the proximal and the distal terms are then largely different objects, joined together by tacit knowing. This is not so when we know a whole by integrating its parts into their joint appearance, or when the discovery of a theory integrates observations into their theoretical appearance. In this case the proximal term consists of things seen in isolation and the distal term consists of the same things seen as a coherent entity.

But tacit knowing does exercise in both cases its characteristic powers of integration, merging the subsidiary into the focal, the proximal into the distal. We may say then that in tacit knowing we always attend *from* the proximal *to* the distal term.

In subordinating the subsidiary to the focal, tacit knowing *is directed from the first to the second.* Since this functional relation is set up between two kinds of awareness, its directedness is necessarily conscious. Such directedness coincides then with the kind of intentionality which Franz Brentano has claimed to be a characteristic of all manner of consciousness.[4] This vectorial quality of tacit knowing will prove important.

We have seen that by attending from the proximal to the distal, we cause a transformation in the appearance of both: they acquire an integrated appearance. A perceived object acquires constant size, colour and shape; observations incorporated in a theory are reduced to mere instances of it; the parts of a whole merge their isolated appearance into the appearance of the whole. This is the *phenomenal* accompaniment of tacit knowing; which tells us that we have a real coherent entity before us. It embodies the *metaphysical claim* of tacit knowing. The act of tacit knowing thus implies the claim that its result is an aspect of reality which, as such, may yet reveal its truth in an inexhaustible range of unknown and perhaps still unthinkable ways.

My definition of reality, as that which may yet inexhaustibly manifest itself, implies the presence of an *indeterminate* range of *anticipations* in any knowledge bearing on reality. But besides this indeterminacy of its prospects, tacit knowing contains also an *actual knowledge* that is indeterminate, in the sense that its content *cannot be explicitly stated*.

We can see this best in the way we possess a skill. If I know how to ride a bicycle or how to swim, this does not mean that I can tell how I manage to keep my balance on a bicycle, or keep afloat when swimming. I may not have the slightest idea of how I do this, or even an entirely wrong or grossly imperfect idea of it, and yet go on cycling or swimming merrily. Nor can it be said that I know how to bicycle or swim and yet do *not* know how to coordinate the complex pattern of muscular acts by which I do my cycling or swimming. I both know how to carry out these performances as a whole and also know how to carry out the elementary acts which constitute them, though I cannot tell what these acts are. This is due to the fact that I am only subsidiarily aware of these things and our subsidiary awareness of a thing *may not suffice to make it identifiable*.

There are unspecifiable subsidiary elements present also in perception and in scientific discovery. We know a person's face and can recognise him among a thousand, indeed among a million. Yet we usually cannot tell how we recognise a face we know. There are many other instances of the recognition of a characteristic appearance—some commonplace, others more technical—which have the same structure as the identification of a person. University students are taught in practical classes to identify cases of diseases and specimens of rocks, plants and animals. This is the training of perception that underlies the descriptive sciences. The knowledge which such training transmits cannot be put into words, nor even conveyed by pictures; it must rely on the pupil's capacity to recognise the characteristic features of a physiognomy and their configuration in the physiognomy.

But does the successful teaching of skills and of the characteristic appearance of a physiognomy not prove that one *can* tell our knowledge of them? No, what the pupil must discover by an effort of his own is something we could not tell him. And he knows it then in his turn but cannot tell it.

This result actually takes me a step beyond the point I had aimed at. It exemplifies not only that the subsidiary elements of perception may be unspecifiable, but shows also that such tacit knowledge can be *discovered*, without our being able to identify what it is that we have come to know. This holds equally for the learning of skills: we learn to ride a bicycle without being able to tell in the end how we do it.

Some fairly recent observations have demonstrated experimentally the process by which we acquire knowledge that we cannot tell. The experiment in question produces a fixed relation between two events, both of which we know but only one of which we can tell.

Lazarus and McCleary [5] have shown this to take place when a person is presented for brief periods with several nonsense syllables and after certain of these syllables he is subjected to an electric shock. Soon the person shows signs of anticipating the shock at the sight of the shock syllables; yet, on questioning, he fails to identify them. He has come to know when to expect a shock, but cannot tell what makes him expect it. He has acquired a knowledge similar to that which we have when we know a person by signs which we cannot tell, or perform a skill by coordinating elementary muscular motions according to principles that we cannot tell.

Lazarus has given the process he discovered the name of *subception* and this has been widely adopted. The connection of subception with gestalt has, however, gone practically unnoticed. In the long-drawn controversy between Lazarus and G. W. Eriksen, which ended in 1960 by Eriksen's confirmation of subception, its connection with gestalt was not mentioned.

For my part, I regard subception as a striking confirmation of tacit knowing, as first revealed by gestalt psychology. I would indeed not rely so much on subception for demonstrating the structure of tacit knowing, had I not established this structure previously, from other, more richly documented evidence.

Psychologists have called subception a process of *learning without awareness*.[6] The description suits our present purpose. If there is learning without awareness, there must be also *discovery without awareness*, since discovery is but learning from nature. The way a novice discovers for himself the characteristic appearance of a specimen is but a minor replica of the act by which that appearance was first discovered by a scientist. Whewell's description of a discovery in mathematical physics (he had Kepler's discovery of elliptic paths in mind) has shown us a typical act of tacit integration at work. Discovery comes in stages, and at the beginning the scientist has but a vague and subtle intimation of its prospects. Yet these anticipations, which alert his solitary mind, are the precious gifts of his originality. They contain a deepened sense of the nature of things and an awareness of the facts that might serve as clues to a suspected coherence in nature. Such expectations are decisive for the inquiry, yet their content is elusive and the process by which they are reached cannot be specified. It is a typical feat of discovery without awareness.

Thus, in the structure of tacit knowing, we have found a mechanism which can produce discoveries by steps we cannot specify. This mechanism may account then for scientific intuition, for which no other explanation is known so far. Such intuition is not the supreme immediate knowledge, called intuition by Leibniz or Spinoza or Husserl, but a work-a-day skill for scientific guessing with a chance of guessing right.

But are all these tacit operations not merely provisional? Are we to abandon the ideal of explicit inference, which alone can safeguard critical reason? My answer is that there is an important area in which explicit thought is ineffectual. No explicit direction can make us see a pair of stereoscopic photographs as one solid image; a person putting on right-left inverting spectacles will go about helplessly for days on end though he knows that he has merely to transpose the things he sees from right to left and from left to right. He will eventually learn to see with inverting spectacles without knowing how he does it. We cannot learn to keep our balance on a bicycle by taking to heart that in order to compensate for a given angle of imbalance a, we must take a curve on the side of the imbalance, of which the radius (r) should be proportionate to the square of the velocity (v) over the imbalance: $r \sim v^2/a$. Such knownedge is ineffectual, unless known tacitly.

We have seen *tacit knowledge* to comprise two kinds of awareness, *subsidiary awareness* and *focal awareness*. Now we see *tacit knowledge* opposed to *explicit knowledge;* but these two are not sharply divided. While tacit knowledge can be possessed by itself, explicit knowledge must rely on being tacitly understood and applied. Hence all knowledge is *either tacit* or *rooted in tacit knowledge*. A *wholly* explicit knowledge is unthinkable.

We can watch the process by which an explicit prescription becomes increasingly effective as it sinks deeper into a tacit matrix. Take a manual for driving a motorcar and learn it by heart. Assuming that you have never seen a motorcar, you will have to identify its parts from the illustrations of the manual. You can then sit down at the wheel and try to carry out the operations prescribed by the text. Thus you will start learning to drive and eventually establish the bearing of the manual on all the objects it indicates and the skills it teaches. The text of the manual is shifted to the back of the driver's mind, and is replaced almost entirely into the tacit operations of a skill.

The speed and complexity of tacit integration far exceeds in its own domain the operations of explicit inference. This is how intuitive insight may arrive at unaccountable conclusions in a flash. This has been pointed out by Konrad Lorenz.[7] While language expands human intelligence immensely beyond the purely tacit domain, the logic of language itself—the way language is used—remains tacit. Indeed, it is easy to show that the structure of tacit knowing contains a general theory of meaning which applies also to language.

When, in the experiment of Lazarus, certain syllables make the subject expect an electric shock, the approaching shock has become the meaning of these syllables to the subject. This view can be generalised, without straining the evidence, to all relations between a subsidiary and a focal term. The elementary motions that serve a cyclist to keep his balance are not meaningless: their meaning lies in the performance they jointly achieve. In this sense a characteristic physiognomy is the meaning of its features, which is in fact what we commonly say when a physiognomy expresses a particular mood. And finally, we may regard the appearance of a perceived object with constant properties as the joint meaning of the clues the integration of which produces that appearance. Such is the *semantic function* of tacit knowing.

A *set of sounds* is converted into the *name* of an object by an act of tacit knowing which integrates the sounds to the object to which we are attending. This is accompanied by a characteristic change in our impression of the sounds. When converted into a word they no longer sound as before; they have become, as it were, transparent: we attend *from* them (or through them) to the object to which they are integrated. Current theories which would explain meaning by the association of sounds with an object, leave unexplained this vectorial quality of meaning which is of its essence.[8]

There is a parallel to this transformation of sounds into words in the conversion of an object into a tool. Someone using a stick for the first time to feel his way in the dark, will at first feel its impact against his palm and fingers when the stick hits an object. But as he learns to use the stick effectively, a transformation of these jerks will take place into a feeling of the point of the stick touching an object; the user of the stick is no longer attending then *to* the meaningless jerks in his hand but attends *from* them to their meaning at the far end of the stick.

I have spoken of the subliminal clues of tacit knowing which cannot be experienced in themselves and of marginal clues which, though clearly visible, may not be identifiable. But we have met now also a number of instances where tacit knowing integrates *clearly identifiable* elements and have observed the way the appearance of things changes when, instead of looking *at* them, we look *from* them to a distal term which is their meaning.

Once established, this *from–to* relation is durable. Yet it can be seriously impaired at will by switching our attention from the meaning to which it is directed, back to the things that have acquired this meaning. Turn your attention on a word you have spoken;

repeat it several times, attending carefully to the sound you produce and to the motion of your tongue and lips, and the word will
regain its sensuous body and lose its meaning. The same is true of
a skilful performance. By concentrating attention on his fingers, a
pianist can paralyse himself; the motions of his fingers no longer
bear then on the music performed, they have lost their meaning.

We can identify then two alternative structures—omitting for the
moment their necessary qualifications. So long as you look *at* X,
you are *not* attending *from* X to something else, which would be
its meaning. In order to attend *from* X to its meaning, you must
cease to look *at* X, and *the moment you look at X again you cease
to see its meaning.* Admittedly, meaning is tenacious; once it is
established, its destruction is not always feasible and is hardly ever
complete, but it *would* be complete, if we could look at X again
fully as an object.

In *Personal Knowledge*, I have described the destruction of the
meaning of X when switching our attention back to X, as due to
the *logical unspecifiability of* X. But this does not show how the
destructive powers of this shift of attention arise. To speak of this
destruction as 'the paradox of the centipede', as Arthur Koestler
does, also fails to make this clear. What happens is that our attention that is directed *from* (or through) a thing to its meaning is
distracted by looking *at* the thing. We shall presently see that to
attend *from* a thing to its meaning is to *interiorise* it, and that to
look instead *at* the thing is to *exteriorise* or *alienate* it. We shall
then say *that we endow a thing with meaning by interiorising it
and destroy its meaning by alienating it.*

Consider once more the process of perception; how we attend
from a large number of clues—some at the edge of our vision, others
inside our body—*to* their meaning, which is what we perceive. This
transposition of bodily experiences into the perception of things
outside, appears then as an instance of the process by which we
transpose meaningless experiences into their meaning at a distance
from us, as we do when we use tools or probes.

It may be objected that many of the feelings transposed in the
act of perception differ from those transposed in the use of tools
and probes, by not being noticeable before their transposition. But
Hefferline (1959) has shown that spontaneous muscular twitches,
unfelt by the subject, can be as effective as the nonsense syllables

of Lazarus in foreshowing punishment.[9] And Russian observations, reported by Razran (1961), have established the same fact for intestinal stimulations.[10] This exemplifies the way subliminal events inside our body are transposed by the act of perception into the sight of things outside.

It has been said that perception cannot be a projection, since we have no internal experiences to project into things perceived. But we have established that projection of this type does take place in various instances of tacit knowing, even when we do not originally sense the internal processes in themselves. I would venture, therefore, to include in tacit knowing also the neural traces in the brain on the same footing as the subliminal stimuli inside our body. We may say then, quite generally, that wherever some process in our body gives rise to consciousness in us, tacit knowing will make sense of the event in terms of an experience to which we are attending.

This answers an old question. Imagine a physiologist to have mapped out completely all that takes place in the eyes and brain of a seeing man. Why do his observations not make him see that which the man sees? Because he looks *at* these happenings, while the subject attends *from*, or through, them *to* that which they mean to him. If the subject were to watch his own nervous system in a mirror, he would see there no more than the physiologist does. What we have here is a curtailment of meaning by *alienation*. The alienated view is not quite meaningless in this case, because the visual apparatus has a meaning as a mechanism of vision. To make the situation clear, imagine one person, looking through a telescope and absorbed in admiring the moons of Jupiter, while another watched him using the telescope and observed the laws of geometrical optics. We are touching here on the problem of Cartesian dualism.

The way the body participates in the act of perception can be generalised further, to include the bodily roots of all knowledge and thought. Our body is the only assembly of things known almost exclusively by relying on our awareness of them for attending to something else. Parts of our body serve as tools for observing objects outside and for manipulating them. Every time we make sense of the world, we rely on our tacit knowledge of impacts made by the world on our body and the complex responses of our body to these impacts. Such is the exceptional position of our body in the universe.

Phenomenology contrasts this feeling of our body with the view of the body seen as an object from outside.[11] The theory of tacit knowing regards this contrast as the difference between looking *at* something and attending *from* it at something else that is its meaning. Dwelling in our body clearly enables us to attend *from* it to things outside, while an external observer will tend to look *at* things happening in the body, seeing it as an object or as a machine. He will miss the meaning these events have for the person dwelling in the body and fail to share the experience the person has of his body. Again we have loss of meaning by alienation and another glimpse of Cartesian dualism.

I have shown how our subsidiary awareness of our body is extended to include a stick, when we feel our way by means of the stick. To use language in speech, reading and writing, is to extend our bodily equipment and become intelligent human beings. We may say that when we learn to use language, or a probe, or a tool, and thus make ourselves aware of these things as we are of our body, we *interiorise* these things and *make ourselves dwell in them.* Such extensions of ourselves develop new faculties in us; our whole education operates in this way; as each of us interiorises our cultural heritage, he grows into a person seeing the world and experiencing life in terms of this outlook.

Interiorisation bestows meaning, alienation strips of meaning; when the two are applied alternately, they can *jointly develop* meaning—but this dialectic lies beyond my subject here.

The logical relation that links life in our body to our knowledge of things outside us can be generalised to further instances in which we rely on our awareness of things for attending to another thing. When we attend from a set of particulars to the whole which they form, we establish a logical relation between the particulars and the whole, similar to that which exists between our body and the things outside it. In view of this, we may be prepared to consider the act of comprehending a whole *as an interiorisation of its parts,* which makes us dwell in the parts. We may be said to live in the particulars which we comprehend, in the same sense as we live in the tools and probes which we use and in the culture in which we are brought up.

Such indwelling is not merely formal; it causes us to participate feelingly in that which we understand. Certain things can puzzle us; a situation may intrigue us—and when our understanding removes our perplexity, we feel relieved. Such intellectual success gives us a sense of mastery which enhances our existence. These feelings of comprehension go deep; we shall see them increasing in profundity all the way from the I—It relation, to the I—Thou relation.

I shall start by taking up a loose end, left behind when analysing the meaning of a word as a name for a single object. We shall ask how a name can come to designate a *group of things*, like a species of plants or animals. This is the ancient problem of universals. It can be summed up in the question: What is a man like to whom the concept of 'man' refers? Can he be both fair and dark, both young and old, brown, black and yellow all at the same time? Or, if not, can he be a man without any of the properties of a man? The answer is that in speaking of man in general we are not attending to any kind of man, but relying on our subsidiary awareness of individual men, for attending to their joint meaning. This meaning is a comprehensive entity, and its knowledge is wiped out by attending to its particulars in themselves. This explains why the concept of man cannot be identified with any particular set of men, past or future. The concept represents all men—past, present, and future —jointly, and the word 'man' applies to this comprehensive entity.

The metaphysical claim of tacit knowing requires that this entity be real. This is confirmed by the fact that the members of a species are expected to have an indefinite range of yet undisclosed properties in common; this is the intension of the class formed by the species. Being real, the classing of living beings into species is fundamental to biology. Moreover, the distinctive nature of the human species underlies all social ties, all emotions between men, and between men and women; all conceptions of responsibility; indeed our whole life as men. Thus do we dwell in our conception of a species.

Indwelling becomes deeper as we pass from the conception of a species to the knowledge of individual living beings. The main points of such knowledge were established long before the rise of science. Life and death were known before biology; sentience and insentience, the difference between intelligence and mindless stupidity, were all recognised before they were studied by science; the knowledge of plants and animals, of health and sickness, of birth, youth and old age, of mind and body, of organs and their functions, of food, digestion, elimination and many others, is immemorial. Such pre-scientific conceptions have formed the foundations of the biological sciences and still represent their major interests. Modern biology has vastly developed these ancient insights and thus confirmed their profundity.

Moreover, biologists still know these fundamentals by the same integrative powers by which they were first discovered before science, and they use similar powers for establishing their own novel biological conceptions. Morphology, physiology, animal psychology—they all deal with comprehensive entities. None of these entities can be mathematically defined and the only way to know them is by comprehending the coherence of their parts.

To appreciate this achievement, remember once more how our eyes integrate a thousand rapidly changing clues into the appearance of an object of constant shape, size and colour, moving about before us. We have to multiply the complexity of this action many times, to approach the intricacy of the integrations performed in establishing our knowledge of life and of living shapes and functions.

This integration is guided by the active functions of the living we are observing. A lion swooping down on the back of a fleeing antelope coordinates its impressions and actions in a highly complex and accurate way within a second. The naturalist watching the lion mentally integrates these coordinated elements into the observation of the lion hunting its prey. Some vital coordinations, like embryonic development, are much slower than this, but no less rich in coordinated details; the study of physiological functions fill many volumes; the coordinations performed by human intelligence are unlimited.

There are no mathematical expressions covering the shape of a lion and the way he pounces on an antelope; nor any that cover a million characteristic shapes and coordinated actions of numberless other living beings. None of these shapes and swiftly moving correlations are precisely definable.

I have said that we integrate these shapes and correlations by the tacit powers of perception. I may add, that our perception of living beings consists largely in mentally duplicating the active coordinations performed by their functions. To this extent our knowledge of life is a sharing of life—a re-living, a very intimate kind of indwelling. Hence our knowledge of biotic phenomena contains a vast range of unspecifiable elements and biology remains, in consequence, a descriptive science heavily relying on trained perception. It is immeasurably rich in things we know and cannot tell.

Such is life and such our knowledge of life; on such grounds are based the triumphs of biology. But this is repugnant to the modern biologist. Trained to measure the perfection of knowledge by the example of the exact sciences, he fells profoundly uneasy at finding his knowledge so inferior by this standard. The ideal of the exact sciences, derived from mechanics, aims at a mathematical theory connecting tangible, focally observed objects. Here everything is above board, open to public scrutiny, wholly impersonal. The part of tacit knowing is reduced to the act of applying the theory to experience, and this act goes unnoticed; while the fact, that tacit powers predominate in the very making of discoveries, is set aside too as forming no part of science.

The structure of biology is very different from this ideal. We know a living being by an informal integration of its coherent parts. Such knowledge combines two terms, one subsidiary, the other focal, that are known in different ways. The particulars of living beings are known as such by attending *from* them to their joint meaning which is the life of the organism. And this includes the sensomotoric centre of the animal as well as the human mind, as the bearer of intelligence and responsibility. Thus the *tangible focal objects* of exact science have been *split into two halves*. We have the tangible bodies of living beings that are not viewed focally, while at the focus of our attention we have such intangible things, as life and mind. Both of these halves are equally distasteful to the modern biologist, who finds their very duality unscientific and intolerable.

But tacit knowing is indispensable and must predominate in the study of living beings as organised to sustain life. The vagueness of something like the human mind is due to the vastness of its resources. Man can take in at a glance any one of 10^{40} brief sentences. By my definition, this indeterminacy makes the mind the more real, the more substantial. But such reality can be discerned only by a personal judgment: its knowledge is personal. The same is true of our subsidiary awareness of the organs and behaviour of a living being, by which we bring these to bear on its life or on its mind at the focus of our attention. All tacit knowing requires the continued participation of the knower and a measure of personal participation is intrinsic therefore to all knowledge, but the continued participation of the knower becomes altogether predominant in a knowledge acquired and upheld by such deep indwelling.

An attempt to de-personalise our knowledge of living beings would result, if strictly pursued, in an alienation that would render all observations on living things meaningless. Taken to its theoretical limits, it would dissolve the very conception of life and make it impossible to identify living beings.

My argument will gain in sharpness by narrowing it to the knowledge of another mind. We know another person's mind by the same integrative process by which we know life. A novice, trying to understand the skill of a master, will seek *mentally* to combine his movements to the pattern to which the master combines them *practically*. By such exploratory indwelling the novice gets the feel of the master's skill. Chess players enter into a master's thought by repeating the games he played. *We experience a man's mind as the joint meaning of his actions by dwelling in his actions from outside.*

Behaviourism tries to make psychology into an exact science. It professes to observe—i.e., *look at*—pieces of mental behaviour and to relate these pieces explicitly. But such pieces can be identified only within that tacit integration of behaviour, which behaviourists reject as unscientific. The actual result of a behaviourist analysis is to paraphrase this integration by the explicit relation of some of its quantifiable fragments. Such a paraphrase can be badly misleading, as in Pavlovian conditioning, which identifies *eating* with *the expectation to be fed,* because both of these induce a secretion of saliva. The behaviourist analysis is intelligible only because it imitates, however crudely, the tacit integration which it pretends to replace.

The claim of cybernetics to generate thought and feeling, rests likewise on the assumption that mental processes consist in explicitly identifiable performances which, as such, would be reproducible by a computer. This assumption fails, because mental processes are recognised to a major extent tacitly, by dwelling in many particulars of behaviour that we cannot tell. But we would rightly refuse to ascribe thought and feeling to a machine, however perfectly it would reproduce the outward actions of mental processes.[12] For the human mind works and dwells in a human body, and hence the mind can be known only as working and dwelling in a body. We can know it only by dwelling in that body from outside.

But could we not conceive of the body as a neurophysiological machinery performing the manifestations of the mind? The answer is, that feeling, action and thought have mental qualities which we perceive by the same principles of tacit knowing by which we perceive the phenomenal qualities of external objects. All these qualities would vanish if we watched, how parts of the human body carry out the performances of the mind. We had an example of this when we noted, that looking at the neurophysiological mechanism of vision, we do not see what the subject sees. We have now before us the full range of the dualism of which that case was a particular instance.

But I shall show that for the case of organisms the dualism of looking *at* and *attending from,* has a substantial foundation in the existence of distinct levels in the organism. The structure of tacit knowing has its counterpart in the way the principles determining the stability and power of an organism exercise their control over its parts. This is true also for machines; so to simplify matters, I shall deal first with machines. The result can then be generalised to the mechanical aspect of living beings and from there to the entire heirarchy of an organism.

Let me choose as an example of a machine the watch I wear on my wrist. My watch tells me the time. It is kept going by its mainspring, uncoiling under the control of the hair spring and balance wheel; this turns the hands which tell the time. Such are the operational principles of a watch, which define its construction and working. The principles cannot be defined by the laws of nature. No parts of a watch are formed by the natural equilibration of matter. They are artificially shaped and sagaciously connected to perform their function in telling the time. This is their meaning: to understand a watch is to understand what it is for and how it works. The laws of inanimate nature are indifferent to this purpose. They cannot determine the working of a watch, any more than the chemistry or physics of printer's ink can determine the contents of a book.

Viewed in themselves, the parts of a machine are meaningless; the machine is comprehended by attending *from* its parts to their joint function, which operates the machine. To this structure of knowing there correspond two levels controlled by different principles. The particulars viewed in themselves are controlled by the laws of inanimate nature, while viewed jointly, they are controlled by the operational principles of the machine. This dual control may seem puzzling. But the physical sciences expressly leave open certain variabilities of a system, described as its boundary conditions. The operational principles of a machine control these boundaries and so they do not infringe the laws of physics and chemistry, which operate within these boundaries.[13]

The same dualism holds for biology. Biologists will tell you that they are explaining living beings by the laws of inanimate nature, but what they actually do, and do triumphantly well, is to explain certain aspects of life *by mechanical principles*. This postulates a level of reality that operates on the boundaries left open by the laws of physics and chemistry.

Such duality opens a perspective to a whole sequence of levels, all the way up to that of responsible humanity, so that this sequence would form a hierarchy of operations, each higher level controlling the margin left indeterminate by the one below it. We can illustrate such a structure by the production of a literary composition, for example of a speech. It includes five levels. The first level, lowest of all, is the production of a voice; the second, the utterance of words; the third the joining of words to sentences; to fourth, the working of sentences into a style; the fifth, and highest, the composition of the text.

The principles of each level operate under the control of the next higher level. The voice you produce is shaped into words by a vocabulary; a given vocabulary is shaped into sentences in accordance with grammar; and the sentences are fitted into a style, which in its turn is made to convey the ideas of the composition. Thus each level is subject to dual control; first, by the laws that apply to its elements in themselves and, second, by the laws that control the comprehensive entity formed by them.

Such multiple control is made possible by the fact that the principles governing the isolated particulars of a lower level, leave indeterminate their boundary conditions for the control by a higher principle. Voice production leaves largely open the combination of sounds to words, which is controlled by a vocabulary. Next, a vocabulary leaves largely open the combination of words to form sentences, which is controlled by grammar; and so the sequence goes on.

Consequently, the operations of a higher level cannot be accounted for by the laws governing its particulars forming the next lower level. You cannot derive a vocabulary from phonetics; you cannot derive grammar from a vocabulary; a correct use of grammar does not account for good style; and a good style does not provide the content of a piece of prose.

A glance at the functions of living beings shows us that they have a broadly similar stratified structure. All living functions rely on the laws of inanimate nature in controlling the boundary conditions left open by these laws; the vegetative functions sustaining life at its lowest levels, leave open, both in plants and animals, the possibilities of growth and leave in animals open also the possibilities of muscular action; the principles governing muscular action leave open their integration to innate patterns of behaviour; such patterns are open in their turn to be shaped by intelligence, and the working of intelligence can be made to serve the still higher principles of man's responsible choices.

Each pair of levels would present its own dualism, for it would be impossible to account for the operations of any higher level by the laws governing its isolated particulars. The dualism of mind and matter would be but one instance of the dualism prevailing between every pair of successive ontological levels.

I expect that the many points at which the views I have sketched out here diverge from those of current philosophic literature, are obvious enough. I shall only try to show that, despite this divergence, they broadly respond to the development of modern philosophy.

Current writings on the history of science have confirmed the view I have put forward years ago, that the pursuit of science is determined at every stage by unspecifiable powers of thought; and I have shown you today how this fact forms my starting point for developing a theory of non-explicit thought. You may call such a theory—using a term coined by Gilbert Ryle—an *informal logic* of science and of knowledge in general. Alternatively, you may call it a phenomenology of science and knowledge, by reference to Husserl and Merleau-Ponty. This would correctly relate my enterprise both to analytic philosophy and to phenomenology and existentialism.

Admittedly, my view that true knowledge bears on an essentially indeterminate reality and my theory of a stratified universe, are foreign to these schools of thought. And again, while knowledge by indwelling is clearly related to Dilthey and existentialism, its extension to the natural sciences is contrary to these philosophies. Similarly, while Kant's categories by which experience of external objects is deemed possible, reappear with me in the active knower participating in all live knowledge, such a knower, responsibly legislating for himself with universal intent, is more like the moral person of the Second Critique than the agent of Pure Reason.

The original intention of Logical Positivism was to establish all knowledge in terms of explicit relations between sensory data. In the course of the last twenty years this programme has been gradually relaxed, by admitting more complex data and making allowance for 'open textures' and 'flexibilities' of the framework. The most recent development in this direction came to my notice in Michael Scriven's assertion that problems of structural logic in science can 'only be solved by reference to concepts previously condemned by many logicians as "psychological not logical", e.g. understanding, belief, judgment'.[14]

I suggest that we transform this retreat into a triumph, by the simple device of changing camp. Let us recognise that tacit knowing is the fundamental power of the mind which creates explicit knowing, lends meaning to it and controls its uses. Formalisation of tacit knowing immensely expands the powers of the mind, by creating a machinery of precise thought, but it also opens up new paths to intuition. Any attempt to gain complete control of thought by explicit rules is self-contradictory, systematically misleading and culturally destructive. The pursuit of formalisation will find its true place in a tacit framework.

In this light, there is no justification for separate approaches to scientific explanation, scientific discovery, learning and meaning. They ultimately rest on the same tacit process of understanding. The true *meaning of* Kepler's Third Law was *discovered* by Newton, when he *explained* it as an outcome of general gravitation. And *learning* by insight has the same three aspects on a minor scale.

The claims of cybernetics represent a revival of logical positivism in its original insistence on strictly explicit operations of the mind. Hence my rejection of a cybernetic interpretation of thought and of a behaviourism based likewise on the assumption that the data and operations of mental processes are explicitly specifiable.

My analysis of machines and living beings entails the rejection of Ernest Nagel's claim to describe machines and living beings in non-teleological terms.[15] Nothing is a machine unless it serves a useful purpose, and living organs and functions are organs and functions only to the extent to which they sustain life. A theory of knowledge based on tacit knowing, does not require that we purify science of references to mind or to the finalistic structure of living beings.[16]

NOTES

1. See my *Science, Faith and Society* (O.U.P., 1946, and as Phoenix Book, expanded, 1964), also *Personal Knowledge,* Gifford Lectures 1951–1952. (New York: Harper, 1964).
2. F. J. J. Buytendijk, *Mensch und Tier* (Hamburg: Taschenbuch, 1958), p. 59.
3. William Whewell, *Philosophy of Discovery* (London: J. W. Parker & Son, 1860), p. 254.
4. Franz Brentano, *Psychologie Von Empirischem Standpunkt* (1874) quoted from edition by Oskar Kraus (Leipzig: F. Meiner, 1942).
5. R. S. Lazarus and R. A. McCleary, *J. Person.* 18 (1949), 191 and *Psychol. Rev.* 58 (1951), 113. These results were called in question by C. W. Eriksen, *Psychol. Rev.* 63 (1956), 74, and defended by Lazarus, *Psychol. Rev.* 63 (1956), 343. But in a later paper surveying the whole field (*Psychol. Rev.* 67 (1960), 279) Eriksen confirmed the experiments of Lazarus and McCleary and accepted them as evidence of subception.
6. C. W. Eriksen, *Psychol. Rev.,* LXVII (1960), 279.
7. Konrad Lorenz in *General Systems,* ed. L. von Bertalanffy and A. Rapoport (Ann Arbor: University of Michigan Press, 1962), p. 50.
8. See e.g. W. V. O. Quine in *Word and Object* (Cambridge: M.I.T., 1960), p. 221. He rejects any reference to intentions as conceived by Brentano.

9. F. Hefferline, B. Keenan, and A. Herford, *Science*, CXXX (1959), 1338–39.
10. G. Razran, *Psychol. Rev.*, LXVIII (1961), 81.
11. This distinction is most widely developed in M. Merleau-Ponty, *Phenomenology of Perception* (New York: Humanities Press, 1962). Eng. Translation of *Phenomenologie de la Perception* (1945).
12. This view was expressed, e.g. by Professor Paul Ziff in *The Feelings of Robots in Minds and Machines*, ed. A. R. Anderson, *Prentice-Hall Contemporary Perspectives in Philosophy Series* (Englewood Cliffs, N. J.: Prentice-Hall, 1964). Other authors contested it. I regard my argument in its favour as decisive.
13. Michael Polanyi, *Reviews of Mod. Physics*, XXXIV (1962), p. 601.
14. Michael Scriven, "Explanation, Prediction and Laws" in *Minnesota Studies in the Philosophy of Science*, Vol. III (Minneapolis: University of Minnesota Press, 1962), p. 172.
15. Ernest Nagel, *The Structure of Science* (New York: Harcourt, Brace and World, 1961), p. 417.
16. I have published simultaneously with this paper a more fully developed statement of my Body Mind theory under the title *The Structure of Consciousness*, in *Brain*, LXXXVIII, part IV (1965), pp. 799–810.

11   The consequences for action

MORTIMER ADLER

Mortimer Adler took up the challenge posed by the cybernetic hypothesis in a 1967 book entitled *The Difference of Man and the Difference It Makes* (New York: Holt, Rinehart and Winston, 1967). Sifting the evidence from evolution and anthropology that the fundamental difference of man lies in the fact that he has the capacity for using language, he accepts, on this basis, the now-famous challenge of the British mathematician, A. M. Turing. The latter argued, in a 1950 article—"Computing Machinery and Intelligence" in *Mind*, LIX (1960), 423–60—that a machine could be built which, in a conversational guessing-game, could deceive its interlocuter into thinking it was human. Its use of language, that is, would lack none of the flexibility and range of a human user. If one accepts language use as the essential difference of personal existence, the success of the Turing test would appear to establish the anthropomorphic thesis about some machines. (One might compare Scriven's discussion of the Turing test on this point.) While Adler does not believe that this conversational test could be passed by a machine, for reasons which he discusses in the book, he is willing to accept the test as being as decisive a resolution as one could have.

In this selection, he discusses some of the practical and moral implications of the test. The discussion is

From Mortimer Adler, "The Consequences for Action," *The Difference of Man and the Difference It Makes,* Chapter 17. (New York: Holt, Rinehart and Winston, 1967.)

unique, I believe, in calling attention to the converse of the usual conclusions drawn. Usually (cf. Scriven) one focuses on the claim that successful machines would be persons. Adler wonders about the consequences for human persons.

Mortimer Adler is Director of the Institute for Philosophical Research, a member of the board of editors of Encyclopedia Britannica, and the author of almost a score of books.

As an initial step toward determining the consequences for action that flow from asserting or denying man's difference in kind, I propose to examine some contemporary views of the matter—the opinions of a number of scientists and philosophers who have faced up to this problem in one way or another.

Let me present first the warning given us by Dr. John Lilly with regard to the possibility that, in the not too remote future, we will be able to engage in a two-way conversation with the bottle-nosed dolphin. If and when this occurs, according to Dr. Lilly, we will have to attribute to dolphins the same kind of intellectual power that we attribute to men and deny to other non-linguistic or non-conversational animals. In other words, though men and dolphins may differ in the degree of their common intellectual power, they will stand on the same side of the line that divides animals that have such power from animals that totally lack it. Men and dolphins together will differ in kind from other animals.[1]

Would this possible state of facts, if realized, have any practical consequences? Dr. Lilly thinks it would. He writes:

The day that communication is established, the [dolphin] becomes a legal, ethical, moral, and social problem. At the present time, for example, dolphins correspond very loosely to conserved wild animals under the protection of the conservation laws of the United States and by international agreement, and to pets under the protection of the Society for the Prevention of Cruelty to Animals.

[But] if they achieve a bilateral conversation level corresponding, say, to a low-grade moron and well above a human imbecile or idiot, then they become an ethical, legal, and social problem. They have reached the level of humanness as it were. If they go above the level the problem becomes more and more acute, and if they reach the conversational abilities of any normal human being, we are in for trouble. Some groups of humans will then step forward in defense of these animals' lives and stop their use in experimentation; they will insist that we treat them as humans and that we give them medical and legal protection.[2]

Let us consider next the view expressed by Professor Michael Scriven of the University of California in his Postscript to an article on "The Mechanical Concept of Mind." He is concerned with the question whether a robot that is successful at playing Turing's game can also pass the test that would require us to attribute consciousness to it. "With respect to all other performances and skills of which the human being is capable," Scriven writes, "it seems to me clear already that robots can be designed to do as well or better." But with respect to this special performance—the one that would be the test of the robot's consciousness—Scriven says that he was not certain at the time of writing the article; however, in the postscript which he added, he tells us that he is, "upon further deliberation, confident that robots can in principle be built that will pass this test too, because they are in fact conscious."[3]

We need not agree with Scriven's prediction about the behavior of some future robot in order to take account of his comment on the practical consequences of his prediction's coming true. On the outcome of his prediction depends, in his judgment, "not only the question of matching a performance, but . . . also the crucial ontological question of the status of a robot as a person and thence the propriety of saying that it knows or believes or remembers. . . . If it is a person," Scriven goes on to say, "of course it will have moral rights and hence political rights."[4]

I turn next to the reflections of Professor Wilfred Sellars on what it means to be a person rather than a thing and on the criteria for drawing the line that divides persons from things. Sellars writes:

To think of a featherless biped as a person is to think of it as a being with which one is bound up in a network of rights and duties. From this point of view, the irreducibility of the personal is the irreducibility of the "ought" to the "is." But even more basic than this . . . is the fact that to think of a featherless biped as a person is to construe its behavior in terms of actual or potential membership in an embracing group each member of which thinks itself a member of the group.

Such a group, according to Sellars, is a community of persons. From the point of view of each of us as an individual, the most embracing community of persons to which we belong includes "all those with whom [we] can enter into meaningful discourse. . . . To recognize a featherless biped or dolphin or Martian [Sellars might have added, "or robot"] as a person is to think of oneself and it as belonging to a community"—the group of those who can engage in meaningful discourse with one another.[5]

I call the reader's attention to the criterion of being a person or a member of the community of persons. It is the same conversational test that Lilly and Scriven use for deciding whether dolphins and robots are persons or things. And that same criterion—conversational ability or ability to engage in meaningful discourse—also operates to differentiate man from brute. In other words, the same line that divides man from brute as different in kind also divides person from thing as different in kind. Furthermore, as Lilly, Scriven, and Sellars all point out, how we treat a particular entity depends on which side of that line we place it. These authors would, therefore, seem to be maintaining that a difference in kind has practical—legal, ethical, and social—consequences.

I would like, finally, to add the testimony of another philosopher, Professor J. J. C. Smart. Professor Smart, like Professor Sellars, is a moderate materialist. Each in his own way argues that conceptual thought can be entirely explained in terms of neurophysiological processes. Hence, both would deny that man differs radically in kind from other animals or machines, and both would affirm the unbroken continuity of nature. But both also appear to maintain that man differs in kind rather than merely in degree from other animals, and that this difference, which is marked by the possession or lack of "conversational ability," also operates to draw a sharp line between persons and things, with the practical consequence of the differential treatment accorded persons and things.[6] Sellars makes all these points more explicitly and clearly than Smart, but it is, nevertheless, instructive to observe Smart moving in the same direction. He writes:

A scientist has to attend seriously to the arguments of another scientist, no matter what may be that other scientist's nationality, race or social position. He must therefore at least respect the other as a source of arguments and this is psychologically conducive to respecting him as a person in the full sense and hence to considering his interests equally with one's own.[7]

The moral obligation of one scientist to another, here recognized by Smart, can be generalized into the moral obligation of one person to another. The other to whom we owe respect, the other whom we ought to treat "as a person in the full sense," is here being defined as the giver or receiver of arguments. Interpreted broadly yet without violence to the essential point, the giver or receiver of arguments is one who can enter into meaningful—one might even say "rational"—discourse. Hence, the line that Smart draws between persons and things is the same line that differentiates man from brute; and, like Sellars and the others, he attaches definite moral consequences—respect and other obligations—to being on one side of this line rather than the other.

2

The foregoing reference to the opinions of Dr. Lilly and Professors Scriven, Sellars, and Smart indicates some practical consequences of opposed answers to the question about how man differs from other animals—in kind or in degree only. These writers all assume that the difference in kind that is established by man's having, and by all other animals' lacking, the power of propositional speech is only a superficial difference. They assume, in other words, that the power of conceptual thought can be adequately explained in neurophysiological terms, and that its presence in man and not in other animals can be explained by the size and complexity of the human brain, which is above the critical threshold of magnitude required for conceptual thought.

On this interpretation of the observed fact that linguistic animals differ in kind from non-linguistic animals, *is man a person rather than a thing?* The answer is affirmative if, as suggested by the above-mentioned writers, the line that divides persons from things can be drawn by such criteria as conversational ability, the ability to engage in meaningful discourse and the ability to give and receive reasons or arguments. By these criteria, men are at present the only beings on earth that are persons. All other animals and machines are things—at least in the light of available evidence. The special worth or dignity that belongs exclusively to persons, the respect that must be accorded only to persons, the fundamental imperative that commands us to treat persons as ends, never solely as means—all these are thought to obtain on this theory of what is involved in being a person.

If in the future we should discover that dolphins, too, or certain robots, are persons in the same sense, then they too would have a dignity, deserve a respect, and impose certain obligations on us that other animals and other machines would not. However, if in the future we should discover that man differs from other animals *only in degree*, the line that divides the realm of persons from the realm of things would be rubbed out, and with its disappearance would go the basis in fact for a principled policy of treating men differently from the way in which we now treat other animals and machines.

Other practical consequences would then follow. Those who now oppose injurious discrimination on the moral ground that all human beings, being equal in their humanity, should be treated equally in all those respects that concern their common humanity, would have no solid basis in fact to support their normative principle. A social and political ideal that has operated with revolutionary force in human history could be validly dismissed as a hollow illusion that should become defunct. Certain anatomical and physiological characteristics would still separate the human race from other species of animals; but these would be devoid of moral significance if they were unaccompanied by a single psychological difference in kind. On the psychological plane, we would have only a scale of degrees in which superior human beings might be separated from inferior men by a wider gap than separated the latter from non-human animals. Why, then, should not groups of superior men be able to justify their enslavement, exploitation, or even genocide of inferior human groups, on factual and moral grounds akin to those that we now rely on to justify our treatment of the animals that we harness as beasts of burden, that we butcher for food and clothing, or that we destroy as disease-bearing pests or as dangerous predators?

It was one of the Nuremberg decrees that "there is a greater difference between the lowest forms still called human and our superior races than between the lowest man and monkeys of the highest order." What is wrong *in principle* with the Nazi policies toward Jews and Slavs if the facts are correctly described and if the only psychological differences between men and other animals are differences in degree? What is wrong *in principle* with the actions of the enslavers throughout human history who justified their ownership and use of men as chattel on the ground that the enslaved were inferiors (barbarians, gentiles, untouchables, "natural slaves, fit only for use")? What is wrong *in principle* with the policies of the American or South African segregationists if, as they claim, the Negro is markedly inferior to the white man, not much better than an animal and, perhaps, inferior to some?

The answer does not consist in dismissing as false the factual allegations concerning the superiority or inferiority of this or that group of men. It may be false that, within the human species, any racial or ethnic group is, as a group, inferior or superior. But it is not false that extremely wide differences in degree separate individuals who top the scale of human abilities from those who cluster at its bottom. We can, therefore, imagine a future state of affairs in which a new global division of mankind replaces all the old parochial divisions based upon race, nationality, or ethnic group— a division that separates the human elite at the top of the scale from the human scum at the bottom, a division based on accurate scientific measurement of human ability and achievement and one, therefore, that is factually incontrovertible. At this future time, let the population pressures have reached that critical level at which emergency measures must be taken if human life is to endure and be endurable. Finish the picture by imagining that before this crisis occurs, a global monopoly of authorized force has passed into the hands of the elite—the mathematicians, the scientists, and the technologists, not only those who make and control machines of incredible power and versatility, but also those whose technological skill has mechanized the organization of men in all large-scale economic and political processes. The elite are then the *de facto* as well as the *de jure* rulers of the world. At that juncture, what would be wrong *in principle* with their decision to exterminate a large portion of mankind—the lower half, let us say—thus making room for their betters to live and breathe more comfortably?

Stressing "in principle," the question calls for a moral judgment.

Validly to make a moral judgment in a particular case, real or imaginary, we must appeal to a defensible normative principle and one that is applicable to the facts as described. Can we do so in the case that we have been imagining? The facts include not only the scientifically measured ranking of individuals according to degrees of ability and achievement, but also the overarching fact that we have been taking for granted for the purpose of this discussion; namely, that it has been discovered that the psychological differences between men and other animals are all differences of degree. With exceptions that constitute a small minority, men have found nothing morally repugnant in killing animals for the health, comfort, sustenance, and preservation of human life. It seems reasonable to regard as morally sound those policies that have the almost unanimous consent of mankind, including its most civilized and cultivated representatives. By this criterion, we must acknowledge the moral validity of the policy that men have always followed with regard to the killing of animals for the benefit of the human race. If that policy is morally sound, it must reflect a valid normative principle. What is it?

It is indicated by the fact that, with the exception of relatively small numbers of scientists and philosophers, the members of the human race have always interpreted and still do interpret the observation that they alone of all animals have the power of speech as signifying not only a psychological difference in kind between themselves and the brutes, but also the psychological superiority of their own kind. Combining this fact with the policy that men have pursued in their treatment of animals, we can discern the normative principle underlying the action. It is that *an inferior kind ought to be ordered to a superior kind as a means to an end;* in which case there is nothing wrong about killing animals for the good of mankind. The same rule applies to other uses of animals as instruments of human welfare.

Now let us alter the picture by introducing into it the supposition with which we began this discussion—the supposition that it has been discovered that men and other animals differ psychologically only in degree. If, on that supposition, we still think it is a morally sound policy to use animals as means to our own good, including killing them, the underlying normative principle must be that *superiors in degree are justified, if it serves their welfare, in killing or otherwise making use of inferiors in degree.* But that principle, once it is recognized to be sound, cannot be restricted to the relation between men and animals; it applies with equal force to the relation between men of superior and men of inferior degree, especially to those who are at the top and at the bottom of the scale of ability and achievement, since the difference in degree that separates them may be as large as the difference in degree that separates the lowest men from the highest animals. Thus we appear to have reached the conclusion that, given only psychological differences of degree between men and other animals, and given a scientifically established ranking of individuals on a scale of degrees, the killing or exploitation of inferior by superior men cannot be morally condemned.

Is there a flaw in the argument? If there is one, it would appear to lie in the illicit substitution of the relation between superiors and inferiors *in degree* for the relation between a superior and an inferior *kind.* I am not prepared to say that the substitution is illicit, particularly if the superior and the inferior in kind are only superficially different in kind and hence in their underlying constitution differ only in degree. But if the normative principle that subordinates inferiors in kind to the good of their superiors in kind is defensible only when the superiors and the inferiors differ radically in kind, then we cannot validly convert that normative principle into a rule governing the action of superiors in degree with respect to inferiors in degree. Since, in the long history of man's reflective consideration of his action with respect to brute animals, the prevailing view of the difference between human beings and nonhuman animals has always been that it is not only a difference in kind, but also a radical difference in kind, I think it is reasonable to presume that the conscience of mankind has sanctioned the killing or exploitation of animals on this basis, and not on the view that the difference in kind is only superficial. The latter view, as explicitly formulated in this book, represents the position implicitly held by a relatively small number of scientists and philosophers in very recent times. It can hardly be regarded as generating the almost universal moral conviction that there is nothing reprehensible in the killing or exploitation of animals.

The conclusion that we have now reached has both negative and positive corollaries. On the negative side, the practical consequences may be very difficult to live with. If nothing less than the superiority of human to non-human beings that is based on a radical difference in kind between men and other animals can justify our killing and exploitation of them, we are without moral justification for our practices in this regard, should it turn out, as well it may, that the success of a Turing machine in the conversational game decisively shows that the difference in kind is only superficial. Two future possibilities—the one just mentioned or the possible discovery by psychologists that the difference between men and other animals is only one of degree—would leave us with what, after protracted consideration, might turn out to be an insoluble moral problem. We might have to concede that there is no clearly defensible answer to the question whether we ought or ought not to kill subhuman animals. We would then be forced to treat the problem as one of pure expediency, totally outside the pale of right and wrong. And in that case, would not the problem of how superior men should or should not treat inferior men also cease to be a moral problem, and become one of pure expediency? For those of us who still hold on to the traditional belief that moral principles of right and wrong govern the treatment of man by man, the contemplation of that eventuality is as upsetting as the possibility earlier envisaged—that with the discovery that men and other animals differ only in degree, it would be possible morally to justify a future elite in extermi- nating the scum of mankind in a global emergency brought on by population pressures that exceeded the limits of viability.

The positive corollary reveals that some of our traditional moral convictions rest on the supposition that men and other animals dif- fer radically in kind. When we affirm the equality of all human beings in virtue of their common humanity, and subordinate to that equality all the differences—and inequalities—in degree between one individual and another, that affirmation involves more than simply asserting that all men belong to one and the same kind, which can be anatomically or physiologically identified. It involves the assertion that men differ from other animals in kind, not only psychologically, but also radically in their underlying constitution. Their superiority to other animals by virtue of such a radical differ- ence in kind is that which gives their equality with one another as members of the human species its normative significance—for the rules governing the treatment of men by men as well as for the rules governing the treatment of other animals by men. The revolutionary social and political ideal of human equality is thus seen to depend for its ultimate validity on the outcome of the test that will decide which of the competing hypotheses about man is nearer the truth.[8]

3

We have seen that the line we now draw between men as *persons* and all else as *things* would be effaced by the discovery that nothing but differences in degree separate men from other animals and from intelligent robots. But can it be preserved if the difference, while one of kind rather than of degree, turns out to be only a superficial difference in kind and, therefore, one that is ultimately reducible to, or at least generated by, a difference in degree? Can the special dignity that is attributed to man as a person and to no other animal, and can the rights and responsibilities that are usually associated with that dignity, continue to be defended as inherently human if man is not radically different in kind from everything else?

Dr. Lilly and Professors Scriven, Smart, and Sellars have presented us with what I shall call a diminished view of what it means to be a person. For them, men are persons by virtue of their distinctive power of conceptual thought, manifested by propositional speech—and so also will dolphins and robots deserve to be ranked as persons if and when they, too, manifest their possession of conceptual thought by conversational or linguistic performances comparable to man's. In an etymologically warranted sense of the word "rational," talking animals are rational, and non-talking animals are brute; for the Greek word "logos" and its Latin equivalent "ratio" connote the intimate linkage of thought and word that is manifested in propositional speech. But if the difference between rational and brute animals solely and ultimately depends upon a difference in degree that places the talking animal above and the non-talking animals below a critical threshold in a continuum of brain magnitudes, such criteria as conversational ability, ability to engage in meaningful discourse, or ability to give and receive arguments may not suffice to establish men as the only persons in a world of things, with the dignity or moral worth that attaches to personality and with all the moral rights and responsibilities that appertain thereto. This began to become clear in our consideration of the hypothetical case that we explored dialectically in the preceding section. The argument there led us to the conclusion that the age-old prohibition against treating men as we have for ages treated animals, and the basic equality of men that rests not only on their all being the same in kind but also on their superiority in kind to animals, not just superiority in degree, cannot be defended—at least, not adequately —except on the ground that men differ *radically* from other animals and other things.

The reason why this is so can be made clearer by going back to the conception of personality as the bearer of moral worth, moral rights, and moral responsibility, which originated in classical antiquity with Plato and Aristotle and with the Roman Stoics, which developed under the influence of Christianity in the Middle Ages, and which, as reformulated in the eighteenth century, especially by Kant, prevailed in Western thought until very recently. As contrasted with the minimal or diminished view advanced by a number of contemporary writers, the traditional view conceived a person as a rational being with free choice. Rationality by itself—if that is nothing more than the power of conceptual thought as manifested in propositional speech—does not constitute a person. A dolphin or a robot would not have the moral worth or dignity that demands being treated as an end, never merely as a means; would not have inherent rights that deserve respect; and would not have the moral responsibility to respect such rights, if the dolphin or robot was nothing more than a talking animal by virtue of having the requisite brain power for speech. Nor would a man! On the traditional view, a person not only has the rationality that other animals and machines lack; he also has a freedom that is not possessed by them— the freedom to pursue a course of life to a self-appointed end and to pursue it through a free choice among means for reaching that end.

I think the traditional view is correct as against the minimal view that has recently been advanced. Man as a person belongs to what Kant calls "the kingdom of ends" precisely because the end he himself pursues and the means whereby he pursues it are not set for him but are freely appointed and freely chosen by himself. His moral rights and moral responsibility stem from the freedom that is associated with his rationality, not just from his rationality itself. If the power of conceptual thought that constitutes his rationality can, according to the identity hypothesis, be adequately accounted for in neurophysiological terms, then man's rationality does not carry with it the freedom of choice that is requisite for his having the moral rights and responsibility that comprise the dignity of a person. The power of conceptual thought elevates man above the world of sense, the world of the here and now; but the power that elevates him above the world of physical things and makes him a person is the power of free choice which, as Kant puts it, involves "independence of the mechanism of nature." [9] Such independence can be man's only if the psychological power that is distinctive of man involves an immaterial or non-physical factor and can, therefore, operate with some independence of physical causes.

The freedom of free choice is properly called a "contra-causal" freedom when "contra-causal" is understood not as the total absence of causality, but as the presence of a non-physical causality. This does not mean total independence of physical causes; it means only that the act of free choice cannot be wholly explained by the action of physical causes. One of the theoretical consequences of affirming the materialist hypothesis is the denial of free choice. If the brain is the sufficient condition of conceptual thought and if, therefore, there is no reason for positing an immaterial or non-physical factor as operative in man, then man may have other freedoms, just as brute animals do, but he does not have that freedom of choice which makes him the master of himself and of his own destiny— the course he takes in life from beginning to end. Conversely, the affirmation of free choice presupposes the truth of the immaterialist hypothesis, which posits in man the operation of a non-physical factor, needed not only to explain his power of conceptual thought, but also to explain his contra-causal freedom of choice.

The proposition that man differs in kind, not just in degree, from other animals and from machines represents the conclusion that we have reached in the light of all the evidence that is at present available. This proposition may not be overturned by future findings, but if future experiments with Turing machines decisively show that man's difference in kind is only superficial, not radical, the practical consequences would be almost the same as they would be if future evidence showed that man differed only in degree. The distinction between men as persons and all else as things, and with it the attribution of a special dignity and of moral rights and responsibility to men alone, can be sustained only if man's difference is a radical difference in kind, one that cannot ultimately be explained by reference to an underlying difference of degree.

We saw, in the course of the preceding discussion, that the dignity of man as a person and his moral rights and responsibility rest on his freedom to determine the goal he pursues in life and on his free choice of the path by which to attain it. This throws light on the fact that we do not refer to other animals as engaged in the pursuit of happiness. Their goals are appointed for them by their instinctual drives, and the means they employ to reach these goals are provided either by fully developed instinctive patterns of behavior or by rudimentary instinctive mechanisms that require development and modification by learning. If man were just another animal, differing only in the degree to which his rudimentary instinctive mechanisms needed to be supplemented by learning, the pursuit of happiness would not be the peculiarly human enterprise that it is, nor would there be any ethical principles involved in the pursuit of happiness. There can be an ethics of happiness only if men can make mistakes in conceiving the goal that they ought to pursue in life, and can fail in their efforts by making mistakes in the choice of means. Lacking the power of conceptual thought, other animals cannot conceive, and hence cannot misconceive, their goals; only man with the power of conceptual thought can transcend the perceptual here and now and hold before himself a remote goal to be attained.

To this extent, a difference in kind, even if only superficial, is involved in man's concern with living a whole life well, not just with living from day to day. Other animals do not have this problem. This is just another way of saying that they do not have moral responsibility or moral rights. But if there were only one solution to the human problem of living well—the problem of how to make a good life for one's self—and if that solution were determined for each man by causes over which he had no control, then man would not be master of his life, would not be morally responsible for what he did in the pursuit of happiness, and could not claim certain things as his by right because he needed them to achieve his happiness—the happiness he has a right to pursue in his own way.

This last right, the source of all other rights, would not be the fundamental human right that it is, were man not master of his life, not only able to conceive a remote goal toward which to strive, but also able freely to choose between one or another conception of the goal to seek as well as freely to choose the means of seeking it. More than the power of conceptual thought is thus involved in the pursuit of happiness. Freedom of choice is also involved, and with it a radical difference in kind between men and other animals that have no moral problems, no moral rights, and no moral responsibility. Hence, should a Turing machine of the future succeed in the conversational test, as proponents of the materialist hypothesis predict that one will, the moral aspects of human life will be rendered illusory. Of course, unable quickly to shake off the habit of centuries, men may for some time hold onto the illusion that there are better and worse ways to live; but in the long run the truth will prevail, and men will give up the illusion that there is a fundamental difference between living *humanly* and living as other animals live.

This, in my judgment, is the most serious and far-reaching practical consequence of a decision in favor of the materialist hypothesis concerning the constitution of man, and with it a decision that man's difference in kind is only superficial. Only if the immaterialist hypothesis is confirmed by repeated trials and failures of Turing machines in the conversational test, only if man's difference from other animals and machines is a radical difference in kind, will the truth about man sustain a serious concern on his part with the moral problems involved in the pursuit of happiness—the problem of trying to find out what the distinctively human goods are and the problem of engaging by choice in one or another way of life aimed at a maximization of the goods attainable by man.[10]

4

One matter mentioned in the preceding discussion deserves further elaboration. It concerns the role of instinct in human life as compared with its role in the life of other animals. The view we take of the way in which man differs from other animals—in degree only, superficially in kind, or radically in kind—directly affects our understanding of the role of instinct in human life; and so, in the first instance, we are concerned with the theoretical consequences of diverse views of the difference of man. But there are practical consequences, too, though they are 'less immediate; for according as we understand the role of instinct in human life, in one way or another, we may be led to adopt one or another practical policy with respect to the alteration or control of human behavior. A striking example of this is to be found in certain recent popularizations of the findings of ethology concerning the instincts of aggression and territoriality that are operative in fish, birds, and mammals. On the basis of those findings, interpreted in terms of the view that man differs only in degree or at most only superficially in kind, the thesis is advanced that the basic patterns of human behavior underlying the institutions of property, nationalism, and war are determined by these same animal instincts; and, being thus instinctively determined, the human institutions in question are unamenable to alteration or eradication as long as man remains the animal he is.[11]

To state the theoretical problem with clarity, a number of distinctions must be made. First, we must distinguish between that which is innate or unlearned, as indicated by its being species-predictable, and that which is acquired or learned, as indicated by its variable presence or absence in individual members of a given species. Second, we must distinguish between those completely formed instinctive mechanisms that operate effectively without the intervention of learning and those more rudimentary instinctive mechanisms that need to be supplemented by learned behavior in order to be effective in operation. And, third, we must distinguish between instinctive mechanisms, on the one hand, both those that are fully formed and those that are rudimentary, and instinctual drives, on the other hand.

The former are patterns of overt behavior; the latter are conative sources of behavior—sources of energy impelling toward certain biological results. Such are the instinctive drives of sexual or reproductive behavior, self-preservative behavior through feeding or flight, aggressive behavior, and associative behavior. These instinctual drives are innate in the sense of being species-predictable; when activated by specific releasing mechanisms, they impel the animal toward specific objects or conditions that constitute satisfactions of the drive and bring about its temporary quiescence. Though quiescent for a time, the instinctual drive remains as a potency to be aroused again, and when aroused it once again activates patterns of behavior seeking its fulfillment. The behavioral means of fulfillment (1) may consist of fully formed instinctive mechanisms, as in the case of the insects without brains or cerebrospinal nervous systems, and also as in the case of the cerebrospinal vertebrates with relatively small brains; or, (2) they may consist of rudimentary instinctive mechanisms supplemented in varying degrees by acquired or learned patterns of behavior, as in the case of the higher mammals with relatively large brains; or, (3) as in the case of man, the means of satisfying instinctual drives when they are operative may consist of overt patterns of behavior that are products of learning or intelligence.

While there seems to be no question that the instinctual drives found in the vertebrates and especially in the mammals are also present in man, the prevailing scientific opinion is that man has no fully formed instinctive mechanisms for the satisfaction of these drives, nor even rudimentary ones as in the case of other higher animals. The only species-predictable behavior in a mature human being consists of such simple reflex arcs as the pupillary, the salivary, the patellar, or the cilio-spinal reflex, together with such involuntary innervations are produced by the action of the autonomic and sympathetic nervous systems. Men are impelled to overt behavior of certain sorts when in states of fear, anger, hunger, or sexual arousal. This overt behavior will be accompanied by visceral changes—in the glands and in the involuntary musculature—that are set in motion by the autonomic and sympathetic nervous systems. But the behavior itself will consist of voluntary actions that have been learned, that are intelligently organized, and that may be directed to the immediate fulfillment of the drive, to a postponed fulfillment of it, or to its frustration. Such behavior will vary from individual to individual; and in any one individual, it will vary from time to time, though the instinctual drive may be the same and be of the same strength.

The foregoing description of the way in which instinctual drives operate in man as compared with the way in which they operate in other animals is more consonant with the view that man differs in kind than with the view that he differs only in degree; for the difference between the operation of instinctual drives and instinctive mechanisms in other animals and the functioning of instinctual drives in man appears to be one of kind rather than of degree. What other animals do entirely by instinct or by the combination of instinct and perceptual intelligence (i.e., the power of perceptual thought through which animal learning takes place), man does entirely by learning, through the exercise of his perceptual intelligence and especially his power of conceptual thought. The presence of the same instinctual drives in man and other animals does not lead to the same overt performances in man and in other animals when these same drives are operative; nor does the presence of the same instinctual drives in all members of the human species lead all men to behave in the same way when they are activated by the release of instinctual energies.

The power of conceptual thought in man enables him to devise alternative ways of dealing with his instinctual urges. But if all the driving power behind human behavior comes from the instinctual urges that man has in common with other animals, and if man's power of conceptual thought is merely the servant of his instinctual drives, then in its main outlines human behavior is instinctively determined, as animal behavior is to a greater extent and in more detail. For human behavior to be radically different in kind from animal behavior, with respect to the role that instinct plays, man must be radically different in kind from other animals. Not only must the power of conceptual thought enable man to devise diverse ways of dealing with his instinctual urges, but he must have psychic energy not drawn from instinctual sources in order to exercise mastery over them—to sublimate or divert them to non-animal satisfactions, to postpone their gratification for long periods of time, or to subdue and frustrate them entirely if he so chooses. No other animal manifests such mastery of its instinctual urges. In Freudian language, no other animal suffers the discomforts or pains that result from domesticating and civilizing its instincts. Both civilization and its discontents belong only to man: civilization with its technology, its laws, its arts and sciences, because man alone has the power of conceptual thought that produces these elements of human culture; the discontents of civilization, born of the frustration, prolonged postponement, or sublimation of instinctual urges, because man alone exercises some voluntary control over the instinctual drives that he shares with other animals.

Surprising as it may seem, Freud's account of the relation between man's intellect and his instincts presupposes that man differs radically in kind from other animals. I say this with full knowledge that Freud himself, if explicitly asked the question about how man differs, would give one of the opposite answers—either that man differs only in degree or that his difference in kind is only superficial. No other answer fits Freud's explicit commitment to the principle of phylogenetic continuity, and his equally strong commitment to a thoroughgoing determinism that precludes free choice. Nevertheless, when we read *Civilization and Its Discontents*, we find many passages difficult to understand unless man is radically different from other animals that have the same instinctual drives; such as the following:

> Sublimation of instinct is an especially conspicuous feature of cultural evolution; this it is that makes it possible for the higher mental operations, scientific, artistic, ideological activities, to play such an important part in civilized life. If one were to yield to a first impression, one would be tempted to say that sublimation is a fate which has been forced upon instincts by culture alone. But it is better to reflect over this a while. Thirdly and lastly, and this seems most important of all, it is impossible to ignore the extent to which civilization is built up on renunciation of instinctual gratifications, the degree to which the existence of civilization presupposes the non-gratification (suppression, repression or something else?) of powerful instinctual urgencies. This "cultural privation" dominates the whole field of social relations between human beings. . . . *It is not easy to understand how it can become possible to withhold satisfaction from an instinct.*[12]

I have italicized the last sentence quoted because I want to call attention to the question that must be answered. *How is it possible for us to withhold satisfaction from an instinct?* What power in us enables us to do so? Freud's answer to that question is, in my judgment, very revealing. It is given in the following passage:

> We may insist as much as we like that the human intellect is weak in comparison with human instincts, and be right in doing so. But neverthe-

less there is something peculiar about this weakness. The voice of the intellect is a soft one, but it does not rest until it has gained a hearing.
Ultimately, after endlessly repeated rebuffs, it succeeds. This is one of the
few points in which one may be optimistic about the future of mankind,
but in itself it signifies not a little. And one can make it the starting-point
for yet other hopes. The primacy of the intellect certainly lies in the far,
far, but still probably not infinite, distance.[13]

The foregoing explanation of how men are able to withhold
satisfaction from instincts, and to exercise mastery over them in
other ways, attributes an autonomy and causal efficacy to the human
intellect which it could have only if the power of conceptual
thought were an immaterial or non-physical power. Only if he possessed such a power would man be able to choose between diverse
ways of gratifying his instincts; be able to decide whether to gratify
them or not; and be able, in addition, to seek the gratification of
desires that are not rooted in his instinctual urges at all, but arise
from the capacities for knowing and for loving, as only an animal
with the power of conceptual thought can know or love.[14] Thus,
Freud's account of civilization and its discontents and his statement about the power of the human intellect in relation to man's
animal instincts appear to lead to a conclusion that runs counter
to his own commitments to determinism and to phylogenetic continuity; namely, the conclusion that man differs radically in kind
from other animals by virtue of having a non-physical power that
gives him freedom of choice and that has sufficient independence of
instinctual energies to gain mastery or exercise control over them.

We find the same conclusion implicit in Konrad Lorenz' recent
book on aggression; and there, as in Freud, its implicit presence
is obscured and contradicted by many things that are explicitly
said to the contrary. Lorenz acknowledges the uniqueness of man
by virtue of his power of conceptual thought.[15] In addition, he attributes to man, because of his rationality, a "responsible morality"
that is not possessed by other animals, and tells us, as Freud does,
that "we all suffer to some extent from the necessity to control our
natural inclinations by the exercise of moral responsibility." [16] In
his discussion of the "behavioral analogies to morality," he clearly
indicates that what morally responsible men do by reason, other
animals do solely by instinctive mechanisms.[17] Nevertheless, he
explicitly denies autonomy to reason; i.e., denies that man has in

his constitution any power sufficiently independent of instinctual energies to exercise mastery over them.

By itself, reason can only devise means to achieve otherwise determined ends; it cannot set up goals or give us orders. Left to itself, reason is like a computer into which no relevant information conducive to an important answer has been fed; logically valid though all its operations may be, it is a wonderful system of wheels within wheels, without a motor to make them go around. The motive power that makes them do so stems from instinctive behavior mechanisms much older than reason and not directly accessible to rational self-observation.[18]

Reason, or the power of conceptual thought, has no driving energy of its own, and no causal efficacy of its own; all its commands or prohibitions draw their effective force "from some emotional, in other words, instinctive, source of energy supplying motivation. Like power steering in a modern car, responsible morality derives the energy which it needs to control human behavior from the same primal power which it was created to keep in rein." [19]

Because, like Freud, Lorenz is committed to determinism and to phylogenetic continuity, he leaves us with the puzzle of how reason and responsible morality can operate to thwart instinctual drives if they lack autonomy, i.e., if all their energy derives from instinctual sources. In addition, there is the further puzzle of how man can have moral responsibility without having a freedom of choice that involves some measure of independence of animal instincts. These puzzles vanish if one holds the view that Freud and Lorenz cannot adopt, because it is irreconcilable with their basic commitments— the view that man differs radically in kind from other animals, and that he has the power of conceptual thought and contra-causal freedom of choice by virtue of having a non-physical or immaterial factor in his make-up, a factor that has a certain measure of autonomy and causal efficacy.

5

The reader should not need to be reminded that, at this stage of our inquiries, we do not *know* whether man's difference in kind is superficial or radical; we do not *know* whether the materialist hypothesis or the immaterialist hypothesis is nearer the truth. Such arguments as can be advanced in support of one or the other hypothesis have already been examined; I have not, in the foregoing discussion of the role of instinct in human life, offered any new arguments for the immaterialist hypothesis. My sole purpose has been to see the alternative practical consequences that would follow from a future decision in favor of one hypothesis or the other. Let me summarize what has now become clear.

On the one hand, if man has an immaterial or non-physical factor operative in his make-up and if, with that, he has freedom of choice and some measure of independence of his animal instincts, then the resultant discontinuity between man and other living organisms would require us to desist from trying to explain human behavior by the theories or laws that we apply to the behavior of subhuman animals. In spite of the fact that the same instinctual drives are operative in man and other animals, the radical difference in kind between them would mean that instinct does not play the same role in human life that it plays in the lives of other animals. Man would have a mastery over his instincts that no other animal has; and he could have rational goals, ideals envisaged by reason, beyond the satisfaction of his instinctual needs. We might then look upon the future of man with the optimism that both Freud and Lorenz express, but we would have grounds for that optimism which they cannot reconcile with their scientific convictions.[20]

On the other hand, if determinism and the principle of phylogenetic continuity hold true in the case of man, as they would if man differs only superficially in kind from other animals, then the laws governing and the theories explaining the behavior of subhuman animals would apply without qualification to human behavior. In spite of the fact that man differs in kind by virtue of having the power of conceptual thought, instinct would play the same determining role in human life that it plays in the lives of other animals; and, in that case, we cannot be optimistic about the future of the human race, for so long as man is governed by his animal instincts, his behavior cannot be altered in its broad outlines and in its basic tendencies.

NOTES

1. See John Lilly, *Man and Dolphin* (Garden City, N.Y.: Doubleday, 1961), Chapters 1 and 12. Cf. Lilly's more recent book: *The Mind of the Dolphin: A Nonhuman Intelligence* (Garden City, N.Y.: Doubleday, 1967).

2. *Ibid.*, pp. 211–212. Considering Dr. Lilly's prediction that, if dolphins and humans engage in conversation and thus appear to share a common intellectual power, some groups of men will probably advocate that we treat them as we treat human beings, a reader of this book in manuscript suggested to me that the opposite result might also occur. It is just as likely, he wrote, that some group of men "will take the view that a large part of the human race is *no better* than dolphins, and should therefore cease to have the rights currently accorded to human beings. In effect, this was the argument of the Germans with respect to Poles and Jews. Without denying that the Poles and Jews were biologically human, the Nazis maintained that they were in other respects sub-human, and more like animals or things. In short, the effect of the discovery that men do not differ in kind from animals is just as likely to promote malevolence toward some human groups as benevolence toward dolphins or other animals that are found not to differ in kind from men."

I have nothing to say about the relative probability of Dr. Lilly's prediction or my friend's prediction of the actual consequences that might follow from the discovery that men and dolphins do not differ in kind. I have no way of estimating which guess is shrewder or more likely to be true. When I consider the practical consequences of man's being different in kind from other animals—or, in the case of the dolphins, perhaps the same in kind—I am concerned *only with what ought or ought not to be the result of one or another state of facts, not with predictions of what might or might not actually result.* In other words, by *practical* consequences, I mean *normative consequences*—consequences in the form of the normative conclusions that we reach in the light of the facts as ascertained, not consequences in the form of actions taken, regardless of whether or not they can be justified in the light of the facts and sound normative principles.

My friend obviously understood Dr. Lilly to be doing no more than making a prediction. I understood him to be considering the legal and ethical problem that the human race will have to face if and when dolphins show themselves to have the power of conceptual thought. I, therefore, read him as taking the position that if and when it is ascertained, as a matter of fact, that dolphins and men do not differ psychologically in kind, justice will require us to treat dolphins as persons and accord to them the same rights that we accord to men as persons. The action predicted by my friend would not be justified by the facts as ascertained, if they were subsumed under the normative principle that all persons (i.e., all living organisms that have the power of conceptual thought *in any degree*) ought to be treated in the same way—as persons, not as things. Nazi policies with regard to Poles and Jews, or similar policies with regard to Negroes, which have long prevailed and are still not eradicated, cannot be justified by the facts (that all human beings have the power of conceptual thought to some degree, and that every human being, even the least, therefore differs psychologically from the most intelligent animal) when those facts are subsumed under the correct normative principle that, as a matter of right or justice, all human beings ought to be treated in the same way (as persons rather than as things), and accorded the rights of persons. If the facts were otherwise—if men and other animals differ only in degree, and if some men are superior to other men in degree, as much as if not more than some men are to some animals—then Nazi policies in the treatment of Poles and Jews, or segregationist policies in the treatment of Negroes, would not be, *prima facie*, wrong as a matter of principle; the only question to be determined would be the question of fact about the inferiority of Jews or Poles to Germans, or Negroes to white men.

3. Michael Scriven, "The Mechanical Concept of Mind," in *The Modeling of Mind*, ed. Kenneth M. Sayre and Frederick J. Crosson (Notre Dame: Univ. of Notre Dame Press, 1963), p. 254.
4. *Ibid.* Cf. Hilary Putnam, "Minds and Machines," in *Dimensions of Mind*, ed. S. Hook (New York: Collier, 1961), pp. 138–64. Donald M. MacKay, "From Mechanism to Mind," in *Brain and Mind*, ed. J. R. Smythies (New York: Humanities Press, 1965), pp. 180–190.
5. Welfrid Sellars, *Science, Perception and Reality* (New York: Humanities Press, 1963), pp. 39–40.
6. For Professor Smart's views, see *Philosophy and Scientific Realism* (New York: Humanities Press, 1963), pp. 153–54; and cf. *ibid.*, pp. 93–105, 111–16, 119–125. For Professor Sellars' views, see *Science, Perception and Reality*, pp. 6, 15–17, 30–34.

7. *Philosophy and Scientific Realism,* p. 155.

8. In a brilliant essay, Jacques Maritain outlines the importance of the question of man's differences for the conception of human equality, showing how divergent conceptions of the equality of men stem from divergent views of man as a species and how they give rise to divergent normative recommendations (see "Human Equality," in *Ransoming the Time,* trans. H. Binsse (New York: C. Scribners, 1941), pp. 1–32). Among its other current projects, the Institute for Philosophical Research is engaged in the dialectical clarification of the idea of equality in Western thought. Even at this early stage in the work, it has become clear that the central and controlling issue in the whole discussion is constituted by conflicting views about the specific equality of men as persons in relation to all the inequalities that arise from their individual differences, and that these views are resolvable into conflicting views of the difference of man.

9. Emmanuel Kant, *Critique of Practical Reason and Other Works on the Theory of Ethics,* trans. T. K. Abbott (New York: Longmans, Green, and Co., 1927), 6th ed., p. 180. Cf. *ibid.,* pp. 46–53; and Emmanuel Kant, *Critique of Teleological Judgment,* trans. J. C. Meredith (Oxford: Clarendon Press, 1928), pp. 99–100. The Christain conception of personality, like Kant's, involves an element of immateriality. The Christian dogma that man is made in the image of God, Who is pre-eminently a person, attributes personality to man as reflecting the divine being in this respect, i.e., immateriality.

10. I have treated these problems at greater length in another book of much earlier date (see M. Adler, *A Dialectic of Morals* [New York: F. Ungar Pub. Co., 1941], Chapter IV, esp. pp. 58–59). While I would revise what is there said in many respects were I to address anew to the problems of moral philosophy, as I hope to do in a book I am now working on, the point made there would remain essentially unchanged, at least so far as they bear on the relevance to morality of the way that man differs from other animals.

11. See Robert Ardrey, *The Territorial Imperative* (New York: Atheneum, 1966); and also his *African Genesis* 1961). Both books are engaging popularizations of the findings of ethology, full of fascinating stories of animal behavior; but both are also flagrant examples of special pleading for the questionable thesis that instinct governs human life exactly as it does animal life. The truth of that thesis depends upon how man differs from other animals; if man differs even superficially in kind from other animals, it is in important respects false; if man differs radically, it is wholly false. In his zeal to explain human behavior and human life in terms of animal instincts, Ardrey

does not pause to consider the facts bearing on the question of how man differs. He assumes the truth of the answer that suits his ad hoc rhetoric. The fact that books of this sort are dismissed for what they are by the scientific community does not prevent them from bemusing and misleading the laymen who read them for the enjoyable animal stories they contain and uncritically swallow the thesis along with the stories.

12. S. Freud, *Civilization and Its Discontents*, trans. by J. Riviere (New York: J. Cape and H. Smith, 1930), p. 63. Cf. Chapter III, *passim*.

13. S. Freud, *The Future of an Illusion*, trans. by W. D. Ronson-Scott (London: Hogarth, 1928), p. 93.

14. Freud's attribution of an intellectual power to man that is not possessed to any degree by other animals is all of one piece with his theory of distinctively human erotic love, as contrasted with the sexuality of other animals, a sexuality that is devoid of love even when it involves the instinctive inhibition of aggressive behavior and so gives the *appearance* of tenderness and benevolence. Nevertheless, for Freud every form of human love is erotic, either overtly sexual or a sublimation of sexuality. But if the human intellect has the autonomy that it would have to have in order to control the instincts and to sublimate them, and if that, in turn, depends on the intellect's transcendence of physical causality, then, contrary to Freud's theory of love, the non-erotic forms of human love (such as the *amor intellectualis dei* of Spinoza, the appetitive character of which takes its special form from intellectual cognition rather than from sense-perception) would be explicable without reference to sex, sexuality, or sublimation.

15. Konrad Lorenz, *On Aggression* (New York: Harcourt, Brace and World, 1966), pp. 238 ff. Though Lorenz discusses free will in relation to "the laws of natural causation" governing human and animal behavior, he shows little or no understanding of free choice (see *ibid.*, Chapter 12, esp. pp. 225, 228–229, 231–232). An excellent critical review of the book by S. A. Barnett points out the illicit use that Lorenz makes of superficial analogies between human and animal behavior, and also the inconsistencies into which he falls by his effort to plead a case beyond what the acknowledged facts will support (see *Scientific American*, CCXVI, No. 2, [February, 1967]). *Ibid.*, pp. 135–37.

16. *Ibid.*, p. 254. Cf. *ibid.*, pp. 240–54.

17. See *ibid.*, Chapter 7, esp. p. 110.

18. *Ibid.*, p. 248. In another place, Lorenz refers to "the functions of reason and moral responsibility which first came into the world with

man and which, provided he does not blindly and arrogantly deny the existence of his animal inheritance, give him the power to control it" (*ibid.*, p. 215).

19. *Ibid.*, p. 247.
20. See especially Lorenz' concluding chapter, "Avowal of Optimism," in *ibid.*, pp. 275 ff.